THE ULTIMATE
Small Business
Marketing Toolkit

All the Tips, Forms, and Strategies
You'll Ever Need

Beth Goldstein

McGraw-Hill

New York Chicago San Francisco Lisbon London Madrid
Mexico City Milan New Delhi San Juan Seoul
Singapore Sydney Toronto

The McGraw·Hill Companies

1 2 3 4 5 6 7 8 9 0   DOC/DOC   0 9 8 7

ISBN-13: P/N 978-0-07-149809-8 of set
            978-0-07-147718-5

ISBN-10: P/N 0-07-149809-5 of set
            0-07-147718-7

All worksheets © Marketing Edge Consulting Group, LLC.

McGraw-Hill books are available at special quantity discounts to use as premiums and sales promotions, or for use in corporate training programs. For more information, please write to the Director of Special Sales, Professional Publishing, McGraw-Hill, Two Penn Plaza, New York, NY 10121-2298. Or contact your local bookstore.

This book is printed on acid-free paper.

Library of Congress Cataloging-in-Publication Data

Goldstein, Beth.
  The ultimate small business marketing toolkit / by Beth Goldstein.
      p. cm.
  ISBN 0-07-147718-7 (alk. paper)
1. Marketing—Management. 2. Small business—Marketing. I. Title.
HF5415.13.G58 2008
658.8—dc22
                                                            2007004626

CONTENTS

ACKNOWLEDGMENTS

When my editor, Donya Dickerson, first approached me with the concept of writing a book about small business marketing, she handed me the opportunity to turn a long-held ambition into reality. I thank Donya for having confidence in me and enabling me to realize my dream.

Like most new business ventures, this project proved to be even more thrilling and exhausting than I could ever have predicted. It truly took a community to help me create this toolkit. I am forever grateful to the many friends, relatives, and colleagues who supported me throughout the process and provided me with the insight and the energy necessary to put all the pieces together. I'd also like to recognize those individuals who tirelessly reviewed chapters and milestones at various stages, taking them on planes, trains, and even vacations out of the country to provide me with timely and critical feedback. Without their incredible knowledge and expertise, this book simply would not exist. Many thanks to Dale Bornstein, Cecilia Caferri, Dennis J. Ceru, Michael Epstein, Harvey Gertman, Mitchell Goldstein, Ruth and Arthur Goldstein (aka Mom and Dad), Holly Intravia, Tina Pfeiffer, Peter Russo, and Greg Stoller.

A special thanks to three friends who each played a major role in the creation of this book. First, to Robert Block, who helped me get the first words and chapters down on paper. Next to Jeffrey Korn, whose support, unique engineering perspective, and ability to make me laugh kept me going to ensure I got the final chapters completed and off to my editor on time. And finally to Paul Horn, who stayed with me every step of the way, reviewing each chapter and guiding me through the process so that I could turn my vision into reality.

I'd also like to honor the experts and business owners in the book who willingly and openly shared their stories, expertise, and knowledge, and allowed us to peek inside their businesses. Thanks to Joanna Alberti, Jonathan Bachman, Jon Boroshok, John Canestraro, Lyn Christiansen, Alyssa Dver, Torsten Ludwig, Luis Lugo, Robin Malone, Raul Medina, Renee Pallenberg, Paul Regensburg, Elizabeth and Eric Schuster, Christopher Sole, and Edward Urquhart.

A particular acknowledgment to my dog, Biscotti, who was often the victim of chapters overflowing from the printer, which landed on him as he occupied the sunny spot in my office under the office equipment.

Finally, to the two most important people in my life, who made the greatest sacrifice throughout the last months of writing this book. They rarely complained as their mom stated one too many times, "I'll be there in a minute, just as soon as I finish this chapter." To Ben and Jacqui, the greatest dreams I could imagine. I love you very much!

)) DEDICATION

This book is dedicated to
the cutest aspiring entrepreneurs I know
and my greatest inspiration in life,
my children, Benjamin and Jacqueline Weiner.
Thanks for your hugs, support,
and never-ending love.

AUTHOR'S NOTE

In a competitive marketplace, time is a key factor in determining success. Because of limited resources (both financial and human), one major mistake can spell doom for an organization. Operating on a limited budget, as most entrepreneurial organizations do, leads to a high level of creativity, drive, and passion, but it also underscores the challenge that sales and marketing experts face as they try to perform their roles. Facing a shortage of critical resources such as time, money, and people with relevant experience, these entrepreneurs must achieve a pioneering level of creativity to ensure that they are providing benefits that their customers truly value. That's where true entrepreneurial spirit takes charge, and that's the force explored in this book.

During the winter of 2000, Boston University approached me to develop a course on entrepreneurial marketing for graduate business students. My objective in developing this course was twofold: first, to educate current and future business owners about entrepreneurial marketing techniques, and second, to highlight for them the importance of developing a complete marketing program that incorporates strong customer-focused sales and marketing strategies. This book not only includes many of the "learning lessons" incorporated in my course, but it also demonstrates how launching a customer-focused approach will enable an organization with a viable product or service to compete effectively against the most seasoned, successful companies.

Interspersed throughout the book are stories of success and failure, many of them chronicling my clients' own experiences. I present real-world business cases combined with in-depth assessments of the myriad of sales and marketing tools available. I interviewed CEOs, sales and marketing directors and consultants, and business owners from a variety of organizations and industries. The book includes more than four dozen worksheets to help guide you through the process of developing a customer-focused marketing program.

By the end of the book, you will have gained the insights and tools necessary to develop and deliver a cost-effective sales and marketing program that will support you through economic ups and downs and won't require an entire department of managers to launch. You'll learn which tactics to use and when, and what skills are necessary to successfully grow your business. Equally important, you will be prepared and motivated to put that knowledge to work for your business immediately. Enjoy the journey!

INTRODUCTION

*I honestly think it is better to be a failure at something you love
than to be a success at something you hate.*

—George Burns

What does it really take to make a business successful? This is not an easy question to answer, as each entrepreneur has a different definition of success. I was recently exchanging e-mails with my friend Robert, who, as a successful retail entrepreneur and a graduate of one of the top business schools in the United States, has a special interest in this topic. When I inquired about his marketing strategy, his response was simple: "The key to a successful business is customer service and retention. That is so much more important than marketing. We both know it costs several times more to find a new customer than to retain a current one."

Fortunately, he couldn't see my jaw drop. I could feel my chest tighten as I stared at my computer screen in disbelief. He had basically dismissed what I do every day as a marketing consultant. I took a deep breath and wrote back, "How can you know what good customer service is if you don't perform the marketing activities that tell you what your customers need and expect from you?" He replied, "Like what? Sending junk mail?"

But as I thought about it, I realized that many business owners would probably agree with him, failing to see how marketing and sales are linked. When many people hear the word *marketing*, they automatically think of activities like creating advertisements or sending direct mail. As a marketing consultant, I have heard this misconception more times than I can count. I am continuously educating my clients, my colleagues, and even my friends about what marketing consultants actually do.

Marketing and customer service are integrally connected, related, and required for optimal business success. Marketing is similar to putting together a complicated puzzle. Each piece contains information that makes sense only when you see the finished product.

In a broad sense, marketing consists of two ongoing activities: (1) understanding your customers' needs, and (2) developing products, services, and communication strategies to meet those needs. If you perform the critical up-front tasks of researching, testing, and getting to know your customers, you'll avoid jamming the pieces together and making some costly errors. Too many people waste time creating ad campaigns or sending direct mail haphazardly, because that's what they think they're supposed to do to "promote" their companies. These outreach activities should be your *last* step. Strategic marketing first requires research into defining your customers. Before you launch a marketing strategy and spend money on tactics, like direct mail and advertising, you need to figure out who your customers are and why they buy from you.

Ultimately, marketing is about *growth*—growth of your product mix, growth of your customer base, growth of your profits, growth of your image, and growth of investment dollars. The key to enhancing your bottom line is understanding what makes your customers tick so that you can provide top-quality customer service to meet their needs. That is the very soul of marketing. Clearly the quality of your products is important. But by becoming customer-focused, you will strengthen your business model and become a fierce competitor. In an increasingly tough marketplace, your success depends upon understanding what makes your customers tick and enhancing your business model to meet their needs.

With that goal in mind, think about your business purely in terms of your customers and ask yourself:

- How much do I know about my customers?

- Why do they buy from me?

- What benefits do my products or services provide?

- How do my customers find out about my company's products or services?

- What can I do to increase their satisfaction with my company?

- Who else are they buying products or services from?

- What other products or services can I offer them to satisfy their needs?

Can you answer these questions? By the time you finish with this book and its worksheets, *you will*!

A FANTASTIC VOYAGE

Look at this book as a fantastic voyage into the minds of your customers. It will give you the hands-on guidance required to cost-effectively create and launch an integrated sales and marketing program that defines your customers' needs so that *you* can maximize your business's growth—and all on a budget. If you're an entrepreneur, a small business owner, or an employee whose job depends on understanding and serving customers' needs, then this book was written for you.

Throughout the book, you will read real-life stories of success and failure, some of them chronicling my clients' own experiences, and others focused on the myriad of inspirational entrepreneurs and owners of successful companies whom I have had the opportunity to learn from over the years. You will read about a variety of effective sales and marketing strategies. You will discover what distinguishes the flourishing companies from the disappointments and recognize a strong prevailing theme: the winners are those that understand their customers and spend their marketing dollars accordingly.

YOUR APPROACH

How can you make the most of this book? This book is a true toolkit, just like the type that holds hammers, nails and screwdrivers. Sometimes you will need to use all the tools in your kit to accomplish a task; other times you may simply need a hammer and nails. But before you can determine which tools you'll use, you must first define the project, look through your toolbox to see what tools you have available to you, and then come up with a plan to complete the task at hand. Use a similar approach with your business. Think about the challenges that lie ahead, then open this book and familiarize yourself with the "tools" it contains. Read the chapters and complete the worksheets that apply directly to your business. Like a traditional toolkit that you use over and over again to accomplish different goals, this book is designed to help you both now and in the future.

To simplify the process for you, I have divided the book into easy-to-follow milestones. Each milestone will get you one step closer to creating a marketing program that reinforces and supports a customer-focused business approach. Each chapter contains worksheets that are specifically related to the topics discussed in that chapter to help you apply the ideas to your current or potential business venture. You can complete a few of the worksheets or all of them, depending on what challenges and opportunities you are facing in your business. This book is designed to support individuals who are new to the concept of marketing, as well as experienced marketers. Please use the CD included in this book and check my consulting firm's Web site, Marketing Edge Consulting Group, LLC, www.m-edge.com/ultimate/, for the most up-to-date copies of the worksheets. Drop me a note if you would like to share stories of how you've used the worksheets or let me know how your business is going. You can e-mail me at Ultimate@m-edge.com.

FLOW OF THE BOOK

Milestone 1 begins with a discussion of your vision and your entrepreneurial spirit. Before you can begin to launch or grow a business, it is critical that you clearly understand your goals, your passion, and your reason for being in your chosen business. Once you understand this, you can begin to assess your customers' needs and begin to define who your customers are and what their goals and passion are. Milestone 2 focuses on conducting the research required to fully understand your customers and outlines how to accomplish this on a shoestring budget. Milestones 3 and 4 are designed to help you assess the marketplace that you operate within and identify the obstacles and how to overcome them, as well as determine the best ways to maximize the opportunities. Milestones 5 through 7 are about deployment, using the tools necessary to determine which specific marketing strategies will help you best reach your customers. This includes everything from direct mail, advertising, and online marketing to important personal sales and networking skills, something that every entrepreneur must excel at. Milestone 8 is about execution. How do you take the knowledge that you've gained and, as the folks at Nike would say, "Just Do It!"? This section focuses on how to lay a strong foundation, using your resources, your passion, and your knowledge wisely to start the process of creating a winning marketing strategy.

By the time you complete the book, not only will you have a solid understanding of your customers, but you will be ready to implement a strategic marketing program to expand your business. Also, you will have a toolkit available to you when future challenges arise. Remember, this book is not designed to sit on your bookshelf and gather dust. It's a tool for you to use on an ongoing basis, for years to come, to help you grow your business and execute solid sales and marketing programs.

MILESTONE 1

HOW WELL DO YOU KNOW YOURSELF AND YOUR CUSTOMERS?

Milestone 1 begins with the concept of helping you identify your goals, vision, and passion, which are required if you are to grow your business. With this passion and commitment to going forward established, we then move from determining how well you know yourself in Chapter 1 to seeing how well you know your customers. Chapters 2 and 3 focus on helping you develop a customer profile, determine your customers' lifetime value, and understand your customers' key behaviors, traits, and characteristics. By the end of this milestone, you are very likely to embrace the notion that running a business is all about your customers, not simply about your products and services. If you do not clearly understand and define who your customers are and how you provide value to them, your business will not be the success you want and need it to be.

The worksheets included in Milestone 1 are:

■ Worksheet 1.1: Business Vision and Goals Worksheet

■ Worksheet 1.2: Seven Strategies to Jump-Start Your Business

■ Worksheet 2.1: Developing a Customer Profile

■ Worksheet 2.2: Customer Questions to Ask

■ Worksheet 3.1: Customer Lifetime Value (LTV) Form

■ Worksheet 3.2: Total Individual Value of a Satisfied Customer

■ Worksheet 3.3: Customer Growth Projection

■ Worksheet 3.4: Customer Differentiation Worksheet

CHAPTER 1

ARE YOU READY?
BUSINESS VISION AND THE ENTREPRENEUR

If I have ever made any valuable discoveries, it has been owing more to patient attention than to any other talent.

—Isaac Newton

Business success is composed of 10 percent vision, 25 percent passion, and 65 percent perspiration. Is that a scientifically proven statistic? Definitely not! However, having worked with entrepreneurs for years, I've noticed that when these three critical elements don't exist in precisely the right proportions, the warning lights for failure begin to blink. Your business vision may get you started, but without passion and commitment to the work required to make it happen, it will fall apart rapidly. Having a strong vision is important, but it's not the only element that's needed for success.

BUSINESS CLOSURE IS NOT ALWAYS FAILURE

Early in my career, I helped close down a graphic design business. I say this not with shame, remorse, or feelings of failure, but with pride because I played a role in helping the owner realize her ultimate dream. (*Hint:* it wasn't running her current business.) One of my first consulting gigs, this project involved my teaming up with a respected management consultant to help a boutique graphic design firm develop a business and marketing plan that would allow the company to move to the next level. We spent weeks studying the firm's business model, interviewing its design team, and reviewing its operations and sales pipeline.

At the end of the consulting engagement, we presented the owner with a model for growth that had a very strong sales component and that required her daily involvement with managing and selling the company's services (or hiring somebody full-time who could be devoted to this effort). We explained how long her sales cycle was and how many clients she needed if she was to maintain and pay her staff of three designers and a business manager (in addition to herself). After careful review of the plan, she thanked us and stated: "You have helped me make a critical decision. I am going to close the business."

Clearly this was not the reaction we expected. But she went on to explain that she was an artist at heart, and she had found that running a business was taking her away from what she loved most, which was creating art. The business had grown because she and her team had been providing high-quality design work for clients, but being a manager or a salesperson wasn't her dream. She simply wanted to paint and design.

What's the lesson here? Without passion on the part of the business leader, a business is doomed to fail. Company owners must be vested not just in the business but also in their role in the business. If this designer/owner could not afford to hire a manager or didn't want to have somebody else run the business operations, then it wasn't worth her time and effort to continue to operate. Years later, she is much happier and even more successful as an artist on her own.

DRIVE AND MOTIVATION

Many well-conceived business plans have never seen the light of day in terms of becoming viable businesses simply because the entrepreneurs lacked drive and motivation. On the other hand, mediocre business concepts driven by passionate and committed individuals have propelled many a company to success. It's simply not enough to have a great idea. You have to be motivated, driven, and willing to put sweat equity into its execution, or your dream is likely to flounder.

In addition, without a clear vision of where you want to go, all the passion and drive in the world may not be enough to get you to your destination. Launching a business is a journey to be experienced by those entrepreneurs who can maintain both their vision and a level of flexibility, understanding that their hard work and drive will one day pay off and they'll be successful business owners.

A COMPANY'S VISION

How do you understand a company's vision and make sure that everybody aboard shares that vision and the passion to succeed? It's important that you understand not only where the company is going, but where it has been and how it is currently perceived. In fact, everybody in your company must understand this.

The following is a list of questions that you should ask yourself, your employees, and your business partners. These questions need to be asked regardless of what stage your business is in. Whether your firm has been operating for 10 years or was just launched, it's essential that you continually assess your vision, your passion, where you are, and where you want to be.

1. What are the two most important business goals for our *company* to achieve in the next 6 months, 12 months, 2 years?

2. What are the two most important business goals for our *department* to achieve in the next 6 months, 12 months, 2 years?

3. What external challenges, if any, do we face in making these things happen?

4. What internal challenges, if any, do we face in making these things happen?

5. What three strategies have we already launched to achieve these goals?

6. Describe the target audience for our business, including what motivates people to buy from our company.

7. What are the top three problems that our business solves for our customers?

8. When prospects think about our company, what word(s) do we want to have pop into their heads?

9. Who are our main competitors, and how are they perceived by our customers and/or prospects?

10. What sets our business apart from our competitors?

11. What are the main objections that we have heard from business prospects, and what steps have we taken to overcome them?

Based on the responses to these questions, you can begin to clearly understand whether there is a shared vision among the key players inside your business and business partners and others who support you outside of your business. Don't take answering these questions lightly. This is hard work, and it should not be done in a single session. These answers will drive your business model and influence your opportunity for growth. This is part of the hard work that needs to be completed to ultimately achieve the success that you desire. So take your time and do the research required to answer these questions that define your business.

BOSTON UNIVERSITY'S ONLINE CERTIFICATE IN ENTREPRENEURSHIP

In early 2005, three colleagues and I began developing an Online Graduate Certificate in Entrepreneurship program (management.bu.edu/exec/elc/online.shtml) for Boston University. These colleagues, Gregory Stoller, Lyn Christiansen, and Dennis J. Ceru, and I were all seasoned entrepreneurs and adjunct professors. We struggled to figure out the best way to teach entrepreneurship through an online medium. We knew that we could not teach passion or hard work, but helping students achieve their goals was an important objective. We used material that we teach in actual classrooms, but we had to figure out how to convey the message via this new medium.

In addition to creating the courses, marketing the program to the "right" audience was a top priority. We needed to identify and attract the best mix of entrepreneurs and *aspiring* entrepreneurs to the online classes. One successful idea that we came up with to locate and interact with prospective students was to create a Webinar entitled, "Seven Strategies to Jump-Start Your Business." This heightened awareness of the certificate program gave us a chance to explain its value, and we obtained new students for the program.

In the next section I share with you the seven key strategies that lie at the heart of entrepreneurial ventures and that are critical to a business's success. Once you have reviewed these, complete the worksheets that accompany this chapter and spend some time deciding whether you have the vision, the passion, and the energy required to launch a business successfully, now or in the future.

SEVEN KEY STRATEGIES TO JUMP-START YOUR BUSINESS

STRATEGY 1: KNOW WHERE YOU'RE GOING

Strategy, especially entrepreneurial strategy, is directional and changing. It is often viewed as an art rather than a science. Therefore, it is essential that you have a solid grounding and a basic sense of why you are investing your time and energy in this venture. Make sure you know where you expect and hope to end up. Before you begin the journey, ask yourself these questions:

- Why do I want to start this business?

- Is it the business idea that I love, or is it the idea of running the business? These are very different things. For example, I know somebody who loved vacationing at bed and breakfasts so much that she decided to buy one. Running a B&B and vacationing at one turned out to be two very different experiences. You don't want to make a major financial commitment like purchasing an inn, only to discover that running it was not exactly what you had in mind.

- What do I personally want to gain from the business?

- What are my real strengths as an entrepreneur?

- What are my limitations?

- What is my directional strategy?

- Where do I want the business to be three to five years from now?

- Does this vision fit with my career goals?

STRATEGY 2: MAKE SURE THE ENTREPRENEURIAL PATH FITS YOUR PERSONALITY AND LIFESTYLE

Running your own business is quite different from working at somebody else's firm. The rewards are higher—but so are the risks. Are you ready for the changes that entrepreneurship will bring? If you decide that you'd like to be your own boss for lifestyle reasons, that's great. But there's one serious caveat: make sure the business can be profitable enough to allow you to maintain the lifestyle that you're accustomed to or are striving to create. If you launch this business as your sole source of income, make sure it can provide you with the financial means that you require.

Questions to ask yourself include the following:

- Who do I want to be when I grow up?

- *Why* am I doing this?

- What will this do *for* me?

- What will this do *to* me?

- Will this business allow me to maintain my lifestyle?

- Does this business fit my personality and interests?

)) STRATEGY 3: ANALYZE YOUR FINANCIAL REQUIREMENTS CAREFULLY

Many business experts will tell you that it typically takes three times as much time and twice as much cash to implement a business model as most entrepreneurs originally projected. Here are some guidelines and questions to ask yourself:

- Since many sources of funding are "one-time" and nonrepeatable, will I have enough money to launch my business?

- How can I borrow, use, and spend only what I absolutely must until my business is up and running?

- How can I defer as many expenses as possible until I am generating revenue?

- What steps can I take to avoid losing ownership of my business at an early stage to partners, suppliers, consultants, or anybody else who is interested in owning a share of it?

- Do I have the financial means to carry the business?

- How will I support myself (and perhaps my family) until my business is profitable?

- Can I get financial assistance from friends, venture capitalists, professional financiers and banks, family, angels, or others?

STRATEGY 4: DON'T UNDERESTIMATE THE AMOUNT OF TIME AND RESEARCH REQUIRED TO DETERMINE THE BUSINESS'S FEASIBILITY

There's a huge difference between a great idea and a bona fide company. Individuals create feasibility plans to decide if this is a go or no-go situation. These are not full-blown business plans, but they still require an enormous investment of time and effort.

A feasibility study typically involves examining various areas such as customer needs and profiles, marketplace conditions, internal strengths and weaknesses, competition, partnership opportunities, and any other factors that might affect your success. Make sure you clearly understand the amount of research that is required to make this determination. Questions you should be asking yourself include the following:

■ Have I thought through all the consequences of running the business?

■ How much do I really know about the industry and the competition?

■ Have I done all the work required to fully understand the challenges and opportunities in the marketplace?

■ How robust is my business idea?

■ What additional research do I need to conduct to determine if this is a viable business or just a great idea?

》》

STRATEGY 5: EMBRACE THE NOTION THAT IT'S ABOUT THE CUSTOMER—NOT THE PRODUCT

The bottom line for any credible business is that you need to be solving a problem for customers or creating an opportunity for them, or they won't have a need to buy your product, service, or solution. You can have the best-designed products in the world, but if there's no market for these products (i.e., no defined customers) and no real reason for people to buy them, then you won't launch successfully or maintain long-term profitability. Ask yourself these questions:

■ What is my call to action and how will it get my customers to buy from me?

■ How well do I know my customers' needs?

- Why do my customers buy from me?

- Who are my most valuable customers?

- Do these customers share common needs and characteristics that make it easier to identify them?

- Why do these customers value my product or service?

- How will I stay close to my customers?

❯❯ STRATEGY 6: PUT TOGETHER THE BEST TEAM

Investors often prefer an A-rated team with a B-rated idea to a B-rated team with an A-rated idea. Why? Because ideas can be tweaked more easily than can a team without enough experience, passion, or expertise. Remember that you will need different *skills* at different *times* in your business's life to complete different *jobs*. In addition to employees, you will need the right advisors and directors to help you round out your expertise. Make sure that prospects or customers are part of your team to ensure that you truly achieve a high level of customer value. Ask yourself the following questions:

- Do I have an A or a B team?

- Do the people on my team have the right mix of experience and skills, and are they in the right positions to support the goals of the company?

- Do I know what the right mix is?

- Have I outlined expectations clearly, set appropriate guidelines, and provided clear incentives to achieve the goals my business needs to not only survive, but to thrive?

- Does my team have access to the right tools (software, hardware, and training) to get their jobs done to the highest standards of quality and delivery?

- Why will the right people join me—what's in it for them?

- What will I do if the team doesn't work out?

- What type of business advisors do I need to launch this business?

- How can I get customers or prospects involved in the business to serve as advisors?

- What other types of support will help me succeed?

STRATEGY 7: BE FLEXIBLE

Growing a business is a marathon, not a sprint. Most business plans change considerably between the first writing of the plan and the actual launch of the business, so take your time and plan wisely. Often your first direction and strategy will not end up being the strategy or set of plans that will get you to your final goal. That's OK, but you need to be adequately prepared, psychologically and financially, for the long journey. Ask yourself these questions:

- Can I maintain my commitment to my business concept, model, and strategy if circumstances change?

- Can I employ appropriate flexibility to adjust to changing market, environmental, and business demands?

- Am I willing to adjust to evolving market, customer, and business demands?

- How often can I change?

- Is my team willing to change course?

- Will my business advisors and investors support change?

STRATEGY 8 (BONUS): UNDERPROMISE AND OVERDELIVER—GIVE THEM MORE THAN THEY ASKED FOR

Like most consultants, my philosophy has always been to underpromise but to do everything within my power to deliver more than the client expected. In keeping with this philosophy, I have provided eight, instead of seven, strategies in an effort to overdeliver on the promise. Ideally, you will believe that you've gotten more value than you expected.

The eighth strategy is

Surround yourself with experts and seek support and education to ensure your success. You do not need to go down this path alone.

Are you ready? Do you have the passion, vision, and commitment required to make your business succeed? If you do, now let's see how well you really know your customers.

WORKSHEET 1.1

BUSINESS VISION AND GOALS WORKSHEET

Each member of your business should answer these questions, and then you should review the responses to see where your vision and goals are aligned and where they are disconnected.

What are the two most important business goals for our *company* to achieve in the next 6 months, 12 months, 2 years?

What are the two most important business goals for our *department* to achieve in the next 6 months, 12 months, 2 years?

What external challenges, if any, do we face in making these things happen?

What internal challenges, if any, do we face in making these things happen?

What three strategies have we already launched to achieve these goals?

(Worksheet continues on next page.)

Describe the target audience for our business, including what motivates people to buy from our company.

What are the top three problems that our business solves for our customers?

When prospects think about our company, what word(s) do we want to have pop into their heads?

Who are our main competitors, and how are they perceived by our customers and/or prospects?

What sets our business apart from our competitors'?

What are the main objections that we have heard from business prospects, and what steps have we taken to overcome them?

WORKSHEET 1.2

SEVEN STRATEGIES TO JUMP-START YOUR BUSINESS

QUESTIONS TO ASK YOURSELF

STRATEGY 1: WHERE AM I GOING?

Why do I want to start this business?

Is it the business idea that I love, or is it the idea of running the business?

What do I personally want to gain from the business?

What are my real strengths as an entrepreneur?

What are my limitations?

What is my directional strategy?

Where do I want the business to be three to five years from now?

Does this vision fit with my career goals?

STRATEGY 2: DOES THIS PATH FIT MY PERSONALITY AND LIFESTYLE?

Who do I want to be when I grow up?

(Worksheet continues on next page.)

Why am I doing this?

What will this do *for* me?

What will this do *to* me?

Will this business allow me to maintain my lifestyle?

Does this business fit my personality and interests?

STRATEGY 3: FINANCIAL REQUIREMENTS

Since many sources of funding are "one-time" and nonrepeatable, will I have enough money to launch my business?

How can I borrow, use, and spend only what I absolutely must until my business is up and running?

How can I defer as many expenses as possible until I am generating revenue?

What steps can I take to avoid losing ownership of my business at the early stage to partners, suppliers, consultants, or anybody else who is interested in owning a share of it?

Do I have the financial means to carry the business?

How will I support myself (and perhaps my family) until my business is profitable?

Can I get financial assistance from friends, venture capitalists, professional financiers and banks, family, angels, or others?

STRATEGY 4: BUSINESS FEASIBILITY

Have I thought through all the consequences of running the business?

How much do I really know about the industry and the competition?

Have I done all the work required to fully understand the challenges and opportunities in the marketplace?

How robust is my business idea?

What additional research do I need to conduct to determine if this is a bona fide business or just a great idea?

STRATEGY 5: IT'S *ALL* ABOUT YOUR CUSTOMERS

What is my call to action, and how will it get my customers to buy from me?

How well do I know my customers' needs?

Why do my customers buy from me?

Who are my most valuable customers?

Do these customers share common needs and characteristics that make it easier to identify them?

Why do these customers value my product or service?

How will I stay close to my customers?

(Worksheet continues on next page.)

STRATEGY 6: PUT TOGETHER THE BEST TEAM

Do I have an A or a B team?

Do the people on my team have the right mix of experience and skills, and are they in the right positions to support the goals of the company?

Do I know what the right mix is?

Have I outlined expectations clearly, set appropriate guidelines, and provided clear incentives to achieve the goals my business needs to not only survive, but to thrive?

Does my team have access to the right tools (software, hardware, and training) to get their jobs done to the highest standards of quality and delivery?

Why will the right people join me—what's in it for them?

What will I do if the team doesn't work out?

What type of business advisors do I need to launch this business?

How can I get customers or prospects involved in the business to serve as advisors?

What other types of support will help me succeed?

STRATEGY 7: FLEXIBILITY

Can I maintain my commitment to my business concept, model, and strategy if circumstances change?

Can I employ appropriate flexibility to adjust to changing market, environmental, and business demands?

Am I willing to adjust to evolving market, customer, and business demands?

How often can I change?

Is my team willing to change course?

Will my business advisors and investors support change?

STRATEGY 8: BONUS

What will I do to overdeliver to ensure that my customers are thrilled with the products and services that they receive from my company?

CHAPTER 2

DEVELOPING A CUSTOMER PROFILE

One secret of success in life is for a man to be ready for his opportunity when it comes.

—Benjamin Disraeli

During the Internet frenzy of the late 1990s, I worked with a publicly held company that had developed an impressive array of software products. It was a growing organization offering cutting-edge applications. I was hired to create a series of marketing brochures for the launch of a new communications tool.

I began this engagement by holding a meeting with the company's marketing team to better understand who the customers and prospects were. What I thought was a simple request for details about customers turned out to be a question for which no answers could be found. Why was this? Shouldn't the marketing team be able to give me detailed information about the company's customers? In this case, it couldn't do so because the marketing team and the salespeople did not share customer information. Each group had vital pieces of the customer puzzle, but they were not willing to share these pieces of data with each other, so there was no complete picture to be seen.

WHERE CUSTOMER KNOWLEDGE LIVES

In this company, the data "lived" only in the individual database and mind of the salesperson serving a target geographic market. For some unknown reason, these salespeople guarded their information like a closely held secret, keeping it from the marketing department. There may not have been actual locks and chains on the data, but for all intents and purposes, that was the situation. Therefore, creating a customer profile or defining the company's customers became a daunting task. I quickly realized that this company had greater challenges than the need for a few new brochures. It clearly needed an overhaul of its sales and marketing approach, with integration between the two groups.

Unfortunately, too many companies have similar breakdowns between the sales and marketing departments. Others haven't taken the time to research and really define who is using their products or services and for what purposes they are using them. This lack of crucial knowledge about customers can be detrimental to the success of any business. Ultimately, for any marketing program to work, the first step is to know who your customers are and why they value your company.

GETTING TO KNOW YOUR CUSTOMERS

How can you create products based on your customers' needs when you don't know who your customers are? The short answer is: you can't, or at least you can't do it very well. Clearly the best way to avoid a significant mistake like this is to ensure that the communication lines are open at every touch point with your customers. If your business has salespeople or customer service representatives, then make sure there is a system in place to collect their information and analyze it for trends in customer needs. To have a complete and accurate picture, these data must be received and communicated to and from all functions and levels within your organization.

Even if you're too small to have separate sales, marketing, and customer service departments, data about your customers still need to be collected. No business is so small that it can afford to lose such vital information. Simple customer relationship management (CRM) systems don't have to cost a lot of money and can prevent or plug up the holes through which data are leaking. Of course, even if you collect these data, you still need to make sure that they get into the hands of every person involved in making decisions related to meeting your customers' needs. This critical information will allow you to put together the pieces of your customer profiles.

CUSTOMER PROFILES

What's included in a customer profile? Basically profiles are descriptions of your customers' values, beliefs, and decision-making processes. It's important that you understand the products and services that you offer customers. But it's even more important that you understand *what* your customers value and *why* so that you can be certain that you are fulfilling those needs. Of course you need to know your products, but it's not the features of the products that are critical. It's the benefits that really matter, because they reflect what the products mean to your customers and how they satisfy their needs. That question can be answered only when you have a solid customer profile that demonstrates who your customers are and what is important to them.

KEY QUESTIONS TO CONSIDER

So, where do you begin? The first step is to answer some key questions about your customers:

- Who is your typical customer?

- What's important to your customers?

- Compared to what your competition offers, what makes your products or services more valuable to your customers?

- What are five common needs that your customers share?

- What are the top three problems that you solve for your customers?

- What opportunities are you creating for your customers when they purchase your products or services?

- What are your customers' decision-making processes (meaning, what issues do they consider before they purchase your products or services)?

- Why do your customers value your products and/or services?

- How do your customers find out about your products and/or services?

- If a consultant were to interview your top three customers, what would they say about your company? How would they describe your products and/or services?

- What influence does price play in your customers' decision to purchase products or services from you?

- What customer touch points exist in your business?

- What is the message conveyed at each of these touch points, and are these messages consistent?

Some of you may find it easy to answer these questions. Many of you, however, may find yourselves struggling. If so, you might be more focused on your products or services than you are on your customers. I recognize the fact that no one operates in an ideal world and that many companies have actually launched their businesses without completely understanding their customers' needs. However, you can sustain growth for only so long before this miscalculation begins to have a negative impact on your business. You must know your customers so that you can understand how your products, or rather the benefits of your products, satisfy their needs.

Let's consider a very simple business model. You are running a small coffee shop, and you believe that the reason customers frequent your shop is that you have the best coffee in town. However, the real reason they visit your shop is that they love the bagels. If you don't know this important piece of information and you decide to use a different bagel baker to save money, your revenue could decrease dramatically. On the other hand, if you understand how important the bagels are and recognize the lesser role the coffee plays, you could save money by switching to a less expensive coffee brand and avoid damaging your profit margin. That's valuable information to know, and it shows how important it is to base your strategy on meeting your customers' needs rather than on product options.

B2B VERSUS B2C

I'm often asked, "Is there a difference between B2B (business-to-business) and B2C (business-to-consumer) marketing?" Throughout this book, we will review marketing strategies and ideas for working with both types of customers. A B2B marketing strategy addresses the needs of a company that sells to other companies, such as a software firm that designs programs purchased by CIOs (chief information officers) of small organizations. A B2C marketing program involves a direct-to-consumer product, such as selling biscuits to dog owners.

If you are asking yourself the right questions to understand customers' motives, needs, and concerns, then the work you need to do to market to each group properly should not change. However, your questions may need to be slightly altered. For example, if you are trying to understand the needs of somebody purchasing dog biscuits, you may have only one decision maker to understand. However, if you're selling software, then your sale might be more complicated because you have users, purchasers, and other individuals whose influence on the final purchasing decision must be understood. Therefore, it's important to keep this in mind when defining your customers. However, just because you have a B2C strategy doesn't mean that the strategy is going to be simple. There can be just as many decision makers in a B2C situation as there are in a B2B one. Therefore, understanding how individuals make decisions is more important than the type of business model that you create.

PRODUCT INFORMATION FLOW

So, what is the best way to learn about your customers and their needs? Let's look at an ideal business model, where information flows back and forth. In this scenario, data move from the customer to the sales team to the marketing department and finally to the product development team, which then creates products and solutions designed to meet those customers' needs. Then the information should flow back to the sales team to allow the salespeople to do their job and sell the products.

You can use the information that you continually gather to develop products that meet your customers' needs as they change and evolve over time. This free flow of information from product development to customers and back will allow you to grow your business for the long term. Whether for a beauty salon or a software start-up, every business model will benefit from using this flow of information. This is guaranteed to be a much more effective approach than creating products without customer research to back them up.

Even the most experienced and sophisticated organizations don't always grasp the value of addressing customers' needs and how this contributes to growth. Ironically, analyzing and reacting to your customers' needs when developing products is easier than developing products based on engineers' or programmers' interests. So, why do so many companies get it backward? Because we've all been taught: product, product, product. One of my goals is to turn that notion upside down and show you how even a small business can develop an intimate understanding of its customers and, by doing so, better address their needs, without spending a fortune on research, consultants, or even technology.

GET OUT OF YOUR CHAIR AND OUT OF YOUR OFFICE

What is the best way to get inside the heads of your customers? Nothing beats the experience of simply getting out of your office and spending time with customers. Without doing that, it's impossible to truly understand what they value. Unfortunately, too many presidents, CEOs, and, yes, even marketing directors spend the majority of their time in their offices, caught up with the daily operations of their businesses, and miss amazing opportunities to be out there with their customers on a regular basis.

Without truly knowing what customers think, value, and want from you, you won't be able to grow and sustain your business. If you are currently a business owner, it is likely that you have figured out that the best way to understand your customers is to spend time with them, learning about the issues and challenges that they face. This is one of the fastest, and simplest, ways to grow your business. If you're not meeting with customers and prospects on a regular basis, then I challenge you to not waste any more time. Open up your calendar right now and include this critical activity in your "must do" list.

GETTING IT RIGHT AT THE BANK

Clearly, not all companies have lost their way when it comes to understanding customers' needs. One strong performer is Guilford Savings Bank (GSB), located in southern Connecticut. GSB relies on its image as a "hometown bank with a personal touch." When you call the bank, you immediately speak with a *real* person, not an automated voice system that directs you to push a number for service.

When I met Renee Pallenberg, the marketing director at GSB, the bank was searching for a firm to help it launch a customer telephone survey. The bank's managers were adamant about not exposing customers to anything that would have overtones of telemarketing, and they wanted to conduct their survey in-house, with bank employees making the calls.

We were able to develop a method of training the staff to conduct the survey, maintaining their strong customer-focused touch. The goal of the survey was to increase the managers' knowledge of how the bank met and did not meet its customers' expectations. They were interested in every aspect of the bank's relationship with its customers, including interactions with tellers, customer service representatives, and bank executives.

The results of the survey confirmed the bank's commitment to taking care of its customers' needs. Its customers gave it an almost perfect score: 4.9 out of 5.0 for employees' professionalism and courtesy, and an overall satisfaction ranking of 4.8 out of 5.0. In the banking industry, that's practically unheard of. Clearly GSB's customer-focused philosophy works; managers listened to feedback about services that their customers desired and spent the next year addressing those—until it was time to launch the survey again. The managers created a continual loop of information, flowing from product/service development and delivery to customer needs and back again. That's the type of information flow that is critical if a business is to succeed.

This flow of information must not be a one-time event. It is something that must happen intensely on an annual or biennial basis. It's essential to have systems in place that provide your company with timely feedback. For example, many companies, including GSB, conduct exit surveys with customers who leave to ensure that the reason they are leaving is not related to a problem at the bank. This system ensures that you don't wait a year or longer before discovering a trend or a recurring problem or need that is unfulfilled.

Every quarter, PricewaterhouseCoopers conducts a survey on business trends, entitled Trendsetter Barometer. In one survey, it interviewed 402 CEOs of companies identified by the media as the fastest-growing U.S. businesses over the last five years. The goal was to find out what these CEOs believed would bring the most profitable returns on their investments. The categories that received the highest rankings were (1) quality of service to customers, (2) product improvements or extensions, (3) information technology, (4) advertising and sales, and (5) new product lines. "Quality of service to customers" was cited by 87 percent as being very important to growth, with 63 percent ranking it as one of the top three factors in terms of importance to growth. These successful CEOs clearly understood that customer service is the key to rapid growth, high ROI, and profitability.

DOING IT YOURSELF

You may be thinking to yourself, "I'd love to run a customer survey and learn what my customers think about me, but how can you expect me to do this when I can't afford to hire a marketing firm? Can I really do it myself?" Of course you can. In fact, the more personalized the approach, the more effective the survey is likely to be, as customers will recognize that it's you asking them, not a third party who doesn't necessarily speak their language. Of course, if you do hire a marketing firm to assist you, then it's critical that you be involved in the development, use of language, and delivery of the survey to ensure that your customers feel a strong connection with your company.

Throughout this book, you will hear stories about many companies, including those of undercapitalized entrepreneurs and poor graduate students, that successfully conducted research and launched surveys and focus groups on a modest budget.

First, let's review the types of questions that you need to answer about your customers:

- *Pain points/challenges*. Except in the health-care industry, "customer pain" does not refer to a true physical pain, but refers instead to a problem or challenge that must be fixed. What pain can you resolve for your customers?

- *Opportunities*. Does your product open doors for your customers or offer them the ability to further grow their businesses? Are you creating an opportunity for them to improve their lives? What are you helping them do better? How can you move up the value chain?

- *Location*. Is your business located in a place that's convenient for your customers or makes sense for their lifestyle? Sometimes businesses open a storefront because they got a really good deal on the monthly rent or because it's the only location they can afford. If your customers can't find you, whether you're on the street or in the virtual community of the Internet, then it doesn't matter how targeted your products and services are.

- *Behavior and decision-making processes*. What behaviors or habits influence your customers' purchasing process? Do your customers need specific information before they make a decision? Do they conduct a lot of research before they purchase your product, or is your product an impulse purchase? Is timing a factor? Who is involved in the purchase decision? Do you know who their customers are?

■ *Spending patterns.* Do certain times of year influence your customers' spending patterns? Does a lifestyle change, such as getting married or having a baby, influence their decision?

■ *Price sensitivity.* How much does price influence your customers' decision? How important is their perception of the value of your product linked to the price? You can price too high or too low, so you need to be careful in answering this question. What are the trade-offs between price, features, and performance?

Let's say you're the owner of a dog-walking service called Biscotti's Canine Encounters. Your day begins at dawn with your first round of visits to your customers' homes to walk their canine companions. You work throughout the day, walking and playing with these beloved pooches, and wrap up around 6 p.m. with your final visits. Here's how you might address these questions:

■ *Pain points/challenges.* Your customers (the pet owners, not the dogs) hate to leave their pets alone all day while they go to work. There is real angst involved with this separation, so you help ease their tension by providing their much-loved dogs with the opportunity to frolic with other dogs and relieve their bladders. You might even be preventing the dogs from destroying their owners' homes if they have separation anxiety and hate being left alone.

■ *Opportunities.* You're allowing the owners the opportunity to maintain hectic schedules, and sometimes even their jobs, because they know that their pets are cared for during the day. You provide peace of mind for the owners, who can come home each evening to happy, well-exercised dogs.

■ *Location.* Your customers are primarily unmarried thirtysomethings living in condos in a city. Since understanding where they live and work plays an important role in where and how you offer your services, you have built your business by networking with folks in condominiums and apartments where dogs are allowed and with providers of other convenience-oriented services that are promoted to this target group (e.g., dry cleaning pickup services like Zoots that focus on the same types of individuals).

- *Behavior and decision-making processes.* You have found that most of your customers rely on their veterinarians to help them find support for their dogs, but that some also work with local animal trainers. They also shop in pet boutiques and rarely go to large pet stores like Petco to look for solutions to their canine dilemmas. This can help you build your business by understanding the sources they rely on when they make decisions.

- *Spending patterns.* Most of your customers have dogs that are at least a year old, but a few have puppies and are looking for services for the first time. You make sure you know the time of year when most puppies are born to help you determine when you might be getting new customers. You have also learned that wintertime is more stressful for your customers' pets, and they tend to require your services more than they do in the summer. This is important in terms of staffing your business.

- *Price sensitivity.* These owners will spend a significant portion of their disposable income on their pets, since they fill the role of beloved children. Therefore, you need to make sure that you're not priced too low or your customers' perception of the value that you offer is likely to be diminished, leading them to wonder if you are qualified or any good at your job, and if they can really trust you with their companion.

Even in a simple business model like running a dog-walking service, you can see that the questions are not difficult to answer. The tricky part is figuring out what questions to ask *without* assuming that you know the answers.

FROM DOG WALKERS TO INTERNATIONAL ENGINE COMPONENT MANUFACTURERS

How easy is it to get these data? If you spend time thinking creatively about how you can get in front of prospects or customers to ask them the right questions, then it shouldn't be that complicated. For example, I recently conducted a customer survey with a client of mine who has been in the engine components industry in Europe for many years. The company is well established but had just recently begun conducting customer surveys on a regular basis. I met with the company's managers to discuss the annual survey and suggested adding a few more customer-focused questions, such as, "What publications do you read before making purchasing decisions?" My client had not thought about asking that type of question because the company was very focused on getting feedback about how its products met its customers' needs.

When the surveys were compiled, the responses to the question "What publications do you read before making purchasing decisions?" completely surprised my client. He was not advertising or publishing articles in a specific journal because of his personal impression that it wasn't highly regarded in the industry. Just looking at the publication, I would have agreed with him. However, his customers let us know that this specific journal was their greatest source of information before they made purchasing decisions. Now he had to think about how many other assumptions he was accidentally making without validation from customers. The good news was that it wasn't very difficult to correct this mistake. We simply needed to ask the right questions. Once we recognized the importance of this publication to customers, my client began advertising in the publication and providing potential new customers with knowledge about the company that they didn't have access to before. He also learned that he should not make assumptions about customer behaviors and decision-making processes.

LESSONS LEARNED

It is important that you think beyond your preconceived notions about your customers' values and interests and make a strong, concerted effort to learn their true needs so that you can better serve them. You clearly don't need to hire a marketing consultant to think of questions to ask. You simply need to modify your thinking and focus on what you *don't* know or perhaps what you assume you know about your customers. It's important that you be objective about your business. Be careful that you aren't so close to your product that you start to see your own assumptions as universal truths. That is one of the greatest dangers a marketing manager or anybody responsible for customer outreach can make. It creates barriers to understanding who your customers are and inhibits growth.

CHECK IN WITH YOUR CUSTOMERS

Even if you've been in business for a number of years, it's critical that you constantly *check in* with your customers to see how their needs have changed over time. There are many variables that influence customers' needs over time, and you need to be aware of those current and future needs if you are to grow your business. Simply take the time to step back and look at your business objectively. Force yourself to ask your customers questions about their needs, even if you are 100 percent convinced that you know the answers. I suspect some of the responses will surprise you. We'll review specific questions related to conducting research and creating surveys in Milestone 2.

Before you complete the worksheets that accompany this chapter, let's examine the various sources you can use to obtain customer information, often referred to as customer touch points. They involve getting information internally as well as externally and include the following:

- Your sales team

- Inbound/outbound call centers

- Web sites and blogs

- Point of sale

- Surveys

- E-mail communication

- Accounts payable

- Shipping departments

- Research and development

- Marketing literature

- Direct-mail campaigns

- Exhibit material

- Advertisements

We'll review these in depth throughout the book. However, you will note that the common thread is that all of these sources are points where you connect with your customers. Where do you connect with your customers? Begin to create a list; depending on the complexity of your business, you may be surprised at how many touch points there are. Obviously these vary from business to business, but the basic information that you need to uncover remains consistent.

(Worksheets start on next page.)

WORKSHEET 2.1

DEVELOPING A CUSTOMER PROFILE

Who is your typical customer? In 50 words or less, describe your most valuable customer(s).

What's important to your customers?

Compared to what your competition offers, what makes your products or services more valuable to your customers?

What are five common needs that your customers share?

1.

2.

3.

4.

5.

What are the top three problems that you solve for your customers?

1.

2.

3.

What opportunities are you creating for your customers when they purchase your products or services?

What issues do your customers consider before they purchase your products or services?

Why do your customers value your products and/or services?

How do your customers find out about your products and/or services?

If a consultant were to interview your top three customers, what would they say about your company? How would they describe your products and/or services?

How does pricing influence your customers' decision to purchase products or services from you?

List all of the customer touch points that exist in your business and the message that is communicated to your customers at each point. These may include

Touch Point (communication point with customer)	Message Relayed About Your Company and How You Value Your Customers
Your sales team	
Inbound/outbound call centers	
Web sites and blogs	
Point of sale	
Surveys	
E-mail communication	
Accounts payable	
Shipping departments	
Research and development	
Marketing literature	

(Worksheet continues on next page.)

Touch Point (communication point with customer)	Message Relayed About Your Company and How You Value Your Customers
Direct-mail campaigns	
Exhibit material	
Advertisements	
Other _____	
Other _____	

Are the messages conveyed at these touch points consistent with the value you provide? If not, why not and what can you do to solve that problem?

Describe the flow of information in your company from customers to sales, marketing, and operations/development. How does this affect your decision-making strategies?

WORKSHEET 2.2

CUSTOMER QUESTIONS TO ASK

Pain points/challenges. What pain can you resolve for your customers?

Opportunities. Does your product open doors for your customers or offer them the ability to further grow their businesses? Are you creating an opportunity for them to improve their lives? What are you helping them do better? How can you move up the value chain?

Location. Is your business located in a place that's convenient for your customers or makes sense for their lifestyle?

Behavior and decision-making processes. What behaviors or habits influence your customers' purchasing process? Do your customers need specific information before they make a decision? Do they conduct a lot of research before they purchase your product, or is your product an impulse purchase? Is timing a factor? Who is involved in the purchase decision? Do you know who their customers are?

Spending patterns. Do certain times of year influence your customers' spending patterns? Does a lifestyle change influence their decision (e.g., such as getting married or having a baby)?

Price sensitivity. How much does price influence your customers' decision? How important is their perception of the value of your product linked to the price? What are the trade-offs between price, features, and performance?

CHAPTER 3

DETERMINING CUSTOMER LIFETIME VALUE

There are no secrets to success. It is the result of preparation, hard work, and learning from failure.

—Colin Powell

At the end of George Orwell's *Animal Farm*, the farm animals come to live by a single commandment, "All animals are equal, but some animals are more equal than others." The same might be said about your customers. Not that I'm comparing your customers to animals, but some of them are more equal, or shall we say more important, than others. Being able to identify those who provide greater value to you is critical to your success.

INEQUALITY

Does it make you uncomfortable to think about your customers as being "unequal"? When starting a business, it is only natural to think that having more customers means greater success. Unfortunately, this isn't always true. For many businesses, there are certain customers who cost more money to obtain or to keep than they are worth. They have a low ROI (return on investment). The example that follows illustrates how different customers with different returns to your business affect your growth.

Dan, a computer networking expert, had a split fee structure, charging his clients either an annual retainer (which ensured 24-hour support for any network problems they had) or a fixed project fee for specific projects. His clients ranged from very small businesses with fewer than 10 employees to firms with 75 to 100 employees. When Dan first launched his business, he networked at local business association meetings to establish a client base. He hadn't really focused on any specific target market. He simply wanted to get as many clients as possible, and he reasoned that the more clients he had, the greater his profitability would be. As his business grew, however, he discovered key differences between the two groups of clients he had acquired. Many of his small business clients were on retainer, and some of these clients were demanding a significant amount of his time to service their accounts. Since he was being paid through a retainer, the actual hourly rate that Dan was earning from them was less than half the rate he charged the project-based clients. On the other hand, it took a lot more time and effort to locate and close deals with these project-based clients (where his hourly fee was based entirely upon the effort required).

Dan wasn't sure where he should focus his time, so we calculated the "lifetime value" of his clients. We discovered that although obtaining the project-based clients took more time and effort and their projects required a lot of time to complete, these clients generated a significantly higher return on his marketing investment than the retainer clients. Next, we studied each of Dan's services to figure out if any of them naturally lent themselves to additional follow-on projects that could produce supplementary revenue from his established client base. These were legitimate services that made sense for his clients and simply required Dan to present these options to them. We uncovered a few new profit centers, but Dan couldn't offer these services without additional staff, and he wasn't ready to add employees. Finally, we analyzed the size of his clients' businesses and the industries they were in. We determined that midsize service firms like law firms and medical practices were generating the greatest revenue for his business.

This was an enlightening process. It helped Dan rethink the value that each of his customers provided to him. It also gave him the opportunity to reflect on how he was spending his "marketing" time so that he could better align his marketing efforts with his business goals. As a result, he stopped attending general business association meetings and began focusing on attracting midsize companies in the service industries through a direct sales effort. He spent less time and money on his marketing effort and more time with his clients, and he began to land additional clients who provided him with a greater ROI. In addition, as his business grew, he was able to contemplate hiring employees so he that could offer more services to his current clients. Dan clearly had a valuable service-based business that was greatly enhanced by developing a better understanding of his customers and their lifetime value to him.

FINDING YOUR IDEAL CUSTOMER

Let's step back for a minute and discuss the customer profile you developed in the previous chapter. Are you satisfied with your ability to create a profile? Was this process more difficult than you anticipated, or were you able to answer all of the questions? The task of creating customer profiles can be quite challenging. If it was relatively easy for you, then you're among the fortunate ones: your business has customers who are virtual clones of one another. Good for you. Your task is much easier. But for many businesses, their customer base has more diversity than they expected. This makes the task that much more challenging, and frequently more rewarding.

How do you filter out those prospects that are not right for your organization? All that's required is some simple math calculations. Let's review how much value each customer brings to your organization. First, note that there are three basic ways for you to increase your organization's sales revenue:

1. Increase the number of customers you serve

2. Increase the sales revenue generated by each customer

3. Increase the frequency of each customer's transactions with your company

Is it really that simple? Yes and no. There are always going to be additional factors that influence your growth, such as the cost of serving a customer once you have landed the account, as we saw in Dan's case. However, understanding how these three basic concepts affect your company will help you understand the importance of constantly reviewing and analyzing your customers' needs to increase your value to those customers.

Let's look at an example showing the three ways previously mentioned in which you can grow your business: increasing the number of customers, increasing the sales revenue per customer, and increasing the frequency of customers' transactions. Basically this refers to how many customers you have now, how much they spend with you over a period of time (usually a year is a good benchmark), and how often they purchase from you (perhaps once a year or once a week).

JACQUI'S SHOE BOUTIQUE

To really understand how these concepts work with your knowledge of your customer, let's study the following example from Jacqui's Shoe Boutique, an upscale shoe store located in Boston, Massachusetts.

Sales Potential for Jacqui's Shoe Boutique

Jacqui's Shoe Boutique	Number of Customers	Average Sales/Visit	Visits/ Purchases per Year	Sales Revenue	Growth
Current	100	$200	2 visits	$40,000	
10% increase	110	$220	2.2 visits	$53,240	+33%
15% increase	115	$230	2.3 visits	$60,835	+52%
10% decrease	90	$180	1.8 visits	$29,160	-27%

Jacqui currently has 100 customers who shop at her store an average of twice a year and spend an average of $200 each time they visit. So, each customer spends $400, which generates total sales revenue of $40,000 each year.

100 customers x $200 sales x 2 visits = $40,000

Let's say you have been hired as a top-gun marketing consultant to help Jacqui grow her business. You are confident that you can improve these figures, so you create a direct-mail piece (we won't include that cost so as to keep this model simple). Your marketing effort pays off and generates a 10 percent increase in each of the following areas: the number of customers Jacqui has, the amount they spend each visit, and their frequency of visits. By increasing all three variables by 10 percent each, you would intuitively expect to generate a 30 percent growth in revenue. However, you benefit from a multiplier effect, and you generate a 33 percent increase.

110 customers x $210 sales x 2.2 visits = $53,240

53,240/40,000 = 1.33 or 133%

This scenario demonstrates how important it is to understand customers' motivations and values so that you can focus your efforts on increasing their satisfaction with your business and concurrently improve their value to you.

MULTIPLIER EFFECT

If you've ever been in a room with young children, you quickly realize that two children do not make twice as much noise as one, but rather they seem to triple the cacophony of sound emanating from the room. While this phenomenon is apparent with children, it is not so obvious in a business environment. Therefore, you need to understand how to increase the *euphonious sound* of your own cash register.

How can you do this? Let's look back at our first example. After Dan identified his customers' lifetime value, he had information that he could use to grow his business. Before, he had been basically shooting from the hip in terms of his marketing strategy. Knowledge is power, and after uncovering knowledge about his customers, Dan was empowered by having two options: seek new customers (which he chose to do) or increase the amount of revenue his current customers were generating by adding services. This formula gave him control over his decisions. It can also empower your business, giving you real knowledge that you can use to make logical and aligned marketing decisions.

DETERMINING WHAT A CUSTOMER IS WORTH TO YOU

What is customer lifetime value? This formula calculates how much revenue *each* customer generates for you. This number includes not only the customer's own purchases, but also the purchases of individuals whom he or she refers. In some businesses this referral amount may be small. But in businesses that operate on heavy volume and rely on customers "telling friends" about their products or services, this can have a significant impact on success or failure.

The table on the next page outlines the individual impact that each customer has on Jacqui's business. We'll read this table from the upper left corner and then head down. Let's begin with Jacqui's current situation. As you can see in the column called "Current Situation," her shoe business is doing well, and her average sale is $200 per visit with two visits/purchases per year. Each customer stays with her for five years (on average), providing her with gross sales of $2,000 over the customer's lifetime.

$200 sales x 2 visits/year x 5 years = $2,000

Jacqui's customers are also very satisfied and refer three new prospects during their lifetimes; 75 percent of these referred prospects become customers. This generates an additional $4,500 in sales revenue.

3 prospects x 75% x $2,000 sales = $4,500

Therefore the total value of one satisfied customer is $6,500, which consists of the $2,000 that the customer spends plus the $4,500 that the customer's referrals generate. Now, if Jacqui can increase the amount of money that each typical customer spends or the frequency of these visits, this increase will have a strong bottom-line impact on her business. If she increases the amount of money each customer spends by just 12 percent, her customer's lifetime value increases to $7,280. However, if she can increase both sales revenue and frequency by 12 percent each, her customer's individual lifetime value will increase more than 25 percent, from $6,500 to $8,154.

Individual Customer Lifetime Value

Individual Impact Each Customer Has on Your Business	Current Situation	12% Sales Increase	12% Sales Increase + 12% Frequency Increase
Average sale amount	$200	$224	$224
Visits per year per customer	2	2	2.24
Number of years customer buys from you	5	5	5
Gross sales per customer per year	$400	$448	$502
Gross sales over customer's lifetime	$2,000	$2,240	$2,509
Number of referrals per customer	3	3	3
Percent of referrals who become customers	75%	75%	75%

(Continued on next page.)

Individual Customer Lifetime Value (Continued)

Individual Impact Each Customer Has on Your Business	Current Situation	12% Sales Increase	12% Sales Increase + 12% Frequency Increase
Number of referrals who become customers	2.25	2.25	2.25
Five-year gross sales from new referrals	$4,500	$5,040	$5,645
Total value of satisfied customer	$6,500	$7,280	$8,154

Now imagine how much more money Jacqui will generate if she can increase the total number of customers visiting her store. The possibilities are endless. How does marketing influence this? Let's say Jacqui realizes that a certain brand of shoes is very popular among 30- to 45-year-old business professionals. If she increases the variety of shoes that she offers to these key customers and does a monthly mailing to them promoting this shoe, then she can increase not only the number of times her customers visit the store but also the number of shoes that they purchase. This increases their average sale amount and hopefully increases their referral rates because Jacqui understands their needs and the needs of their friends and colleagues. This scenario should help convince Jacqui, and you, that knowing what drives your customers to buy from you will have a strong and lasting impact upon your business.

CUSTOMER DIFFERENTIATION

Naturally, your business model and the type of customers that you attract play a critical role in your revenue model. Therefore, the final step in analyzing your customers' value to your business begins with understanding how different businesses view their customers. The figure that follows shows customer needs relative to their value to your business.

■ On the horizontal axis, we have "Customer Needs," reflecting what *customers want* from you.

- On the vertical axis is "Customer Value to Your Business." This refers to what *you get* from your customers.

How these two elements relate to your business plays an important role in determining your marketing strategy.

Customer Value to Your Business	A Online Cookie Store	B Dan's Networking Consulting Practice
Highly Differentiated		
Similar	C Cookie Kiosk	D Marketing Edge Consulting Group, LLC
	Similar	Highly Differentiated

Customer Needs

Let's review the four quadrants, beginning with Quadrant A: Online Cookie Store. This business sells cookies online, and it has a wide range of customers whose needs it serves. Some individual customers buy a few cookies each year, and other customers are major businesses like restaurants or schools that buy thousands of cookies each month.

- *Customer needs.* The business provides the same product to each customer, except in varying amounts, so the needs are quite similar (there's no variety in the actual product).

- *Customer value to your business.* The value of these different customer groups to the business varies tremendously and is therefore highly differentiated. In terms of pure revenue generated, the major purchasers are much more valuable to you than the individual purchasers.

Now let's look at Quadrant B: Dan's Networking Consulting Practice. Dan offers networking consulting practices to a variety of clients.

- *Customer needs.* Dan's clients have very different needs.

- *Customer value to your business.* Their value to him is very different.

Next is Quadrant C: Cookie Kiosk. This kiosk in the mall sells one type of chocolate chip cookie, and 99 percent of its customers buy only one or two cookies on each trip to the mall.

- *Customer needs.* Customers have very similar needs.

- *Customer value to your business.* Customers have very similar value to the business.

We finally come to Quadrant D: Marketing Edge Consulting Group, LLC. As a marketing consultant, I have a variety of clients ranging from small start-ups to midsize manufacturers and financial institutions.

- *Customer needs.* Each client hires me for a different reason. Some clients require a marketing plan; others simply want to launch a survey, create a brochure, or conduct research. Therefore, my clients' needs are highly differentiated.

- *Customer value to your business.* I have a mix of clients with varying demands and working styles. I don't necessarily prefer the clients with simple projects, since I have discovered that the more challenging projects can be the most rewarding. As a result, I prefer a mix. Therefore, my overall rating of my customers' value to me falls into the *similar* box, but it is close to the border of the *differentiated* box.

WHY BOTHER?

You may be asking why determining your business's quadrant even matters. Dan didn't think it mattered at first. He initially believed that his clients gave him the same value regardless of the services they purchased from him. Once he recognized the truth about his clients' unique value, he was empowered to adjust his marketing and business strategy. This gave him more time to focus on expanding his relationships with those clients who were able to generate the most revenue for his business.

Learning your position on this chart will empower your decision-making ability and help you better focus your marketing strategy. The greater the difference in the value you receive from your customers (some customers are more equal than others) and the more individual or differentiated their needs are, the more customized your marketing tactics need to be. This should influence all of your marketing campaigns, since you want to ensure that you spend your limited time focusing on the customers who will help you succeed in the shortest amount of time.

WORKSHEET 3.1

CUSTOMER LIFETIME VALUE (LTV) FORM

Complete this for each target customer. You may need to make multiple calculations, depending on the variety of your clients.

Target Customer #1 _____

A. How much does your target customer spend on each purchase from your
    company? $_____

B. Annually, how often does your customer make a purchase from your
    company? _____

C. How many years does your customer stay with your company? _____

D. How many new customers will he or she refer to your business? _____

E. What percentage of referrals become clients? _____%

    A $_____ x B_____ x C_____ = gross sales over customer's lifetime
    $_____ (F)

    D _____ x E_____% x F $_____ = gross sales from new
    referrals $_____ (G)

    F $_____ + G $_____ = total lifetime value of a satisfied
    customer $_____

(Worksheet continues on next page.)

Target Customer #2 _____

A. How much does your target customer spend on each purchase from your company? $_____

B. Annually, how often does your customer make a purchase from your company? _____

C. How many years does your customer stay with your company? _____

D. How many new customers will he or she refer to your business? _____

E. What percentage of referrals become clients? _____%

    A $_____ x B_____ x C_____ = gross sales over customer's lifetime
    $_____ (F)

    D _____ x E_____% x F $_____ = gross sales from new
    referrals $_____ (G)

    F $_____ + G $_____ = total lifetime value of a satisfied
    customer $_____

WORKSHEET 3.2

TOTAL INDIVIDUAL VALUE OF A SATISFIED CUSTOMER

In the first column, calculate your present situation based on your current customers' behavior from Worksheet 3.1, including sales amount, visits per year, the number of years they buy from you, and their referrals to your business.

Next, see what happens when you increase by 10 percent their individual sales amount, frequency of purchase, or years they stay with your company. You can also do this for smaller or higher percentages. This will give you both the current and the future total value of a satisfied customer.

	Current Situation	10% Sales Increase	10% Increase in Frequency of Purchase	10% Increase in Number of Years They Buy from You
Average sale amount				
Visits per year per customer				
Number of years customer buys from you				
Gross sales per customer per year				
Gross sales over customer's lifetime				
Number of referrals per customer				

(Worksheet continues on next page.)

	Current Situation	10% Sales Increase	10% Increase in Frequency of Purchase	10% Increase in Number of Years They Buy from You
Percent of referrals who become customers				
Number of referrals who become customers				
Five-year gross sales from new referrals				
Total value of satisfied customer				

WORKSHEET 3.3

CUSTOMER GROWTH PROJECTION

Using the figures from your customer lifetime value, let's determine how you can grow your business.

A. How much does your target customer spend on each purchase from your company? $_____

B. Annually, how often does your customer make a purchase from your company? _____

C. How many years does your customer stay with your company? _____

    A $_____ x B_____ x C_____ = gross sales revenue per year $_____

Which of these factors can be easily manipulated to grow your business?

Identify three strategies that you could deploy that will have a dramatic impact on your potential customers and increase your value to them.

1. Strategy_____

   _____

   Impact:

   Amount spent by each customer increased by _____%.

   Frequency of purchase by each customer increased by _____%.

   Number of total customers increased by _____%.

(Worksheet continues on next page.)

2. Strategy_____

    _____

    Impact:

    Amount spent by each customer increased by _____%.

    Frequency of purchase by each customer increased by _____%.

    Number of total customers increased by _____%.

3. Strategy_____

    _____

    Impact:

    Amount spent by each customer increased by _____%.

    Frequency of purchase by each customer increased by _____%.

    Number of total customers increased by _____%.

Situation	Number of Customers	Average Sales per Year	Frequency per Year	Sales Revenue	Growth %
Current					
1. _____% increase					
2. _____% increase					
3. _____% increase					

WORKSHEET 3.4

CUSTOMER DIFFERENTIATION WORKSHEET

Name the top three customer needs that you fulfill.

1.

2.

3.

List the different customer groups that you have and the value they provide to you.

1.

2.

3.

Plot your position on the chart below, thinking about your customers' need in terms of how they relate to each other (are they very similar or very different?) and also how different their value is to your business.

Customer Value to Your Business	A	B
Highly Differentiated		
Similar	C	D
	Similar	Highly Differentiated

Customer Needs

How does your position on this chart influence your marketing strategy?

What can you do to increase your most important customers' value to your business?

MILESTONE 2

RESEARCH ON AN ENTREPRENEUR'S BUDGET

The goal of conducting research is to uncover important and previously unknown knowledge about your customers and the marketplace. Milestone 2 focuses on the various methods you can employ to gather this information and turn it into knowledge that will help you grow your business. We begin with a discussion of the types of questions you should be asking and the data you should seek. The key lesson to learn is how to increase your chances of obtaining consistent and valuable responses that will assist you in making essential business decisions. In Chapter 5, we cover primary research techniques that will help you reveal and recognize critical information and explain the value of customer surveys conducted on a tight budget. We wrap up this milestone by showing you how you can improve the reliability of your data and study the before and after versions of an actual survey conducted by an entrepreneur.

The worksheets included in Milestone 2 are:

- ■ Worksheet 4.1: Customer Information Checklist

- ■ Worksheet 4.2: Customer Information Framework

- ■ Worksheet 5.1: Survey Design

- ■ Worksheet 5.2: Survey Questions

- ■ Worksheet 6.1: Survey Success Checklist

CHAPTER 4

TURNING DATA INTO KNOWLEDGE

Searching is half the fun: life is much more manageable when thought of as a scavenger hunt as opposed to a surprise party.

—**Jimmy Buffett**

Many small businesses and entrepreneurs protest that they don't have the funds required to conduct customer research. My response is simple: you're wrong. The fact is, you don't need the budget of Coca-Cola or Microsoft to conduct "proper" market research. Research can be conducted with very limited funds as long as you clearly identify the specific information you need in order to make vital business decisions and develop a concrete plan to achieve these objectives.

STANDARD RESEARCH TECHNIQUES

You may already be familiar with some of the research practices used by marketers to understand and define their customers and prospects. These include focus groups, surveys, concept testing, market analysis, segmentation, and many others. All are time-tested ways of better understanding your customers and your market opportunities. However, when conducted by professional research firms, these techniques can be quite expensive and can quickly drain an entrepreneur's budget. Since many managers assume that they must hire professionals to conduct these activities in order to feel confident with the data, market research techniques are sometimes overlooked or skipped entirely in the start-up phase of a business. I've had several business owners tell me, "Well, I can't afford to hire a consultant or research group. Besides, I already understand the market well enough, so why waste time and money? I'm not going to find out anything I don't already know." My goal in this chapter is to dispel this widely held false impression and help you define what information you need, what questions you need to ask, and how to turn the data into knowledge so that you can make wiser business decisions.

TURNING INFORMATION INTO KNOWLEDGE

In Milestone 1, we defined information that you need to have about your customers and/or prospects. However, it is important to note that the essential element that separates the successful companies from the struggling ones is their ability to turn this *information* about customers' needs into *knowledge* that can be used to make sound business decisions. Information and knowledge are vastly different. Simple facts alone cannot help you grow your business. You need to turn those facts—the raw data— into knowledge by adding your own analysis and research, and then use this knowledge to create value for your business. If you cannot use the knowledge effectively, then conducting the research is not worth your time and effort because it won't help your business grow. In fact, it might actually harm your business because raw data used improperly can lead to very poor business decisions. I say this not to discourage you from conducting research and creating knowledge but instead to emphasize the importance of not merely conducting the research but of also using the knowledge wisely to benefit your business.

Information ➔ Knowledge ➔ Value ➔ Growth

EVEN THE SMARTEST MAKE MISTAKES

Before we talk specifically about research techniques, let me share a story about a former client's experience with research. A few years ago, he and his fiancée identified a gap in the market for designer laptop bags for professional women and decided that a survey would be a good way to learn more about the interest in the market for this product. This client is a bright and talented entrepreneur who is always coming up with new and interesting ideas for products and who has been quite successful in his career. He decided that if he and his fiancée could clearly identify the type of bag or bags that women would want, they might be able to develop a thriving business. Sounds logical, right? He asked me to participate in an online survey that he had written and provide him with feedback about the survey. His goal was to use the survey to determine the feasibility of his idea. He launched his survey and received hundreds of responses. Here are just a few of the several dozen questions that appeared on the survey:

1. Do you carry your laptop often?

2. Do you like pockets on your bag? Do you like them on the inside or the outside of the bag? Both or not at all?

3. What kind of handle does your laptop bag have (hand carry, strap, backpack)? Which do you prefer?

At first glance, his questions might appear to be on target, but when you ask yourself what he will do with the answers, you begin to realize that he wasted a lot of his valuable and limited time developing this survey, since the answers could not give him the information he needed to identify market demand.

VAGUE QUESTIONS MADE SPECIFIC

Regardless of the research method you use, the most critical first step is figuring out what knowledge you want to gain so that you ask the right questions. Let's study the questions my client asked to learn what was, and what was not, achieved with his research technique. Question 1, "Do you carry your laptop often?" is very vague. The answer anyone will provide will depend entirely on how she personally defines the word *often*. If I think *often* is once a month and the next respondent believes it is twice a day, then the answers are going to be irrelevant and misleading because my client did not define *often* for his participants. There are two possible consequences of this vagueness. First, my client may realize that the question is useless, and that he's wasted time and money preparing a pointless question. Or, second, he may use his own definition of *often* to reach a conclusion about the frequency with which women carry a laptop bag, in which case he is making a costly business decision based on an incorrect understanding of market demand. Neither possibility is helpful. An alternative question could be the following:

1. How often do you carry your laptop with you (daily, two to three times a week, once a week, a few times a month, less than once a month)?

This is much more specific and will begin to give him the knowledge that he is seeking.

Now let's look at question 2, "Do you like pockets on your bag? Do you like them on the inside or the outside of the bag? Both or not at all?" This reminds me of a riddle from a Dr. Seuss book. There are too many things being asked in this question, and this will cause confusion for the respondent, who might simply be answering one or two of the questions. If the respondents don't answer in complete sentences, then you won't know if an affirmative response implied that they like pockets on the inside, the outside, both, or not at all. This question should have been broken down into multiple questions. For example, my client could have asked the following:

2. On a scale of 1 to 5 (with 1 being not very important and 5 being very important), how would you rank the importance of the following accessories as part of your laptop bag?

- Pockets on the outside   1 2 3 4 5

- Pockets on the inside   1 2 3 4 5

- Place for keys   1 2 3 4 5

This series of questions allows him to explore the importance of many types of bag accessories. He can add a variety of features to gauge how important they are to the respondents and compare them with one another to facilitate the design process (if he moves ahead with the business).

Finally, the third question, "What kind of handle does your laptop bag have (hand carry, strap, backpack)? Which do you prefer?" asks respondents about their current handles. This implies that respondents have a preference for one handle style over another. Perhaps they don't care about the handle. The question does not ask if they like their current option, and my client doesn't know if the handle is even important in the decision-making process. If you ask participants how important the handle is and give them the ability to rank their interest and preferences about this feature, then you may end up with better data—data that you can actually use to make business decisions. Questions my client could have used include these:

3. On a scale of 1 to 5, how important is the handle in terms of its style?
   1 2 3 4 5

4. On a scale of 1 to 5, how important is the handle in terms of its functionality? 1 2 3 4 5

5. Please rank the likelihood of your purchasing a bag with the following handle styles (1 = not very likely and 5 = very likely):

- Hand carry   1 2 3 4 5
- Strap   1 2 3 4 5
- Backpack style   1 2 3 4 5

It's important to ask how different features will affect customers' decisions to purchase an item. It's not only what they like, but how likely they are to *act upon* that value or interest.

ASKING THE RIGHT QUESTIONS

By having a clear sense of the information you're trying to obtain and phrasing your questions specifically to elicit those data, you will avoid receiving inconsistent or erroneous responses that could lead you to make disastrous business decisions. This is true with every type of research that you conduct, from running a survey and interviewing prospects to conducting online and offline research. In fact, making a decision based on gut instinct or no information at all could actually be less harmful than making a decision based on inaccurate information. The reason is that you probably wouldn't realize that your information is based on false assumptions, so it would be much more difficult for you to reassess your decision later.

But this is not a reason to panic. The good news is that it isn't that difficult to ask the *right* questions. The goal of sharing my client's story is to ensure that you understand how vital it is to think about the knowledge that you are seeking before you begin any research effort. That's how you develop a solid survey that will give you the answers you need if you are to move forward. You have to begin at the end and ask yourself, "What is the purpose of obtaining this information?" and "How will I use the answer to improve my business?" If you constantly ask those questions and can honestly provide a response that makes logical business sense, then you're heading in the right direction.

We will cover more specific strategies for achieving these goals in the next two chapters. Let's continue this discussion by reviewing the general types of data you'll need to know and compare various techniques for gathering those data.

GETTING TO KNOW YOUR CUSTOMERS

As we discussed in Milestone 1, general data that you need to have if you are to understand your customers include demographic and psychographic factors such as these:

- *Demographics.* These are very factual pieces of data such as

  - Age

  - Gender

  - Ethnicity

  - Education

  - Employment status

  - Income

  - Location—where are your customers located, and how do they find you?

- *Psychographic and behavior influences.* What behaviors or habits influence the purchasing process, and who is involved in that process? These include

  - Spending patterns/usage—examples include certain times of year that influence customers' spending patterns. When do your customers make purchases, and what influences this pattern?

  - Price sensitivity—how much does price influence your customers' decisions?

  - Pain points/challenges—what issues or problems challenge your customers and influence their behavior? What is the one problem that your customers have that you solve for them better than anyone else?

  - Lifestyle, interests, and values

  - Personality traits and attitudes

  - Brand loyalty—are your customers more concerned about price, value, reliability, or something entirely different, such as status or brand appeal?

Of course, the specific data that you need are completely dependent on your business and the customers that you require. How will you gather these data?

PRIMARY AND SECONDARY RESEARCH

There are two basic types of data-gathering techniques: primary research and secondary research. Primary research involves collecting original data, data that you create yourself or that you obtain directly from the source (i.e., your current and/or prospective customers, partners, or industry experts). The advantage of conducting primary research is that it will give you specific information related directly to your business and/or your customers and not just general industry or target market data. This information can be obtained by conducting surveys, interviews, or focus groups, or by examining your internal database and uncovering clues about your customers. We'll review primary research strategies in Chapters 5 and 6.

Secondary research, on the other hand, is one step removed from the direct source. This involves uncovering clues about industry practices and norms and gathering data about customers and the marketplace in general. The word *general* is the key here, since these data may not be specific enough to allow you to make any critical business decisions, or you may need to confirm their relevance to your business. The sources of secondary research, in most cases, are publications, documents (government and non-government), newspapers, magazines, associations, journals, and articles. This type of research might include government studies, chamber of commerce statistics, surveys conducted by trade associations or industry-affiliated organizations, and rankings carried out by other reputable organizations. We'll review secondary research techniques in Chapter 7.

So how do you decide which type of research to conduct? Typically, you will need to conduct both types. Of course, if you have an established database of customers and prospects, then the task of obtaining specific customer data will be easier, provided you have been collecting the right information. If you haven't been collecting valuable information, such as how customers heard about your product, but have been gathering only basic facts like addresses and phone numbers, then the most sophisticated database system is not going to help you make any decisions. In addition, if you are trying to understand trends in the industry or spending patterns that influence your business, then you will definitely need to conduct secondary research.

BOSTON PEDORTHIC CASE STUDY

A few years ago, I became acquainted with the CEO of Boston Pedorthic (www. bostonpedorthic.com). This start-up specializes in helping patients feel better on their feet by creating custom foot orthotics, customizing shoes, and making modifications to shoes. Targeting competitive athletes, geriatrics, pediatrics, and ordinary people who spend too much time on their feet, Boston Pedorthic was quietly making inroads in the field. But Boston Pedorthic wanted to raise awareness of the company, especially among refer- ring clinicians—a critical audience, but one that was difficult to reach. To bet- ter understand what sales and marketing tools would work best to capture the attention of busy medical professionals, I studied the company's position in the industry to help define its unique value proposition to its customers. Areas reviewed included (1) secondary research like industry trends that affected the company's business and the external challenges that it faced and (2) the strategies that the company was currently using to target its audience, as well as profiles of its target audience.

Combining these data with secondary research—from industry associa- tions, trade organizations, and competitors that have a reputation for "best in class"—we were able to articulate what Boston Pedorthic's position and value in the marketplace were. This positioning allowed us to determine how Boston Pedorthic could set itself apart from its competition and identify what the medical community needed if it was to confidently recommend a product. The raw data were developed into insight and knowledge that allowed us to then develop a promotional tool that would be both engaging and educational for the referral sources. It was an interactive CD that demon- strated the benefits of using Boston Pedorthics's services/products and showed how they satisfied patients' needs.

WHAT YOU NEED BEFORE YOU CONDUCT RESEARCH

Since primary research involves going to the source of the data, it's critical to understand what those data should consist of. You can begin this process by first determining what specific information you need and then deciding where that information lives or can be found. If you have been tracking data about your customers and prospects for a while, you're in the fortunate position of being able to uncover valuable information by mining your own database. On the other hand, if you're new to the industry or have not been doing a very good job of tracking the data, then you will have to use other creative methods that we'll discuss later in this chapter.

First, let's assume that you've been collecting information about your customers. Perhaps you have been tracking customer and/or prospect data in a customer relationship management system (like ACT, File Maker, or Goldmine) designed for small businesses, or even in a simple Excel spreadsheet. Ideally, you will have more than basic demographic data. Do you know what your customers have purchased? Can you use this information to track trends in products purchased by certain groups or to determine if the timing of certain purchases is related to specific demographic data like age or gender? It is critical to review your database, not only to gain knowledge, but also to understand where gaps exist so that you can think about how to fill them.

Imagine that your five most important customers are sitting in a room with you. What questions would you ask them about their purchases, their needs and interests, and the factors that influence their decision-making processes? Hopefully you already know how they found your company, what they have purchased, and why they purchased those products from your company. If you don't have this information, though, these should be among the first questions you ask.

What other questions do you want to have answered? I suggest you create a *wish list* of information that you *need* in order to grow your business. You will probably want to know how well you are servicing your customers' needs and inquire about products that they have purchased from other companies. In addition, you might ask them to rank your value to them or how likely they are to purchase products from you in the future. Or ask them who they think the "best in class" company in the industry is and what that company is doing to meet their needs. Past purchases can also be a good predictor of future spending. If you're able to determine all of the factors that go into your customers' purchasing decisions, then you have a better chance at determining future buying trends. One critical point that I'd like to emphasize is to be careful that you don't assume that you already know the answers to these questions. If you make this assumption, you will risk making erroneous decisions that can negatively affect your business's future. It's always safer to ask than to assume.

CREATING A PRODUCT BASED ON CUSTOMER BEHAVIOR

Here is an example that illustrates how data can be used to create knowledge and influence product development. Let's say you are a credit union serving the local community. Perhaps your radius is within 25 miles of your eight local branches. You have carefully studied your database, and you realize that there are a lot of new business owners in your area. You also have concluded that within six months of launching their businesses, these owners' need for specific financial products like business insurance, small and large equipment loans, and online business banking increases dramatically.

Since your database indicates the start date of each of these businesses (roughly based on the date the business opened a business checking account with you), you decide to create a new product called the New Business Starter Kit. The kit might be filled with valuable information about growing a business, along with a few brochures highlighting financial products that you offer that will help them grow rapidly. Let's say you mail business owners this Starter Kit approximately 30 days after they open their accounts, congratulating them on launching their businesses and demonstrating how you help them support their growth. This could be a very powerful tool for you to increase revenue and concurrently generate customer loyalty. It's a win-win situation because you can help your customers grow their businesses while you grow yours.

DO YOU NEED A PROFESSIONAL RESEARCH FIRM?

In terms of your time and your need for data, sometimes it makes more sense to hire a professional research firm to gather the information you require. This is truly an issue of how best to use your time. Yes, you really can conduct all or most of the market research you need for your business. However, there are clear business reasons to outsource this research. As with every business decision, there are pros and cons, and I have listed a few here for you to consider when making this important decision. Remember, time is money, and if you can use your time better by outsourcing this task, then it might make more business sense to do so. The positive aspects of hiring an agency are the following:

■ An independent, unbiased opinion

- Possibly faster results

- Greater confidence in the results, since the research was conducted by an outside agency

- Expertise in developing the "right" questions

- Access to knowledge sources that you may not be aware of

On the other hand, the cons of hiring an agency might include these:

- The cost can be prohibitive

- You may not be a priority client, so it may take longer to get results or to get started

- The agency may not uncover anything that you wouldn't have discovered on your own

- The agency may lack expertise in your industry and so may not completely understand your research needs (although this should not be a problem with a reputable firm)

RESEARCH IN DOUBLE

Many years ago, I worked with an Internet-based start-up that wanted to test its new Web site before launching it. The CEO of the company wanted to hire a pure market research firm specializing in web optimization to help him determine whether the design of the site made it easy to navigate, but the marketing director and I were not convinced that this was absolutely necessary given the firm's limited budget. Since the target audience for this firm was mothers who were using the Web to make local purchases, we believed that we could compile reliable results almost as well as a specialized marketing research firm could. The CEO agreed to allow us to conduct our own research before he spent a large portion of his budget on a specialty research firm. The marketing director and I developed a series of questions regarding the ease of use of the Web site and the flow of the information and its *value* to Web visitors.

Working in our favor (which is not always the case) was the fact that we had ready access to the target audience. This allowed us to easily organize an informal focus group. Hosting a dinner party at the marketing director's house, we invited about half a dozen women (whom the marketing director knew were in our target demographic) to review the site and give us specific feedback about its ease of use. Our objective was to find out if users found the site easy to navigate.

We presented the site to them at dinner, watched them conduct searches, and asked a series of prepared questions about the ease of use and navigation of the Web site. We conducted this within a few days of, rather than a few months of, determining that we needed more information about the site's value to end users. (Typically it takes a research firm a few months to go from hire to report completion.) The knowledge gained from our "experimental" focus group led us to the conclusion that the Web site was indeed too complicated for a typical user. We presented our findings, along with a list of recommendations, to the CEO.

The CEO was pleased with our findings, but he wanted additional confirmation. So he hired a Web optimization market research firm to conduct more formal focus groups. The CEO, the marketing director, and I sat behind one-way glass mirrors and watched "professional researchers" uncover the exact same results that we had discovered in our informal group, held over a pasta dinner at the marketing director's house. It took several months from hiring to conducting the research to obtaining the final report, and we unfortunately learned nothing new or valuable. By the time the final report was delivered, we had already revised the Web site based on the knowledge we had gained over dinner (and by watching the focus groups through the one-way mirrors).

Let me be clear: I have the utmost respect for specialized market research firms. The good ones do an outstanding job, and this firm was exceptional. If you have a budget that allows you to hire a professional research firm, I say, wonderful. However, the lesson of this example is that if your budget is limited and your need is immediate, you can feel confident that you can conduct reliable research on your own, without depleting your entire marketing budget. The key is to be careful and to ask the right questions.

WORKING WITHOUT A DATABASE

What can you do if your database isn't valuable or if you haven't collected that kind of information about your customers in the first place? Relax. You do have alternatives that will help get you up to speed. Some options include the following:

- Purchase a mailing list of prospective customers. It is usually quite easy to buy a list of prospects that fit into your customer/prospect profile. You can work with a company like USAData (www.usadata.com), infoUSA (www.infousa.com), or Dun & Bradstreet's Zapdata (www.zapdata.com), or you can find a magazine or newspaper that focuses on your industry and see if its list is available for rent or purchase. Then use this list to survey customers or to mail prospects a sample of your product to gauge their interest. Once you hear back from them, you *own their name* (you can communicate with them again without renting the list), and they become part of your new knowledge base. This is important for future research.

- Work with a noncompeting partner company that has a database of similar customers. Such a company might be willing to share its knowledge about its customers' needs and/or interests, or even give you the ability to communicate with its customers in exchange for your providing something valuable to those customers. For example, let's say you've started a dog-walking business and you want to find out what hours are most desired by the folks who bring their dogs to the local pet boutique (which doesn't offer these services). You can make a deal with the boutique to offer its customers a discount or a free walk for trying your services and answering a few important questions about their needs.

- Invite friends or customers who fit into the right target audience to participate in an informal focus group. If you're not familiar with running a focus group and fear that you will bias the process, then go to a local university or business school and see if you can find a graduate student who is able to help you with it. By doing this, you will not only have a better chance of getting unbiased data but you will also be supporting the educational efforts of the student you work with.

ADDITIONAL RESEARCH STRATEGIES

At this point, you may see that it is worthwhile to conduct research and that this process need not drain your marketing budget. Once you have completed both primary and secondary research, you should ideally have enough knowledge to make strategic business decisions. However, if you discover that you still have only a bunch of facts and none of them can be turned into knowledge, then you should begin to think about the data that you are collecting and what changes you need to make to ensure that you are gathering information that can help guide your future decisions. In the next chapter we will cover the power of surveys to identify and truly understand your customers' needs.

(Worksheets start on next page.)

WORKSHEET 4.1

CUSTOMER INFORMATION CHECKLIST

General demographic information that you may need includes

☐ Age

☐ Gender

☐ Ethnicity

☐ Education

☐ Employment status

☐ Income

☐ Location

☐ Other _____

☐ Other _____

Psychographic and behavioral information includes

☐ Spending patterns/usage

☐ Price sensitivity

☐ Pain points/challenges

☐ Lifestyle

☐ Personality traits

☐ Values

☐ Attitude

☐ Brand loyalty

☐ Interests

☐ Other _____

☐ Other _____

WORKSHEET 4.2

CUSTOMER INFORMATION FRAMEWORK

To complete this assignment, you will need to compile a list of 20 questions that will help you define your customers and/or the industry. Imagine that you are in a room with your top customers and you have the opportunity to ask them anything you need to know about how they make purchasing decisions. Jot down the knowledge that you need to obtain in the table, and, then next to each entry, answer the following three questions:

1. What is your goal in gathering this information (what will you do with it), and how will the knowledge help your business grow?

2. What external/internal methods will you use to obtain the answer? Methods could include survey, focus group, concept test, secondary research, or market segmentation.

3. What are your sources of data? Sources can be an internal database, external documents, or Web sites.

If you cannot think of a good use for the information or how you will obtain the answer, then cross the question off your list. Otherwise, you'll be wasting your time.

Customer Information Required	Goal of Obtaining the Information (what will you do with the info?)	Method	Source
1.			
2.			
3.			

(Worksheet continues on next page.)

Customer Information Required	Goal of Obtaining the Information (what will you do with the info?)	Method	Source
4.			
5.			
6.			
7.			
8.			
9.			
10.			
11.			
12.			
13.			
14.			
15.			
16.			
17.			
18.			
19.			
20.			

CHAPTER 5

PRIMARY RESEARCH: SURVEYS GET YOU TO THE SOURCE

The power to question is the basis of all human progress.

—Indira Gandhi

ARE SURVEYS WORTH THE TROUBLE?

Try to imagine the number of times you've come home, opened your mail, and found a letter (often the two-page, double-sided, single-spaced variety) asking you to complete the "enclosed survey." Whether it was from a political organization, a private business, or a charity, the chances are that you tossed it in the trash. Or perhaps—with the best of intentions—you put it aside in your "I'll deal with this later" pile (where you came across it again weeks or months later while looking for something else).

American businesses spend billions of dollars each year on customer surveys, from traditional mail to Web-based questionnaires to in-person focus groups. Yet many of these businesses have seemingly little to show for their efforts. The average response rate to a mail survey is typically less than a few percent of the entire mailing.

So why do businesses bother with customer surveys, and why should you bother with them, especially with a tight marketing budget? Because, despite the sometimes paltry results, the information you can gain through a carefully designed and executed survey can be invaluable for growing your business. I learned this early in my career when I worked for a newsletter publisher. This company conducted annual surveys for each of its publications and, based on the information it collected from its existing readership, it was able to develop several successful new products and even spin off a "sister" consulting company.

What were the secrets to this company's "survey success"? How can you design and conduct surveys that produce useful results for your business? That will be our focus in the next two chapters. Using some instructive, real-life examples, I'll look at several key questions:

1. What you can expect to learn from a good survey

2. The pros and cons of different survey techniques (direct mail, phone, Web-based, focus group, etc.)

3. Why the length, format, and exact wording of questions are so important

4. What you can do to make your survey more appealing and increase your response rate

5. What other "best practices" you should follow to ensure survey success

TRUE SURVEY BENEFITS

As I mentioned earlier, before launching my consulting business, I worked as a marketing manager for a newsletter publisher. This was an extremely entrepreneurial organization that was very focused on understanding its customers' evolving needs. It used its annual surveys to ensure that it achieved this goal. The information and feedback that the company received from these surveys was powerful and helped it grow its business, developing additional publications, creating seminars and conferences, and even launching a sister organization that provided consulting services in the areas that best addressed its customers' needs. Can all this be accomplished by simply launching an annual survey? Yes, if the survey is a part of your customer-focused business philosophy and is carefully constructed to elicit valuable customer information.

You are hopefully beginning to see how the gaps in your knowledge of your customers and the marketplace can seriously compromise the success of your business. Conducting research and creating feedback loops (such as running annual surveys) can ensure that your message is targeted and your customers are receiving the products and services that they need. According to the U.S. Small Business Administration, only 44 percent of new employer establishments survive for at least four years. Given the preponderance of small businesses that fail, there is no doubt that understanding your customers will give you an advantage in the market.

The benefits of conducting a survey include:

- Giving you the ability to identify current and future customer and prospect needs

- Helping you understand what information customers and prospects need to make purchasing decisions

- Providing you with information such as ranking of preferences or interests

- Allowing you to identify how customers find out about the solution(s) you offer and why they would even want your solution

- Providing a feedback loop to ensure that loyalty and customer satisfaction standards are being met and addressed

- Helping you prioritize new product features or capabilities as they apply to your customers' interests now and in the future

WHAT DRAWS YOU IN?

Although only a small fraction of people respond to any given survey, many of us are likely to respond to at least one survey in the course of a year. What makes us take the time to respond to one, but toss another in the trash? Think about a survey that you've completed recently. Was it a phone solicitation, an e-mail request, or a letter in the mail that grabbed your attention and intrigued you enough to respond? What drew you into the process? Were you interested in the topic? Maybe you were satisfied, or perhaps unsatisfied, with a product or service that the company provided, or maybe you were simply interested in the opportunity to win a "prize" for participating. Or was it that the survey was short and therefore was easy for you to respond to? Keep your response in mind as you attempt to engage your customers in a dialogue. Think about what will capture their attention and get them to respond in a timely manner.

A successful survey depends on getting the following four objectives right:

1. *Format.* Use the delivery method that is most appropriate for your audience and subject to ensure that you achieve the highest response rate.

2. *Word choice.* Choose your words wisely. Ask the right questions in an unbiased and clear manner.

3. *The list.* Send the survey to the appropriate list.

4. *Insights.* Turn data into insights for decision making.

In this chapter, I'll discuss the pros and cons of various survey formats and styles. In Chapter 6 I'll review other strategies that will increase your chances of successfully gaining knowledge from your survey.

ACHIEVING A STRONG RESPONSE RATE

In developing your survey, it is critical that you determine your delivery method and format at the start, since this will influence the rest of the survey. There are benefits to using different types of survey formats for different audiences. As with all good marketing efforts, you make your choice relevant to the needs of your target audience. Here are some different ways you can launch a survey and the advantages and disadvantages of each technique.

TELEPHONE SURVEYS

》 PROS OF CALLING

■ These surveys are most effective when you already have a relationship with the individuals you are contacting, even if they're not current customers. Your success in connecting with your audience will improve if the relationship you already have is by phone or through a personal connection.

■ This method works well if your audience prefers to communicate by phone (perhaps your customers are elderly and will not respond to an online or a mail survey).

- Current customers are typically more open to receiving a call from a business with which they already have a relationship (it gives the impression of being more of a customer courtesy than an imposition).

- One bonus that you occasionally get from phone surveys is the "extra" conversation that is shared once you have your customer or prospect on the phone. You may learn information that you hadn't even thought of asking for that can be very valuable to your business.

)) CONS OF CALLING

- Timing is critical with phone surveys—you need to know when your customers are available and coordinate this with your calling action plan.

- Compared to mail or e-mail surveys, phone surveys are extremely time consuming. The chance that your telephone calls will reach a significant number of respondents during your first, second, or even third attempt may be quite slim. So, your efforts may need to be doubled, and your response rate may be low.

- If you choose to outsource the survey, you may discover that companies that perform these services are more expensive than your budget allows.

- In addition to the expense, outsourcing also tends to limit the information that you get, since a hired agency won't have the same relationship that you have with your customers and may not be as responsive or receptive to the additional information that can be learned by speaking directly with customers. For example, if a customer begins to tell you details about a problem he is having with a product or service, you can respond immediately to address the concern. Even a well-trained firm wouldn't have the knowledge or the ability to respond immediately.

- You may need to purchase phone number access (which is more costly than purchasing just a mailing address), and you need to follow strict state and federal guidelines about telephone solicitations.

NATIONAL DO NOT CALL REGISTRY RULES

Before you make any phone calls, it is essential that you understand how the *National Do Not Call Registry* works. Please note that if the call is for the sole purpose of conducting a survey, it is exempt from this registry. However, if callers claim to be conducting a survey, but they also offer to sell goods or services, they must comply with the Do Not Call provisions. In addition, there are also state laws regulating telemarketing practices.

The National Do Not Call Registry was created in the United States in 2003 and contains a list of phone numbers from consumers who have indicated their preference to limit the telemarketing calls they receive. The registry is managed by the Federal Trade Commission (FTC), the nation's consumer protection agency. It is enforced by the FTC, the Federal Communications Commission (FCC), and state officials. The do not call provisions of the Telemarketing Sales Rule (TSR) cover any plan, program, or campaign to sell goods or services through interstate phone calls. This includes calls by telemarketers who solicit consumers, often on behalf of third-party sellers. It also includes sellers who are paid to provide, offer to provide, or arrange to provide goods or services to consumers. The do not call provisions do not cover calls from political organizations, charities, telephone surveyors, or companies with which a consumer has an existing business relationship. The National Do Not Call Registry covers intrastate telemarketing calls under the FCC's rules. You can find information on the FCC's regulations at www.ftc.gov/donotcall.

Source: www.ftc.gov/bcp/conline/pubs/alerts/dncbizalrt.htm.

GUILFORD SAVINGS BANK SURVEY PROCESS

Remember Guilford Savings Bank, the customer-focused bank discussed in Chapter 2? One reason why its biennial survey is so successful is that before conducting it, the bank always sends out a letter informing customers that the phone survey is beginning, and that they might receive a phone call. This serves two purposes: (1) it lets customers know that they might be called, which increases the response rates, and (2) it gives customers an opportunity to call on their own because they want to voice their opinion to the bank. (Another incentive to respond is that survey respondents are entered into a raffle to win a weekend getaway.) Over the years of working with its customers, the bank has learned that when its customers have a strong opinion (either negative or positive) about a bank service or product, they will become more vocal about it. The bank has always encouraged this feedback and incorporates customer feedback into its business plans, goals, and operational strategy. In addition, when the bank's customer service reps personally make these calls to customers, they sometimes lead to new service purchases because the service reps understand the customers' needs and concerns and are able to inform the customers of products that will meet these needs. An outside agency simply cannot do this as effectively as an employee who is well versed in the products offered by the bank.

MAIL SURVEYS

If you choose to conduct your survey via mail, then it's important to recognize some important factors that can influence your success:

- *Length and style* are essential. If the survey is too long, respondents may take one look and decide it's not worth their time to participate.

- *Getting it open*. If the envelope isn't interesting looking, your response rate might be quite poor because people will simply toss it into the recycling bin. Direct mail, as a format, suffers from low response rates, so you will need to make your survey as appealing, personal, and compelling as possible to ensure that it is read.

- *Be creative*. Some businesses include surveys in regular customer correspondence, while others include them as a self-mailer, thus eliminating the need to open the envelope, since the entire "package" is the survey.

- *Survey response vehicles*. Once you determine the exact mail format, you will need to think about how you will want the survey returned. You can send it by mail and offer a variety of ways to respond, including fax, online, and in the mail. Keep in mind the fact that if you request a mail response, you should always include a business reply envelope (BRE) or some other type of prepaid or stamped envelope. Although this will obviously add to your costs, it should boost response rates.

- *Mailing addresses.* You need to consider how many physical mailing addresses you have. If you're using your own database, this information should be readily available. If not, you will need to determine how you will get names and addresses and what the cost will be if you have to rent or buy these names.

IN-PERSON INTERVIEWS

How many times have you been walking around a local mall when somebody has approached you and asked you to complete a quick survey? Depending on your interest in the product, your planned activities for the day, and sometimes the likeability of the person who approaches you, you might consider participating. This can be a hit-or-miss option for the company conducting the survey. Nonetheless, it is sometimes the best alternative if you're looking for immediate feedback and you also believe that it's important to demonstrate the product. Another benefit of this method is that you have the ability to ask follow-up questions, and you may hear things that you might not otherwise have thought to ask. Of course, the downside is the expense—either of hiring a consultant to conduct the interviews or of the time you'll spend doing the work yourself.

SALLY'S HOMEMADE DOG FOOD

Robin Malone, a graduate student at Boston University's School of Management, recently used an in-person survey to determine the need for her product, Sally's Homemade Dog Food (www.sallysdogfood.com). As a student, she had neither the time nor the budget to mail a survey to prospective customers, and contacting them online didn't make sense for her audience. Robin faced the additional challenge of not having a customer list, since her homemade dog food business was still in its infancy (her full-time job was finishing her MBA). However, she did have the passion and commitment to make the business successful and the support of two fellow students who were determined to help her launch the business. As a team, they decided that approaching dog owners at local dog parks would give them easy access to prospective clients and provide them with a solid understanding of what was important to their customer base (again, the dog owners, not the dogs). This technique proved to be quite effective. I will review their survey at the end of Chapter 6 to see how they refined their questions to learn enough about their prospects' needs to turn data into knowledge to position their business.

ONLINE

Online surveys have many benefits. If your audience is receptive and knows who you are (you don't want to "spam" individuals with whom you are trying to establish a relationship), then an online survey provides the following benefits: affordability, ability to conduct a survey quickly (on the fly), rapid response rate, ease of delivery, and significant cost savings compared to printing and mailing postal mail surveys. In the right circumstances, this method fits very well into an entrepreneurial budget for market research.

One of the key factors in increasing response rates, especially for online surveys, involves sending them from a "known" person or company. Therefore, if you are surveying your own customers, and they frequently correspond with a particular individual within the organization (like a sales manager or customer service rep), make sure your e-mail request is sent from this person.

》 MÄRKISCHES WERK ANNUAL CUSTOMER SURVEY

When I first began conducting customer surveys for Märkisches Werk in Germany, a client of mine, we had two goals: (1) to boost response rates from previous years and (2) to obtain honest, open feedback we could use to better understand customers' needs. Therefore, we chose to have the survey completed online at my company's Web site rather than my client's Web site. However, the challenge in doing this was that Märkisches Werk's customers had no relationship with my business. We knew that if I sent the e-mail request, most of those customers would view it as spam and hit the "delete" button immediately. Therefore, the survey was e-mailed from the marketing director's e-mail account with an explanation that the survey was being conducted anonymously online at my Web site. This increased the open rate for the e-mail request and increased the honesty factor by ensuring confidentiality through completing the survey at a third-party Web site. We also offered a gift (a USB flash drive) for the first 25 individuals completing the survey, since we wanted to encourage customers to complete it quickly. Within a few days we had more than achieved our response rate target, and by the end of the survey process (we sent three requests to customers to complete the survey), we had almost doubled our response rates from the previous year, when the survey had been managed internally. The knowledge we gained provided tremendous insight into the challenges that customers faced in the industry and helped frame my client's business strategy for the upcoming years.

)) CREATING ONLINE SURVEYS

There are many ways to create a survey cost effectively. You can hire a programmer to create an online system for you or use an outside company that specializes in this. There are a variety of companies that support online surveys. Two companies that are quite popular are Zoomerang (info.zoom erang.com) and Survey Monkey (www.surveymonkey.com). Both offer the ability to custom design a survey to meet your needs and help you connect with your customers. Neither is expensive (when I last checked, Survey Monkey offered a monthly subscription of less than $20, which included up to 1,000 responses each month), but you will need to research your options to determine what makes the most sense for your business.

)) KEY BENEFITS OF USING ONLINE SURVEYS

- They can be more engaging than a regular mail survey. You can be very creative with online formats, making them interactive and driving respondents to your Web site, where they might browse once they're done with the survey

- They are usually easier and more affordable to conduct.

- They allow you to inexpensively and easily test different audience reactions or interests in a short period of time.

- Since there are no mailing or print costs involved, you can send different surveys to different or even similar audiences to determine which will provide you with the best response rate. However, this is assuming that you get a decent response from your audience. Inexpensive doesn't matter if people don't respond.

- Since most responses occur within 48 hours of sending out the survey, you won't have to wait long to know how well this style worked for you. If the survey didn't bring you the anticipated response, then you can quickly move to Plan B (assuming that you have a Plan B). It takes a lot longer to realize that your direct mail or telephone survey did not provide you with the data you need.

Finally, it's important to recognize that you don't have to pick just one technique. You can choose a combination of techniques to gain the most knowledge in a short period of time. For example, I recently conducted a survey about the Hispanic market in New England with my business partner, The Hispanic News Press, which publishes *El Planeta* (www.elplaneta.com), a weekly Spanish-language newspaper with a distribution of more than 65,000 readers in Massachusetts, New Hampshire, and Rhode Island. We decided to promote the survey in the paper, allowing readers either to complete the version in the paper and mail in the responses or to go online to answer the questions in the survey. In addition, we took advantage of online marketing capabilities by sending e-communications to readers and supporters of the newspaper. Our goal was to boost response rates through a variety of distribution channels.

An alternative is to vary the techniques that you use from year to year to keep your costs at a reasonable level but still gain the most access to knowledge about your customers' needs. In the next chapter, I'll discuss more specific methods of turning data into knowledge to grow your business.

(Worksheets start on next page.)

WORKSHEET 5.1

SURVEY DESIGN

Based on your knowledge of your customers' interests, needs, and behaviors, consider which formats might work best to increase survey responses. Compare the pros and cons of different formats.

Survey Format	Pros	Cons
Telephone		
Postal mail		
In-person survey		
E-mail survey		
Focus group		
Other _____		

WORKSHEET 5.2

SURVEY QUESTIONS

What knowledge will you seek with each of your questions, and what questions will you ask to obtain this knowledge?

Customer Knowledge	Question	Format (rank, yes/no, check, open-ended question)

CHAPTER 6

IMPROVING THE RELIABILITY OF YOUR DATA

A stumble may prevent a fall.

—Margaret Thatcher, former British prime minister

Early in my career, when I began selling, I quickly learned that if I asked the right questions and simply listened, the prospect would become my teacher. She would tell me what was important to her so that I would know how to "sell" her my product or service. I'll discuss sales techniques in depth in Milestones 6 and 7. However, it's important to note here that the same principle applies with surveys. A well-designed survey can help you create a road map for success because it can reveal who your customers are and let them tell you what you need to do to satisfy their needs. If you ask the right questions, then the respondents will do most of the heavy lifting for you.

There are dozens of ways to improve survey response rates. Here I will explore the various methods you can use to improve your survey response rates and the reliability of your data, including choosing the right words, using the right list, and motivating your participants to respond. After I have discussed these tips, I'll analyze the survey conducted by aspiring entrepreneur Robin Malone to launch her dog food business.

CHOOSE YOUR WORDS WISELY

I previously discussed what you would ask your key customers if they were sitting in a room with you. Now, imagine you once again have this opportunity to question your customers, but this time through an online or mailed survey, not in person. How should you modify your questions to fit the format? Most importantly, your questions have to be absolutely clear and concise. There's no room for ambiguity, since you won't be able to clarify what you really meant to ask. If there is any vagueness in your questions, your responses will be meaningless, since your respondents might have misinterpreted the question; unfortunately, you might not know that.

QUALITY VERSUS QUANTITY

It's also critical that you focus your questions tightly so that you only ask the few, most critical ones. Of course, we'd all love to have 100 questions answered by our current and potential customers. But if you create a survey with 100 questions, it's likely that your response rates will be so low that your results will be useless. If you can get between 10 and 20 focused, key questions answered by 20 or 30 percent of your key prospects and/or customers, then you are quite likely to have enough data points to be able to understand customer needs and trends that will affect your business. So after writing each question, ask yourself: "What will I do with this answer?" If you cannot think of a good use for the response, then eliminate the question.

TEST YOUR SURVEY

Before you launch the final survey, test it with people who match the criteria of your key target audience. Ask them to complete the survey and then describe to you what you are looking for from each question. If there is ambiguity, you need to change the style or wording of the question. You should also test the survey with somebody who knows little about your business. If such a person can understand the questions (even if he's not qualified to answer them), then you very likely have a clear, precise series of questions. Send it to your friends, your children, or even your mother. This is an inexpensive, simple, and usually effective way to determine if you're asking the questions as clearly as possible.

SEND TO THE APPROPRIATE LIST

If you are trying to understand the needs of the customers in your database, then you don't have to think twice about what list you'll be using; you already own it. However, if your current customer list lacks key demographic information (such as gender, age, or simply e-mail or mailing addresses) or perhaps does not represent your audience for a new product, then you will need to identify an appropriate list. There are endless sources of lists, but making sure you get the correct one with the appropriate demographic reach is critical. You can purchase or rent a list from a list source like Dun

& Bradstreet's Zapdata, infoUSA, or USAdata or from a publisher or organization whose target audience matches your demographic profile.

Be sure you review this list very carefully to ensure that the demographics are on target. Even the best-written survey launched in the most appropriate format will provide useless data if your list is not aligned with your target audience. For example, you might sell expensive wellness products (vitamins, supplements) for adults who are interested in their health. Most of your customers are 45 to 70. One of your list rentals is from a magazine called *Senior Health*. Sounds appropriate, right? Not necessarily. If most of the subscribers are over 75 and receiving Medicaid benefits (i.e., they can't afford your products), then they may not be your ideal target market. You have to be careful when renting lists to make sure you find out the demographics of the audience first.

Before I proceed, let's highlight the information that should be in your database. Clearly the customer or prospect's name and basic demographic details should be available to you. In addition, you will want as much information about these people's needs as possible. When you're renting a list, you begin with the general name, address, and phone number, but you use these basics as a starting point and look for more detailed information, such as needs, interests, and lifestyle. If you are using a rented list, you won't own the names (which means that unless you've purchased a multiuse license, you won't be able to use the list again without rerenting it). Thus, you will want to get as many people as possible from that list to "register" with you so that you own their names and they become part of your database.

Here are some methods for enlisting those customers for future communication:

- Offer them something for free if they sign up to receive future information from your company.

- Give them a limited trial offer (if it makes sense with your product or service).

- Send them a free article on a specific topic that is relevant to their needs.

- Run a contest or giveaway associated with the survey and ask for basic information when they enter.

- Send a sample of your product if they give you their name and address.

TURN DATA INTO KNOWLEDGE FOR DECISION MAKING

This objective is critical to your success. If you cannot obtain reliable data that you can analyze and then turn those numbers and statistics into relevant knowledge and insight for making decisions, then it's not worth the effort. This is one of the most important pieces of advice I can offer pertaining to each and every aspect of your marketing strategy, including, but not limited to, surveys. Always think about what you will do with the information you obtain, because if you cannot turn it into usable knowledge, then you have wasted time, effort, and money. As an entrepreneur or small business owner, you certainly don't have time or money to waste.

WAYS TO BOOST YOUR RESPONSE RATES

1. *Keep it simple.* Don't confuse your respondents by asking them to do anything other than complete the survey. This will dilute your message and have a negative impact on your response rates.

2. *Use clear and concise questions.* Make sure that the survey is easy to complete and understand. As with every marketing tool that you create, it's essential that you speak directly to your audience in an easily understandable tone and style. The easier the survey is to complete, the better the response rates will be.

3. *Offer a gift or premium for participating.* Make sure you're offering an item that will be an incentive to your target audience. For example, being entered in a sweepstakes to win a USB flash drive or a weekend getaway can have a strong impact on the number of responses you receive. However, if your audience is made up of octogenarians (people aged 80 to 89) and you offer a technology product like an iPod, you probably won't achieve the results desired (unless they're really savvy or have kids or grandkids who would love the product).

4. *Assure confidentiality.* This is essential. Respondents will be more willing to share honest responses with you if you let them know that what they say will be confidential. For online surveys, if you ask for e-mail addresses, assure the respondents that you will neither sell their e-mail addresses nor use them for any purpose other than to thank them and

let them know if they have won a prize for responding. If the response is at a third-party Web site or is being mailed to a research firm, point out this important information to the recipients. Honest feedback will provide you with the most valuable data.

5. *Thank them.* This basic lesson, which my parents taught me long ago, applies to all business communications. Thanking respondents for their time can only help to further promote your image as a company that cares about its customers.

6. *Tell them why.* Why is it important for you to hear from your audience? Why is it important to your customers to complete the survey? If the survey results are going to help you make decisions that will improve your customers' lives or help you develop products that are specifically designed to meet their needs, let them know that. They can't read your mind, so make sure they know why they're spending their time doing this for you.

7. *Highlight what they will get for responding.* It's important that you not only offer a gift but also clearly explain when, why, and how the winning respondent will receive it, and then follow through on your promises. You clearly want to avoid misunderstandings. Imagine offering a drawing for a weekend getaway but forgetting to deliver the prize. Unfortunately, I've seen this happen with busy entrepreneurs, and it's had obvious negative repercussions. It's easy enough to let the entire survey list (respondents and nonrespondents) know who won the giveaway. This is one more opportunity to communicate with them, and it will hopefully encourage greater response to future requests when people realize that somebody actually won the prize. It's also a great PR opportunity.

8. *Send your request from the highest or most appropriate level in the organization.* If receiving a letter from the company president or customer service director will have a strong impact on response rates, then use this strategy. However, if each customer's individual sales or service rep is more appropriate, then customize the letters so that each person receives a request from his or her direct contact. Make sure there's a way for respondents to communicate with somebody at the company if they have any questions. Give a phone number and e-mail address so that they can get in touch with the right person.

9. *Include a space for comments.* People may want to share additional thoughts with you. You never know what other information the respondents will want to tell you. I've seen these responses turn out to be the most interesting data gathered from the survey because they're unsolicited and provide you with information that you might never have thought of asking for. Customers can have the best suggestions for products and sometimes advertising venues.

10. *Allow them to respond in a variety of ways.* Many times you are tempted to request one method of communication, especially if you are conducting an online survey and your database is set up to receive information and sort it automatically. But the more options you can offer for response, the higher your response rate will be.

11. *Give them something unexpected.* Underpromise and overdeliver works in every venue of business life. If you promise them 10 methods to increase response rates, then give them 11 ways, just as I have done here.

THE SURVEY IS THE MESSAGE

What other factors can influence the success of a survey? First, make sure that the survey is the focal point. You want to be certain that you're not bombarding respondents with distracting material. This is not the time to send sales literature or ask people to respond to an offer. All they should be "required" to do is complete the survey. Not only is this important in terms of response rates, but, as I mentioned previously, the Do Not Call Registry has strict regulations about the difference between survey calls and sales calls, and the two should not be combined.

GIFT IDEAS

As discussed earlier, survey response rates can be significantly boosted by offering the recipients rewards in exchange for participating in the survey. What you offer depends entirely upon your audience.

I recently worked with a credit union interested in surveying its former members to better understand the reasons they left the credit union. Since these were individuals no longer affiliated with the credit union, we were concerned that response rates would be paltry. Therefore, when we mailed the surveys out, we offered the first 25 respondents (who completed the survey online) $25 gas cards. We could tell exactly when the surveys landed in the mailboxes because within hours of their arrival we were flooded with online responses. The newsletter publisher I worked for also did a great job with boosting response rates using "gifts." However, the company didn't give away fancy pens or other trinkets that its customers had no use for. It gave away three-month trial subscriptions to its publications, summaries of survey results, research articles, and back issues of its publications. Many companies also offer the opportunity to win a "valuable" prize, and I've seen crisp, new $1 bills inserted in surveys in advance of their being completed. This is an advance thank-you that everybody receives. It relies on the recipient's ability to feel guilty about spending the money without *earning* it.

THE COVER LETTER

Don't forget the importance of your cover letter, whether it's an e-mail or an actual letter that accompanies your request to complete the survey. Make sure you put the time into creating a well-written and targeted letter that speaks directly to your audience and clearly explains the value of the survey to that audience. This is as important as your elevator pitch for your company. Along with your introduction, the ability of your cover letter to convey your message will help determine the success of the survey.

SURVEY FOLLOW-UP

What happens when you have completed your survey and received valuable feedback, but you suddenly realize that you have more questions or would like to clarify trends that you have seen in the responses? The best way to handle this is to prepare for it ahead of time; include a question asking the respondents if you can follow up with them if you have additional questions. Leaving this door open during the survey process makes the next contact much easier.

If you'd like to follow up, here are a few ideas that you might consider. Of course, all of these strategies work well on their own, without a formal survey preceding them:

1. *Personal interviews.* This is a great method to use if you want to further explore the information revealed in your surveys. This one-on-one

method (via phone or in person) might give you the deeper level of feedback you need to understand your clients. Again, make sure that the questions are focused and unbiased so that you create knowledge.

2. *Focus groups.* A focus group with half a dozen or more targeted individuals can help answer specific questions, especially questions that require visual aids to understand (such as evaluating a product container or design). This is more subjective and open-ended in nature, but it will allow you to compare the responses to the survey in order to validate the results. Unless you have experience in conducting focus groups, I recommend that you use a facilitator who is trained in this method, is unbiased, and has no vested interest in the results. You should be able to locate a graduate student or professor at a local university who can help you run a focus group without blowing your entire marketing budget. However, you need to remember that groups can be subject to groupthink, so if you have the time, money, and ability, you should try to hold several focus groups to ensure that your results are reliable. One last piece of advice: try to make an audio or video recording of the sessions so that you and others can review them later for clarity.

3. *Customer advisory forums.* If you have VIP customers or important prospects whose business and/or loyalty you are trying to win, forming an advisory board made up of some of these individuals can help you achieve two objectives. First, it will provide you with feedback and insight from outsiders whose opinions you value. Second, it will keep these customers or prospects close to your company, and this can only help you grow your business and make more informed, customer-oriented business decisions. Choose a few key individuals who are willing to give you their time to meet on a quarterly or semiannual basis and provide you with feedback. This can be helpful and very insightful. But remember, this group can also be biased, so keep this in mind when reviewing its feedback. In addition, this might be a good networking opportunity for your customers, since they might benefit from knowing other customers of yours (as long as they're not competitors). You might offer the people involved financial compensation for their time, discounts on your products or services, or access to new releases or products before they become available to the mainstream market.

CASE STUDY: SALLY'S HOMEMADE DOG FOOD

A perfect example of using your entrepreneurial energy to get out there and discover who your customers are and what they want is the work done by Robin Malone, one of the winners of the annual Boston University Business Concept Competition. While getting her MBA, Robin was launching a business that provides fresh, all-natural, homemade dog food—a venture inspired by her own dog, Sally, who needed an alternative food to treat a skin condition that she developed as a puppy. Robin could not find any fresh dog food, so after thorough research and working with an animal nutritionist, she created a balanced food that helped Sally. Of course, Robin realized that just because this product worked for her dog did not mean that there was a market for it. She understood that there's a huge difference between a bona fide business idea and simply a good idea, and she needed to conduct research to determine the feasibility of her concept.

Robin began researching the pet food industry to understand where there were product gaps that she could fill. She also spoke with a variety of dog owners to try to assess their level of interest in a homemade dog food. Early results showed an interest in the product. But this secondary research was not enough. Before she invested a significant amount of money into launching this product, Robin wanted to better understand her potential customers' needs. Therefore, Robin, along with two students at Boston University, decided to conduct research that included a formal survey and a focus group. Her initial survey is given here. While you are reading the questions, think about whether the survey passes the "what will I do with this answer?" test. In addition, consider the following:

1. How easy is the survey to complete?

2. How valid are the survey questions?

3. Were all of the questions clear?

4. Were any questions vague or misleading?

5. Do any of the questions assume knowledge that the respondent might not have?

6. Are there additional questions that you think the survey should ask?

7. Are there questions that should be eliminated?

SALLY'S HOMEMADE DOG FOOD DRAFT SURVEY: VERSION ONE

Target audience: dog lovers of any type. The survey is to be conducted at pet stores—large chains and small boutiques.

Product

- Would you buy this product?

- If so, would you feed it to your dog as an occasional treat or as an everyday meal?

- How often would you buy this product, and in what quantities?

- What do you like/not like about the product (e.g., texture, smell, etc.)?

- Do you think your dog would like this food?

- Do you perceive any health benefits to your dog from eating a natural dog food? Any health risks?

Price

- How much would you spend for a 16-oz. container of this product?

- How much more expensive than canned dog food/dry dog food would you expect a product like this to be?

- Do special price promotions drive your purchases?

Packaging (show them the package)

- Does this package communicate what the product is?

- Is there enough/too much color?

- Would you prefer different packaging?

- What else would you include to communicate what the product is?

Consumer Behavior

- How often do you buy dog food?

- How much do you spend per month on dog food?

(Continued on next page.)

- Where do you purchase dog food? Specialty pet store; natural foods store such as Whole Foods or Trader Joes; grocery store; mass retailer such as Wal-Mart; mass pet retailer such as PetCo?

- Do you have freezer space constraints?

- Would you dedicate freezer space for Sally's?

Demographics

- Age and household income

- Main household buyer—who makes buying decisions?

- How many kids do you have?

- How many animals/dogs do you have? Do you have big dogs or small dogs?

Contact/Follow-Up

- Can we call you to follow up?

- Would you be interested in participating in a focus group?

- Name/e-mail/phone

Let's dissect the first two sections of this survey, so that you can understand the concerns I have with these questions. I have provided you with the comments I gave to Robin and her team to help them refocus their final survey. When you have read both the draft survey and the final survey, I am confident that you will see the importance of asking the right questions and using the right method at the right time.

Product

1. Would you buy this product?

    Comment: Asking prospects if they would buy the product as one of your first questions is premature and doesn't provide you with any insight into customer interests and buying behavior. You haven't even established that this person has a need for the product, and you're asking her if she would buy it. Even if all the respondents said yes, this wouldn't really tell you anything valuable because it's a response made under pressure. However, if you ask them about their current buying habits, their need for specific products for their dog, and the likelihood (on a scale) of their purchasing this type of product, then you will have results that you can work with.

Given the scale concept, I would change the wording to "On a scale of 1 to 5 (1 being very unlikely, 5 being very likely), how likely are you to buy this product in the next three months?"

2. If so, would you feed it to your dog as an occasional treat or as an everyday meal?

Comment: This is your second question after showing respondents the product. At this point in the survey, you have not even established what they currently feed their dog, how this product might meet their needs, and if they are even your right target audience. In addition, they might want to feed this to their dog as both a treat and a meal, but you've limited their response to one or the other. I'm not sure this question is valid at this point in the survey. Since you need to limit the number of questions you ask, you might want to eliminate this one at this time.

3. How often would you buy this product, and in what quantities?

Comment: To begin with, these are two different questions. However, even if they're broken into separate questions, the respondent's frequency of purchase may not mean anything, since respondents do not have enough information about the product; they do not know what size it comes in, how long it lasts, and so on. They need a lot more information before they can answer this question with any data that will help you make a decision.

4. What do you like/not like about the product (e.g., texture, smell, etc.)?

Comment: This question also requires a scale system and relevance to respondents' purchasing decision. Perhaps there are aspects of the product that they dislike, but these aspects are not important in the decision-making process. Just because the product has a smell that you don't like does not necessarily mean that you won't buy it. A better way to state this would be to separate product features and ask: "On a scale of 1 to 5, how important is texture to you when

(Continued on next page.)

you purchase dog food?" Then ask about smell and other characteristics. The responses to these types of questions will give you more data, which will help you determine the product features that are most critical in the purchasing decision.

5. Do you think your dog would like this food?

   Comment: Honestly, how will the owner know if the dog will like the product? Is that answer going to give you any relevant information to use? If it doesn't, it should be eliminated, since there are many questions in this survey and you want to be sure that your respondents answer all of the important ones and don't get bogged down with meaningless questions.

6. Do you perceive any health benefits to your dog from eating a natural dog food? Any health risks?

   Comment: How important are health benefits or risks to dog owners, and will these perceptions play a role in the decision-making process? I believe that's really what you want to know. If that's the answer you need, then you should change the wording of the question to read: "On a scale of 1 to 5, how important are health benefits in determining which dog food you purchase?"

Price

7. How much would you spend for a 16-oz. container of this product?

   Comment: Pricing questions are difficult because there are so many variables that influence what a price should be, including perception of value, need, availability of alternatives, and other consumer behavior traits. At this point, it's more important for you to understand how much the respondents currently spend on their dog food purchases than to ask them how much they would spend for this one item. Your responses are likely to range from 50 cents to $15, providing you with completely useless information.

8. How much more expensive than canned dog food/dry dog food would you expect a product like this to be?

   Comment: Are you expecting a percentage, a dollar amount, or something else? What will you do with these responses in a way that will provide you with any relevant data? Price is a combination of cost, perception, what the market will bear, competition, and other factors. Why ask how much more they would expect this to cost if they don't know enough about the product to make that decision?

9. Do special price promotions drive your purchases?

   Comment: Do you think anybody is going to say, "No, I never buy products on sale"? Again, you could use a scale of 1 to 5 and ask, "How much does price influence your purchase?" You're trying to determine how important these factors (price, smell, texture, health benefits, etc.) are to the decision-making process. In addition to using a scale, another way to uncover this answer is to have respondents rank these qualities in order of importance.

Now, take a look at the remaining original questions and think about what recommendations you would have made to Robin to create a valuable survey. When you're ready, review her final survey and see the difference in the types of questions she asked. Once you've completed your assessment of Robin's survey, you're ready to launch your own. The worksheet in this chapter will help you get started.

SALLY'S HOMEMADE DOG FOOD SURVEY: FINAL VERSION

We represent a local company starting a business making all-natural, homemade dog food. This new dog food is *fully-cooked*—it is not a raw or "barf" diet. It is made from all-natural ingredients including ground turkey or beef, beef liver, spinach, carrots, broccoli, barley, brown rice, and oats. This is a fresh product—it's not canned or dry. It will be sold frozen in packaging that can be quickly defrosted in the microwave or refrigerator. We thank you for your time and value your comments and suggestions.

1. How many dogs do you have?

   ☐ 1　　　☐ 2　　　☐ 3　　　☐ More than 3

2. Who makes the pet food buying decision in your household?

   ☐ Myself　　☐ Spouse　　☐ Children　　☐ Vet
   ☐ Other_____

3. What type of dog food do you buy?　(Check all that apply.)

   ☐ Dry　　☐ Canned　　☐ Other _____

4. How often do you buy dog food?

   ☐ Once per month　　☐ Twice per month
   ☐ 3 times per month　　☐ More than 3 times per month

5. Where do you primarily purchase dog food?
   (Check only 1 box.)

   ☐ Small, independently owned pet store

   ☐ Natural foods store (such as Whole Foods)

   ☐ Grocery store

   ☐ Mass retailer (such as Wal-Mart)

   ☐ PetCo or PetSmart

   ☐ Online

   ☐ Other_____

6. Name of store(s) where you purchase dog food:

_____

_____

7. How much do you spend per month on dog food?

☐ Less than $10 ☐ $10 to $50
☐ $50 to $100   ☐ $100 +

Please indicate the extent to which you agree or disagree with each of the following statements:

	Strongly Disagree	Disagree	Neither Agree Nor Disagree	Agree	Strongly Agree
8. Money is no object when it comes to my dog.	☐	☐	☐	☐	☐
9. I think of my dog as a member of the family.	☐	☐	☐	☐	☐
10. My dog's health is as important as my own.	☐	☐	☐	☐	☐
11. My dog deserves only the best-quality food.	☐	☐	☐	☐	☐
12. I am knowledgeable about current dog-related issues in the news.	☐	☐	☐	☐	☐

13. Have you ever fed your dog fresh dog food (not canned or dry)?

☐ Yes   ☐ No   If yes, which brand(s)? _____

(Continued on next page.)

14. Do you perceive any health benefits to your dog from eating a fresh, natural dog food?

☐ Yes ☐ No ☐ Don't know

	Very Unlikely	Unlikely	Neither Unlikely nor Likely	Likely	Very Likely
15. How likely would you be to buy fresh, all-natural dog food as an alternative to dry or canned dog food within the next six months?	☐	☐	☐	☐	☐
16. How likely would you be to dedicate freezer space to frozen dog food?	☐	☐	☐	☐	☐

	Least Important	Somewhat Important	Most Important
17. Price	☐	☐	☐
18. Availability	☐	☐	☐
19. Nutritional value	☐	☐	☐
20. Dog's preference	☐	☐	☐
21. Vet recommended	☐	☐	☐
22. Health considerations of your dog (such as allergies, etc.)	☐	☐	☐

23. Your age

    ☐ Under 18   ☐ 18–24   ☐ 25–34   ☐ 35–49   ☐ 50 +

24. Gender

    ☐ Male   ☐ Female

25. Marital status

    ☐ Single   ☐ Married

26. Do you have children?

    ☐ Yes   ☐ No

27. Household income (optional)

    ☐ Under $15,000   ☐ $15,000 to $34,999

    ☐ $35,000 to $49,999   ☐ $50,000 to $74,999

    ☐ $75,000 to $89,999   ☐ $90,000 +

28. Can we contact you to follow-up?

    ☐ Yes   ☐ No

    Name_____

    Address_____

    City, State, Zip_____

    Phone number_____

    E-mail address_____

29. Would you be interested in participating in a focus group?

    ☐ Yes   ☐ No

30. Comments or suggestions?

    _____

    _____

    _____

(Worksheet starts on next page.)

WORKSHEET 6.1

SURVEY SUCCESS CHECKLIST

After you have drafted your first survey, use the checklist below to make sure you've met these critical objectives:

☐ The survey is the message.

☐ Clear and concise questions.

☐ You know what you will do with each answer.

☐ Gift or premium offered for participating.

☐ Thank-you for participating emphasized.

☐ Explanation of why it's important to complete the survey.

☐ Highlight what people get for responding.

☐ Request sent from the highest or most appropriate level in the organization.

☐ Space for comments included.

☐ Gift offered in advance.

☐ Confidentiality assured.

☐ Variety of response methods offered.

☐ Bonus or unexpected item offered.

☐ You have tested your survey with friends or colleagues to ensure that it's clear and concise.

☐ Do any of the questions assume knowledge that the respondent might not have?

☐ Are any questions vague or misleading?

☐ Are there questions that you can eliminate without negatively affecting the survey?

☐ Are there additional questions that you should ask?

☐ Do questions include a ranking or scale system to ensure that you receive responses that force the respondents to evaluate the likelihood or importance of each question?

☐ Survey follow-up has been prepared for including possible interviews, focus groups, or meetings.

MILESTONE 3

LOOKING OUTWARD, THEN IN

This section begins by looking at what's happening in the market-place and your industry. The first chapter of this milestone includes a list of general business resources and publications that you can use to begin the assessment process. Chapter 8 talks about competitors who provide customers with solutions that are similar to yours, not just similar products or services. The final chapter in this milestone walks you through the process of defining your strengths, weaknesses, opportunities, and threats (SWOT), and ends with a case study highlighting how you can create a strategic plan to address your SWOT analysis.

The worksheets included in Milestone 3 are:

- Worksheet 7.1: Industry Analysis and Strategy

- Worksheet 7.2: Business Research Sites Checklist

- Worksheet 8.1: Competitive Strategy Worksheet

- Worksheet 8.2: Competitive Analysis Worksheet

- Worksheets 9.1 to 9.4: SWOT Analysis

- Worksheet 9.5: Strategic Plan to Address SWOT

CHAPTER 7

SECONDARY RESEARCH: WHAT'S HAPPENING IN YOUR WORLD?

Difficulties mastered are opportunities won.

—**Winston Churchill**

Imagine that you've been running an antiques shop in your local town for the past 20 years. Business has always been good, and you depend on a mix of local clientele and out-of-towners who travel to visit your shop. In the past year, you have begun to notice that some of your regular customers are spending more time browsing and less time buying. When they do make a purchase, they're negotiating harder, cutting your profit margin dramatically. You're not sure what's causing these changes, but they are starting to have an enormous impact on your inventory level and the profit that you're generating. You know that you've got to remedy this situation quickly, or you won't be in business much longer. As profits continue to plummet, you begin to feel panic set in, and you ask yourself: "Can I approach my customers and ask them why their behavior has changed? What is happening, and what could I have done to prevent this situation?"

A BASELINE OF KNOWLEDGE

It is critical that you establish a baseline of knowledge about the world around you, including the industry, the marketplace, and your place and value as they relate to your customers. Therefore, many individuals and organizations begin their research with secondary research strategies.

As discussed in Milestone 2, secondary research involves uncovering clues about industry practices and norms and data about customers and the marketplace in general. The word *general* is the key here, since these data may not be specific enough for you to use to make any critical business decisions, or you may need to confirm their relevance to your business. The sources of secondary research tend to be trade and consumer publications, documents (government and nongovernment), newspapers, and magazines.

HINDSIGHT IS 20-20

It's a cliché, but it's an important truth: if this antiques shop owner had paid more attention to the decrease in local demand and the softening of prices, she might have realized that these changes occurred at the same time that the Internet became easily accessible to the general public. The decrease in demand and prices is strongly related to the availability of antiques online (creating global competition at a very local level). It's essential to understand how the Internet and other powerful distribution channels have upended business models for many organizations. The power of the Web results in an increase in access to antiques, which has the same negative impact on prices that an increase in actual supply would.

It's impossible to produce additional authentic furniture from the 1700s, but with more access to these items, it's as if supply had dramatically increased. Not only are there more sellers (since you can now live in Boston and buy from somebody in Europe without leaving your house), but the purchaser has access to more data about the items and is therefore better educated about their worth, price, and value.

If you as an antiques shop owner had seen the shift and trend earlier, you might have had the opportunity to react by changing your inventory levels or the products you offered (perhaps by offering heavier pieces of furniture that are expensive to ship, deterring buyers from purchasing from nonlocal sources). You could even have decided to go online to expand your customer base. Regardless of the actions you would have taken, you'll probably agree that it's always better to be prepared with information about external forces such as supply, competition, or changes in interest in certain products that can affect your business, from a positive as well as a negative perspective. This will allow you to be proactive and make more informed decisions, rather than being forced to scramble to react to market changes after they have already had a negative impact on your revenue stream.

USEFUL MARKET AND INDUSTRY INFORMATION

Let's take a look at some of the information that's available at your local library or online with the click of your mouse. Here are some questions to address to get you started:

1. What are the key associations and publications in your industry?

2. What companies belong to these associations?

3. For each association, what are the most active companies on the association site? (You can tell this from their support of the site or perhaps their appearance at industry conferences.)

4. Does the association conduct an annual survey of its members or the industry? If yes, can you get access to it?

5. Is anybody advertising at the industry or association Web site? If yes, who are they, and what is their message?

6. What publications does the association produce online and offline? Can you subscribe or review articles that are published?

7. Can you join this association? If yes, what benefits will you get by joining (like access to its annual survey or mailing list)?

8. What annual industry statistics can you find?

9. What conferences are important to the industry?

   • What are the hot topics being discussed at each conference? Who's speaking, and what companies are they from?

   • Can you download presentations or white papers from the conference sites?

   • Which companies are sponsoring these conferences? Visit their Web sites to learn more about them and their role in the industry.

10. What are the trends in the industry? How do these trends affect your business or your understanding of the industry?

11. What newsletters are produced about the industry? Can you get a sample copy of one to determine its value?

12. Identify and describe three competitors in the industry. How do they position themselves in the industry in terms of their value to their customers?

13. What consulting and research firms are respected in the industry? What information do they reveal that is important?

14. What are the buzzwords in the industry? What do they tell you about the benefits that individuals get from working with other companies in the industry?

The best way to understand how research can affect your business is to see firsthand how it's been conducted. One of my graduate students, Cecilia Caferri, was interested in launching a magazine for the Hispanic market entitled *Ola Boston*. Here are the highlights of her industry analysis, which helped her determine how she might position her business to address the attitudes, issues, and challenges in this competitive marketplace.

OLA BOSTON
INDUSTRY ANALYSIS AND STRATEGY—
ONLINE RESEARCH

What are the associations and publications in your industry?

The magazine publishing industry is blessed with two of the most professionally operated and useful associations:

- Magazine Publishers of America (MPA), primarily serving consumer magazines; www.magazine.org

- American Business Media (ABM), addressed to business magazines; www.americanbusinessmedia.com

  Comment: Identifying these publications allowed Cecilia to know what information sources she could count on for valuable magazine publishing news and trends.

What annual industry statistics can you find?

- "Custom Publishing: Opportunities Abound for B2B Publishers." Prepared by The Publishing and Media Group.

- 2004 annual report. Prepared by ABM.

- *The Magazine Handbook: A Compressive Guide for Advertisers, Advertising Agencies and Consumer Magazine Marketers 2005/06.* Prepared by MPA.

(Continued on next page.)

Comment: Although details are not given here, these industry reports helped Cecilia determine how her advertising strategy would work and how B2B publishing operated as a business.

What conferences are important to the industry?

■ The Hispanic Magazine Summit. This event is open to publishers, advertisers, researchers, and media professionals. It will be held October 14–15, 2005, at the Wyndham El Conquistador in Puerto Rico.

■ The American Magazine Conference. This is the annual conference sponsored by Magazine Publishers of America and the American Society of Magazine Editors. This year it will be held October 16–19, 2005, at the Wyndham El Conquistador in Puerto Rico.

■ Magazine Day, Boston. This event will be held on February 8, 2006, at the Westin Copley Place.

Comment: Being able to speak with potential partners, subscribers, and vendors in one location is a major advantage for any aspiring entrepreneur. In addition to attending a few of these shows, Cecilia was able to go to their Web sites and obtain valuable, timely knowledge about trends in the industry and gather a who's who to help her position her own magazine.

What are the trends in the industry?

■ Thirty-five magazine launches were announced in the third quarter of 2005, according to research conducted by MPA. They range in editorial focus and type from magazines serving policemen and law enforcement professionals to titles dedicated to music, archery, and travel. The newest titles include nine new lifestyle magazines, six magazines for women, five titles serving African Americans, and four magazines focusing on the arts and special hobbies. To date, 207 launches have been identified in 2005.

■ The new magazines of 2005 continue to innovate to serve the public, from an uplifting lifestyle magazine for young children who use wheelchairs to a new women's magazine crafted especially for the wives of professional athletes. This year has seen America's diverse population reflected in new magazines, with 23 new titles aimed at African Americans, Hispanics, and Asian Americans.

■ Information about launch announcements is posted on the New and Noted section of the MPA's Web site. Information for the MPA's New and Noted is compiled by the association's Information Services Department, which collects information from a variety of sources, including *Advertising Age, Arrivenet. com, Business Wire Inc., DM News, eMediawire.com, I-News wire.com, Magazinelaunch.com, MagazineYellowPages.com, Media Infocenter.com, MediaPost Communications, Mediaweek, Newscom.com, Newsday.com, The Pocket Guide to New Magazine Launches Specials & Annuals, PR Web, Reuters, Trendcentral.com, Ulrich's Web, Wooden Horse Publishing, WWD,* and assorted publisher press releases.

Comment: Clearly, the magazine industry is growing, with 35 publications launched in the third quarter of 2005. Knowledge of the competition and trends in topics is critical information for an organization considering a launch in a tight market space. Cecilia must be able to use this information to determine her own value-added in this tight space to ensure that she can compete effectively.

OTHER SOURCES OF DATA

In addition to researching industries online, you should also try to find out what companies are actively involved with research or provide consulting or advisory services within these industries. For example, if you're in the high-tech field, you should definitely review what major consulting/research firms like Gartner and Forrester Research have to say about the industry and the trends that they are seeing. Keep in mind that the information gleaned by these firms might be expensive to purchase. It's important to know that many businesses like these produce press releases highlighting important findings or statistics about the industry, based on surveys or research that they conducted. Since their goal is to sell their reports, they want to call attention to the firm's latest report by providing interesting "teaser" facts. These facts may be enough to help you identify key trends and/or information about important businesses and partnerships in the market. But depending on the price of the report, it could be a worthwhile purchase and may be considerably less expensive than hiring a market research firm or spending hundreds of hours trying to obtain the same data on your own.

NEWSLETTERS AS A SOURCE OF INDUSTRY DATA

Many business owners already receive magazines that cover their industry. However, another source that most don't consider or even know about is the newsletter industry. Do a quick online search using a few keywords to describe your industry, and add the word *newsletter* to the search string. It is quite likely that you will uncover a wealth of important resources. Be aware that almost anybody can easily produce a newsletter—especially an online newsletter. Still, there are many legitimate newsletters that could be valuable sources of information. Most legitimate publishers will send you a free trial subscription or a copy of a back issue to help you determine if this publication is worthwhile. This is one area where you get what you pay for. If a newsletter is free, the content will most likely reflect that. The newsletters that cost money typically will contain data that are not easily obtained; many also do not accept advertising, so you will get more objective—and probably timely—data.

OTHER SOURCES OF INFORMATION

In addition to the industry-specific associations, publications, newsletters, and consulting and research firms' reports, a slew of other organizations offer general business data. Here is a starter list of general business resources and publications that you should review.

BUSINESS RESEARCH SITES AND ONLINE RESOURCES

- About.com's List of Business Resources
  (about.com)

- Barron's Annual Reports
  (barronsonline.ar.wilink.com/cgi-bin/start.pl)

- Bureau of Labor Statistics
  (www.bls.gov)

- The Business Technology Network
  (www.brint.com)

- CEO Express
  (www.ceoexpress.com)

- Company Sleuth
  (www.company.sleuth.com)

- Corporate Information
  (corporateinformation.com)

- Dow Jones Business Directory
  (www.dowjones.com/corp/index_directory.htm)

- Edgar Online
  (www.edgar-online.com)

- U.S. government's official Web portal
  (firstgov.gov)

- Hoover's Online
  (www.hooversonline.com)

- Kauffman Center for Entrepreneurial Leadership
  (www.eventuring.org)

- Lycos Companies Online
  (www.companiesonline.com)

- Microsoft Bcentral
  (www.bcentral.com)

- PricewaterhouseCoopers Money Tree Survey
  (www.pwcmoneytree.com)

- The Public Register's Annual Report Service/Online Annual Reports
  (www.annualreportservice.com)

- Service Corp. of Retired Executives (SCORE)
  (www.score.org)

- Statistics USA
  (www.stat-usa.gov)

- Thomas Register of American Manufacturers
  (www.thomasnet.com/index.html)

- U.S. Census Bureau
  (quickfacts.census.gov/qfd/index.html)

- U.S. Nationwide Public Record Search
  (www.searchsystems.net)

- U.S. Small Business Administration (SBA)
  (www.sba.gov)

- University of Michigan Document Center
  (www.lib.umich.edu/govdocs/)

- *Wall Street Journal* Web site for start-ups
  (StartupJournal.com)

- Yahoo Business
  (biz.yahoo.com/research/indgrp/)

BUSINESS PERIODICALS AND NEWSPAPERS

- *American Banker*
  (www.Americanbanker.com)

- *Business Journal*
  (www.businessjournal.com)

- *Crain's NY*
  (www.crainsny.com)

- *Financial Times*
  (www.ft.com)

- *Investor's Business Daily*
  (www.investors.com)

- *Journal of Commerce*
  (www.joc.com)

- *Kiplinger*
  (www.kiplinger.com)

- *Mass High Tech*
  (www.masshightech.com)

- *New York Times*
  (www.nyt.com)

- *Venture Wire Newsletter*
  (www.venturewire.com/register.aspx)

- *Wall Street Journal*
  (online.wsj.com/home/us)

- *Weekly Business Journals*
  (www.bizjournals.com)

BUSINESS MAGAZINES (ONLINE AND OFFLINE)

- *Business 2.0*
  (money.cnn.com/magazines/business2/)

- *BusinessWeek*
  (www.businessweek.com)

- *CFO*
  (www.cfonet.com)

- *Direct Marketing News*
  (www.dmnews.com)

- *Economist*
  (www.economist.com)

- *Electronic Business*
  (www.eb-mag.com)

- *Entrepreneur Magazine*
  (www.entrepreneur.com)

- *Fast Company*
  (www.fastcompany.com)

- *Forbes DigitalTool*
  (www.forbes.com)

- *Fortune*
  (www.fortune.com)

- *HBS Publishing*
  (www.hbsp.harvard.edu)

- *Inc.*
  (www.inc.com)

- *Industry Week*
  (www.industryweek.com)

- *Information Week*
  (www.informationweek.com)

- *Money*
  (www.money.com/money/)

- *Newsweek*
  (www.msnbc.msn.com/id/3032542/site/newsweek/)

- *Red Herring*
  (www.redherring.com)

- *Sloan Mgmt Review*
  (mitsloan.mit.edu/smr/index.html)

- *Smart Money*
  (www.smartmoney.com)

- *Strategy & Business*
  (www.strategy-business.com)

- *Time*
  (www.time.com/time/)

- *US News & World Report*
  (www.usnews.com/usnews/home.htm)

- *Worth*
  (www.worth.com)

Where do you begin? The worksheets in this section are important tools that can help guide you through the process of determining what information you need to seek and how to obtain it.

WORKSHEET 7.1

INDUSTRY ANALYSIS AND STRATEGY

What are the key associations and publications in your industry?

What companies belong to these associations?

For each association, what are the most active companies on the association site? (You can tell this from their support of the site or perhaps their appearance at industry conferences.)

Does the association conduct an annual survey of its members or the industry? If yes, can you get access to it?

Is anybody advertising at the industry or association Web site? If yes, who are they, and what is their message?

What publications does the association produce online and offline? Can you subscribe to or review articles that are published?

Can you join this association? If yes, what benefits will you get by joining (like access to its annual survey or mailing list)?

(Worksheet continues on next page.)

What annual industry statistics can you find?

What conferences are important to the industry?

What are the hot topics being discussed at each conference? Who's speaking, and what companies are they from?

Can you download presentations or white papers from the conference sites?

Which companies are sponsoring these conferences? Visit their Web sites to learn more about them and their role in the industry.

What are the trends in the industry? How do these trends affect your business or your understanding of the industry?

What newsletters are produced about the industry? Can you get a sample copy of one to determine its value?

Identify and describe three competitors in the industry. How do they position themselves in the industry in terms of their value to their customers?

What consulting and research firms are respected in the industry? What information do they reveal that is important?

What are the buzzwords in the industry? What do they tell you about the benefits that individuals get from working with other companies in the industry?

Questions you have that are specific to your business:

1.

2.

3.

4.

WORKSHEET 7.2

BUSINESS RESEARCH SITES CHECKLIST

☐ About.com's List of Business Resources
(about.com)

☐ Barron's Annual Reports
(barronsonline.ar.wilink.com/cgi-bin/start.pl)

☐ Bureau of Labor Statistics
(www.bls.gov)

☐ The Business Technology Network
(www.brint.com)

☐ CEO Express
(www.ceoexpress.com)

☐ Company Sleuth
(www.company.sleuth.com)

☐ Corporate Information
(corporateinformation.com)

☐ Dow Jones Business Directory
(www.dowjones.com/corp/index_directory.htm)

☐ Edgar Online
(www.edgar-online.com)

☐ U.S. government's official Web portal
(firstgov.gov)

☐ Hoover's Online
(www.hooversonline.com)

☐ Kauffman Center for Entrepreneurial Leadership
(www.entreworld.org)

☐ Lycos Companies Online
(www.companiesonline.com)

☐ Microsoft Bcentral
   (www.bcentral.com)

☐ PricewaterhouseCoopers Money Tree Survey
   (www.pwcmoneytree.com)

☐ The Public Register's Annual Report Service
   (www.annualreportservice.com)

☐ Service Corp. of Retired Executives (SCORE)
   (www.score.org)

☐ Statistics USA
   (www.stat-usa.gov)

☐ Thomas Register of American Manufacturers
   (www.thomasnet.com/index.html)

☐ U.S. Census Bureau
   (quickfacts.census.gov/qfd/index.html)

☐ U.S. Nationwide Public Record Search
   (www.searchsystems.net)

☐ U.S. Small Business Administration (SBA)
   (www.sba.gov)

☐ University of Michigan Document Center
   (www.lib.umich.edu/govdocs/)

☐ Wall Street Journal Web site for start-ups
   (StartupJournal.com)

☐ Yahoo Business
   (biz.yahoo.com/research/indgrp/)

☐ Other _____

☐ Other _____

☐ Other _____

☐ Other _____

☐ Other _____

(Worksheet continues on next page.)

BUSINESS PERIODICALS AND NEWSPAPERS

☐ *American Banker*
(www.Americanbanker.com)

☐ *Business Journal*
(www.businessjournal.com)

☐ *Crain's NY*
(www.crainsny.com)

☐ *Financial Times*
(www.ft.com)

☐ *Investor's Business Daily*
(www.investors.com)

☐ *Journal of Commerce*
(www.joc.com)

☐ *Kiplinger*
(www.kiplinger.com)

☐ *Mass High Tech*
(www.masshightech.com)

☐ *New York Times*
(www.nyt.com)

☐ *Venture Wire Newsletter*
(www.venturewire.com/register.aspx)

☐ *Wall Street Journal*
(online.wsj.com/home/us)

☐ *Weekly Business Journals*
(www.bizjournals.com)

☐ Other _____

☐ Other _____

☐ Other _____

☐ Other _____

BUSINESS MAGAZINES (ONLINE AND OFFLINE)

☐ *Business 2.0*
(money.cnn.com/magazines/business2/)

☐ *BusinessWeek*
(www.businessweek.com)

☐ *CFO*
(www.cfonet.com)

☐ *Direct Marketing News*
(www.dmnews.com)

☐ *Economist*
(www.economist.com)

☐ *Electronic Business*
(www.eb-mag.com)

☐ *Entrepreneur Magazine*
(www.entrepreneur.com)

☐ *Fast Company*
(www.fastcompany.com)

☐ *Forbes DigitalTool*
(www.forbes.com)

☐ *Fortune*
(www.fortune.com)

☐ *HBS Publishing*
(www.hbsp.harvard.edu)

☐ *Inc.*
(www.inc.com)

☐ *Industry Week*
(www.industryweek.com)

☐ *Information Week*
(www.informationweek.com)

(Worksheet continues on next page.)

☐ *Money*
(www.money.com/money/)

☐ *Newsweek*
(www.msnbc.msn.com/id/3032542/site/newsweek/)

☐ *Red Herring*
(www.redherring.com)

☐ *Sloan Mgmt Review*
(mitsloan.mit.edu/smr/index.html)

☐ *Smart Money*
(www.smartmoney.com)

☐ *Strategy & Business*
(www.strategy-business.com)

☐ *Time*
(www.time.com/time/)

☐ *US News and World Report*
(www.usnews.com/usnews/home.htm)

☐ *Worth*
(www.worth.com)

☐ Other _____

☐ Other _____

☐ Other _____

☐ Other _____

☐ Other _____

CHAPTER 8

EVERYBODY'S GOT OPTIONS: COMPETITION, SUBSTITUTES, AND INERTIA

*An organization's ability to learn, and translate that
learning into action rapidly, is the ultimate
competitive business advantage.*

—**Jack Welch, former General Electric
chairman and chief executive**

Who is your competition?

Students who come to my office to discuss their business model and insist that there is absolutely "no competition" for their product or service intrigue me. I usually ask them to define what they mean by "competition." What I tend to hear is, "It's a company that has a product or service that is the same as or very similar to mine." And therein lies the confusion, because that is not the true definition of competition. These students have not fully grasped its true meaning. If your competition was limited to companies that have a product or service exactly like yours, the business environment would be a friendlier place. Companies compete on solutions and their value to customers, not merely on products or services. Therefore, competition is about fulfilling a need, not about offering an identical product or service.

Let's say you have a company that has just developed the most extraordinary orange juice. It tastes great and has lots of extra vitamins and calcium, and nobody in the local area produces this exact blend of ingredients. If you think of competition merely in terms of a similar product, you might easily, but unwisely, conclude that you do not have any competition. However, if you think of your product and competition in a broader light, you can readily see that yours is not the only company offering a product whose solutions include the following:

1. It satisfies thirst.

2. It promotes and supports a healthy lifestyle.

3. It helps maintain and develop healthy bones and teeth.

If you think of your product in any of these ways, then you realize that your competition is vast, ranging from any beverage that satisfies thirst to all health products that promote a healthy lifestyle. That would include milk, calcium supplements, vitamins, and other products focused on obtaining and maintaining healthy bones and teeth. By thinking about your product in terms of its benefits, not simply its features, you will have a much more meaningful perspective on your potential competition.

MCDONALD'S VERSUS STARBUCKS

When you think about companies like McDonald's and Starbucks, do you think that they compete with each other? What benefits does each company provide to its customers? Some of you might think of hamburgers and happy meals when you think of McDonald's, while Starbucks makes you think of coffee and perhaps some upscale pastries. These are relatively accurate descriptions of some of the products that the companies offer, but each company also provides other benefits that actually make them competitors. Have you thought of the fact that each offers customers a clean, local place to meet their friends or business colleagues? Many (if not all) of their locations offer Internet access, for a fee. So they actually offer similar solutions to the challenge of finding a place to meet, work, and socialize, thereby qualifying as competitors.

THE RIGHT PERSPECTIVE

Defining your competition is often a matter of perspective, and finding the proper perspective—generally, your potential customer's perspective—may take time and considerable work. Let's look at my company, Marketing Edge Consulting Group, LLC (MECG), as an example. MECG provides strategic sales and marketing services, including market research, marketing plan development, Web design, direct mail, and brochure/sales tool development. Those are the tangible services that I offer, but what my customers ultimately care about is whether I help them grow their business. None of my customers begin their day thinking, "I really want to spend money on developing a direct-mail campaign to send to thousands of potential customers." But they do wake up in the middle of the night pondering the best way to grow their business. Since the solutions I offer help them achieve their business goal, my competition is not limited to "other marketing consultants." It potentially includes all sorts of "experts," from Web designers to sales training coaches to management consultants. In addition, I also compete with the CEO and with other employees who are running the marketing program. Therefore, in order to justify my value to prospective clients, I need to address these bottom-line concerns. They must be confident of their decision to hire a consultant who can help get them to market faster, more efficiently, and in a more cost-effective manner, regardless of the tactical actions taken (such as direct mail and advertising) to achieve these goals.

)) DEFINE YOUR COMPETITION

To figure out who your competition really is, start by asking yourself these questions:

- What needs do my products or services fulfill?

- How else can my current or potential customers have their needs met?

- What companies fulfill this exact need?

- What companies fulfill a similar need?

- What do customers like about their current options?

- Are there gaps in the solutions that other companies offer?

- Are customers open to the concept of switching?

- How loyal are customers to their current options?

- If switching is a challenge, are there improved benefits that my company offers that will help battle inertia?

)) FIRST-MOVER ADVANTAGE

Are there real advantages to being first to market? How important is being first in terms of your competitive position? Clearly the answers to these questions depend on many factors, including the industry you are in, the products or services that you offer, and the number of other companies in the industry trying to gain market share. However, there are certain ideas, and myths, that are typically associated with being first to market. These include

- *Glory.* Yes, if you are the first to offer a cutting-edge technology or service, you can sometimes find yourself in the public eye and can take advantage of press coverage (assuming, of course, that it's positive). However, this glory can quickly turn in the opposite direction if you moved too quickly. Imagine that you've developed a great new product, but it was not quite ready (it is software, and it still has bugs). If you release it anyway to beat possible competitors, the glory could fade rapidly, as customers will be turned off, the press will grow negative, and your reputation will be tarnished.

- *Profits.* If you come out of the gate fighting, then you might gain a lead in terms of generating revenue. But there is no guarantee that being first to the marketplace will secure funding for your business. Nor will it ensure that you will have customers, since being a trendsetter often means that the general population may not be aware of the value you offer. This can be a major stumbling block for some first movers.

- *Access to distribution channels.* By capturing market share and developing partnerships early on, you can gain a strong lead on the activities in your market. Clearly, being the first to work actively with customers, prospects, and partners can be an enormous advantage. If you're ready and willing, you might beat the problem of inertia (the inability to get customers to make changes) by capturing the largest share of customers first, thus leaving your competitors to deal with inertia. If your products are viable and you are satisfying the needs of your customers, then you should be able to keep them. Truly that's the key ingredient to success: winning over your customers and keeping them for life.

)) SECOND-MOVER ADVANTAGE

Now that I've covered some of the benefits of being first to market, it's important to discuss the advantages of being second, third, or even 200th. Some of these include

- *Ability to watch and learn from your predecessors' mistakes.* If you carefully watch your competitors' mistakes as they launch, then you can take advantage of the gaffes they've made. For example, if a competitor's customers are unhappy because the product is too expensive or lacks certain features, you might be able to lure customers away if your products address these problems.

- *Ability to offer a more complete product.* If you're moving in behind the innovator, that company has ideally established a customer base that can be defined and hopefully is accessible. This might give you the opportunity to communicate with these customers so that you can understand the gaps in current product offers and address them by providing a more robust product.

- *The road has been paved.* If the innovators have done a good job, they've created awareness of the product and established a need for it. Therefore, it's not just the trendsetters who are buying your product, but ideally a larger set of customers. This larger target audience should help you get up to speed more rapidly.

- *Improved benefit knowledge.* With a new product, customers or prospects might not always understand how it benefits them. For example, when the Internet was first developed, it was used for educational and government purposes. There weren't any companies conducting business online. However, as the enormous potential and power of the Internet became apparent, the business community jumped in to take advantage of the opportunity.

- *Funding options may be better* if the industry's pioneers have established a clear set of needs. On the other hand, if there are lots of pioneers ahead of you, it may be too late, and the venture capitalists or angels investors may see you as less innovative and too late to the market. In that case, you will be challenged to prove to them that you have a better product/ service or value to offer and are not just another "me too" player.

- *Learning curve advantages.* Ideally, the innovators in the market established the need and helped educate your prospects about the benefits of your products or services. Therefore, your learning curve should be shorter, allowing you to focus on changes and current shifts in the market.

)) WHAT IS INERTIA?

The famed writer Isaac Asimov wrote in *Understanding Physics:* "This tendency for motion (or for rest) to maintain itself steadily unless made to do otherwise by some interfering force can be viewed as a kind of 'laziness,' a kind of unwillingness to make a change." And indeed, Newton's first law of motion is referred to as the principle of inertia, from a Latin word meaning "idleness" or "laziness." Inertia is about the tendency of a body at rest to remain at rest or of a body in motion to remain in motion *unless it is acted upon by an outside force*. What's the implication for your business as an *outside* force? If the body at rest is your potential customer base and it's not willing to switch to your solution, then you will have to figure out a creative way to motivate that body, en masse, to move. Inertia can be deadly for even established companies with great new products. Why? If customers already have their needs met, they may just find it too much trouble to switch—even if their current product or service is just mediocre. The benefits have to be significant enough to go through the "pain" of making a change. Therefore, if there are products on the market that are simply "good enough" for your prospects, then you have to aggressively sell your added value to your prospects or they won't switch.

One powerful example of a creative marketing campaign designed to battle inertia is the "Friends and Family Campaign" developed by MCI back in the 1990s (with the support of a marketing firm based in London called London Ink). MCI knew how difficult it was to get individuals to switch phone service carriers, so it implemented a method that pressured people to get their friends to sign up so that they could all get discounts.

At the time, MCI was the second-largest U.S. consumer long distance company. In late 1990, MCI was under attack from a $400 million negative advertising campaign launched by AT&T, which was hurting its market share. MCI's plan was to create a new consumer long distance service, MCI Friends and Family, to establish itself as a powerful brand in this category. It launched a $100 million advertising and branding campaign, running TV commercials featuring celebrities like George Burns and Elle McPherson to communicate the emotional value of keeping in touch with your friends and family. The result was that MCI's credibility and awareness grew by 25 percent within three months, while awareness of the Friends and Family program shot up to 65 percent of U.S. households within five months. In the first twelve months, MCI signed up 8 million new subscribers and gained 11 market share points worth $550 million.

Source: London Ink (www.londonink.com).

What does the MCI case tell us? Besides the fact that it took a whole lot of money to get people to switch phone carriers, it demonstrates how important it is to "think outside the box" to battle inertia. Can you accomplish that if you don't have the budget that MCI did? Yes, but not without first clearly understanding your customers' behavior. MCI realized that getting folks to switch carriers would be hard, so it had to make switching appealing at an emotional level. MCI focused on the need people have to stay in touch with their families. The campaign encouraged people to sign up their friends and family members on MCI's plan so that they could not only stay in touch but save money. The message was: everybody wins if everyone is on the same plan. I remember the campaign well because my older brother convinced all of us to switch carriers to take advantage of the savings. When I eventually got off this plan (several years later), I felt guilty about my friends and family having to pay more money to stay in touch with me. And that was clearly one of the goals that MCI was going for: to make you think twice about saying no to joining and to feel guilty when leaving.

So-called viral marketing campaigns are effective in combating inertia because one person passes the "message" on to many others, with a spiraling impact and exposure level. When these programs are successful in creating a mass audience, they also can benefit from inertia by making switching brands more difficult. A current example of this phenomenon is the cell phone companies' policies regarding subscriber benefits. Talking to anybody within your own cell phone network is free. When service from one carrier became a problem for me, I ultimately switched carriers—much to the dismay of my parents, who now had to use their "minutes" to talk to me, since we were no longer on the same plan. I felt that I had somehow abandoned them. But the pain caused by my original cell phone carrier was enough to make me go through the process of switching providers. Without a compelling reason to change, though, most customers will simply not do anything and keep the status quo.

» LEAPFROG YOUR COMPETITION

Once you have a better understanding of your competition, it's critical to know how to leapfrog it to survive in the industry and remain a player. Some survival strategies include the following:

- *Differentiate yourself.* Make sure that whatever product or service you provide, it's better than or different from that offered by your competitors. Remember that you need to provide prospects with a compelling reason to switch from what they are currently doing (which may be nothing) in order to grow your business. How do you differentiate yourself or better serve the needs of your customers? Only you can answer that question. If you've done your homework and have a solid customer profile, as well as competitive market research, you should know what unique role your product or service plays in the life of your customer.

- *Better serve the needs of your customers.* How do you accomplish this? Clearly, you have to know what your customers' needs are before you can better serve them. Therefore, ensuring that you understand the real value you provide to your customers can give you an edge over your competitors, who may not have done their homework or are missing some piece of the value chain with their offering.

- *Learn from the innovators in the industry.* What value does or did the first movers in the field provide to customers? You need to ask yourself how you can provide at least comparable positive value and even improve upon that value.

- *Form strategic alliances.* Consider aligning your company with other organizations that provide services targeting the same clients. For many small companies, a strategic alliance is the key to success. This idea will be explored in depth in the next chapter. Once you have a solid understanding of how you compete with other companies, then you can develop a stronger sense of how to position your company so that it will succeed in the market. What are your overall strengths and weaknesses, and how do these affect the opportunities and threats you will face? I will turn attention to these issues in Chapter 9.

WORKSHEET 8.1

COMPETITIVE STRATEGY WORKSHEET

What needs do my products or services fulfill?

Am I a first mover? If yes, what are the

Pros

Cons

If I'm not a first mover, what are the

Pros

Cons

How else can my current or potential customers have their needs met?

What companies currently fulfill these exact needs?

What companies fulfill similar needs?

What do customers like about their current options?

(Worksheet continues on next page.)

Are there gaps in the solutions that other companies offer?

Are customers open to the concept of switching?

How loyal are customers to their current options?

If getting customers to switch is a challenge, are there improved benefits that my company offers that will help to overcome customer inertia?

WORKSHEET 8.2

COMPETITIVE ANALYSIS WORKSHEET

Identify two important companies that offer competitive or substitute products. Visit their Web sites, and answer the questions below.

What is the stated value proposition/customer benefits?

Your company

Competitor 1

Competitor 2

Describe the target audiences.

Your company

Competitor 1

Competitor 2

What partnerships exist? Describe these partners and how you think each company benefits from the relationship.

Your company

Competitor 1

Competitor 2

(Worksheet continues on next page.)

What do press releases reveal about each company and its position in the industry?

Your company

Competitor 1

Competitor 2

Based on this assessment, name three strategies that you will use to position yourself more effectively against these two competitors.

1.

2.

3.

Identify three market segments that you can enter and that your competitors are not dominating.

1.

2.

3.

CHAPTER 9

WHAT ARE YOU REALLY GOOD AT DOING?

Here is the prime condition of success:
Concentrate your energy, thought and capital exclusively
upon the business in which you are engaged. Having begun on one
line, resolve to fight it out on that line, to lead in it,
adopt every improvement, have the best machinery,
and know the most about it.

—Andrew Carnegie

Do you really know what your core competencies or strengths are? Let's revisit Cecilia Caferri, my business school student who is developing a magazine for the Hispanic market called *Ola Boston*. When I asked her about her business's core competencies, she told me the following: "Our strength is the fact that we outsource our magazine's production and printing process, which lowers our overall costs." But when I pushed Cecilia to define and explain why this is a core competency, she came to some interesting conclusions.

Cecilia believed that outsourcing was a strength because it reflected the fact that the company was not locked into high production costs. But when I asked her what this said about *Ola Boston* specifically, she told me that because it was small, it had more flexibility than large magazine publishers, which enabled it to outsource parts of the business to save time and money. I then responded, "OK, you are *flexible* and can *make rapid, cost-effective decisions* such as outsourcing the production. Then your strengths are *flexibility* and *the ability to make rapid decisions*. Outsourcing merely *reflects* your flexibility." Cecilia agreed. And by thinking about this "strength" in a broader light—as flexibility—she was able to think of other ways to ensure that she maintained her flexibility, such as keeping her staffing numbers and overhead low to nurture this core competency and grow her business.

This chapter will explore how you can develop a business strategy that combats external threats and takes advantage of opportunities in the market by acknowledging and taking advantage of your core competencies and strengths and minimizing your weaknesses.

A MORE MEANINGFUL PERSPECTIVE

What do I mean when I say *core competency*? Basically, your core competencies are your company's unique strengths, whether they involve a special patent, marketing savvy, or cost advantages that your organization possesses. Understanding your company's core competencies is critical because these strengths represent areas where you outshine your competition. Being able to honestly evaluate both your strengths and your weaknesses relative to your competition is critical to success. You can use this valuable internal information to defend yourself against threats and take advantage of opportunities that will surface in the marketplace and are beyond your control.

Let's examine your core competencies/strengths and your overall competitive position using a popular business framework called SWOT: strengths, weaknesses, opportunities, and threats. Strengths and weaknesses refer to traits like flexibility, a special expertise or lack thereof, and other internal factors that you have some control over. On the other hand, opportunities and threats are environmental factors like the price of oil, changes in consumer preferences, rising interest rates, and other external events that are much more difficult, or even impossible, to control (but that clearly affect your business).

STRENGTHS

Strengths, also known as core competencies, are areas where your organization stands out from others in your industry. These can include technology (special code or patents that only you possess), marketing/sales savvy, personnel, experience, or cost advantages.

When you're trying to figure out what your strengths are, some questions you might want to ask yourself include the following. To gain a realistic picture of your strengths, it's also important that you ask these questions of your employees, customers, business partners, and industry experts.

- What unique advantages does my company have in the marketplace or industry?

- What does my company do very well?

- What does my company do that surpasses our competitors?

- Is there access to resources or distribution channels or technology that is unique to my company?

- How do individuals within the organization contribute to our success?

- What expertise or unique experience do I or my employees have that will have a positive impact upon our business growth?

- What other strengths does my company have that provide it with a unique advantage in the market?

The strengths that you and your company have are relative to the entire industry. Therefore, if all of your competitors have the same cost position or access to the same distribution channels, then you cannot consider that a strength; it simply becomes a minimum requirement. A good example of this is in the banking industry, where exceptional service is critical to keeping customers (especially as banks find it harder to compete on interest rates alone). Using a customer relationship management (CRM) system to communicate with your clients is a nice-to-have asset, but it is not necessarily something that would be considered a strength, since it has become a minimum requirement rather than an exception for most banks. However, if a bank does something different with the software that allows it to better serve its customers, then the use of this specialized program is turned into a strength or core competency.

WEAKNESSES

Obviously weaknesses are areas in which your company fails to excel or lacks expertise altogether. Therefore, not possessing some of the qualities noted in the strength category can be considered weaknesses if your major competitors have these abilities. But if your competitors don't have these skills either (perhaps everybody's poor at managing changing customer demand), then this may not be a mortal weakness—yet. Important questions to ask yourself to determine your weaknesses include

- Relative to our competitors, what areas are we simply not proficient at?

- Do we lack experience in a vital area such as sales, or do we lack the ability to develop new products that will contribute to our growth?

- Do we have a shortage of people with the right experience, skills, or expertise?

- How much knowledge do we possess about certain markets or industry sectors that are relevant to our business?

- Do we lack technical skills or need improvements in our ability to operate smoothly?

- Are we experiencing production capacity problems because our systems are not working at peak performance?

- Are our manufacturing/production costs too high, yet we are not able to lower them in the near future?

- What other areas need improvement?

It's far easier to admit to your strengths, but a candid appraisal of your weaknesses is important. If you have colleagues or friends whom you trust, ask them if they think your assessment is accurate. If you have employees, their input is vital, too. If you personally are not good at selling, don't delude yourself into believing that you can overcome this simply by being passionately committed to your business. Talking to others may help you see that your competition might be just as passionate—and have a talented sales force as well. However, if everybody in the industry is weak in a certain area (such as limited distribution channels), you may see that this may not be a major weakness *yet*, since it puts you on a level playing field with your competitors. Once you have clearly defined your areas of weakness, then you will be in a better position to determine if they can be turned into strengths.

To get you thinking about how to conduct such an evaluation of your own business, consider Cecilia's analysis of *Ola Boston*'s internal strengths and weaknesses.

STRENGTHS

1. A knowledgeable, well-educated team that is fluent in the language and culture of the Latino community

2. A unique understanding of how to serve the Latino community

3. Flexibility to outsource the production process and other expensive aspects of the business

WEAKNESSES

1. Lack of experience doing business in the United States and in Boston

2. Limited expertise in financial planning and funding issues

3. Lack of significant capital to fund the business

)) OPPORTUNITIES

It's always fun to daydream about business opportunities—a new location, a possible new product line, an expansion through acquisition, or discovering an underserved market.

Opportunities are external factors in the marketplace that you do not control, yet that present you with the ability to grow your business if you position yourself correctly. Opportunities can include strong demand for certain products, lack of satisfaction with available product options, and/or limited competition. Here are some questions to help you identify opportunities in your market:

- Is there strong customer demand in the market for our products or services and the value that we provide to our customers?

- Is there a lack of satisfaction with the products that are currently offered or available?

- Is our competition limited or weak in certain areas that we have not yet addressed or attacked with full effort?

- Is there a lack of competitors or substitute products or services that currently satisfy customers' needs?

- Are there readily available and/or easily accessed distribution channels (e.g., the Internet or the opening of a new trade channel) that we can take advantage of?

- Are there opportunities to easily enter a new or related market?

- What other opportunities are there in the market that will help me launch my business?

- Are switching costs (perceived or real) low?

In Milestone 4, I will discuss an opportunity that was presented to me and the steps that I took to seize it, based on my strengths and weaknesses.

By threats, I mean conditions in the marketplace that make entry or growth less desirable, more difficult, or even risky, including competitors, regulation, tax law changes, new technologies, cheaper overseas labor, and litigation. Threats include obstacles that stand in the way of your company's achieving success because you lack control over them. An example of a threat that is being faced by many businesses today is the movement of production facilities to low-cost countries like India and China. If your competitors now begin to benefit from significantly lower production costs, this could have a major impact on your organization, your pricing scenario, and the industry as a whole. To identify threats to your business, begin by asking yourself questions like these:

- Do barriers to entry, such as limited distribution channels or the closure of certain channels for importing or exporting products, affect my business?

- How much competition is there in the market?

- Are there a lot of substitute products, making it difficult for me to differentiate my value?

- Is my company affected by an increase in the price of supplies or lack of availability of certain supplies required to develop or deliver my product?

- Does inertia affect my business (i.e., people are "happy enough" with the present solution to their problem)?

- What regulations affect my business, now and in the future?

- Have there been any changes in customers' interest in my product or service?

THE INTERNET: THREAT OR OPPORTUNITY?

Here's where your industry research is required. Knowing the trends in the industry, the legal and political environments, and information about distribution channels helps you determine where the threats can be confronted and the opportunities best seized. A great example of this is the commercialization of the Internet in the 1990s. This distribution channel continues to provide opportunities for individuals and companies that would never have had access to customers around the world without its existence.

For example, eBay has created enormous opportunities and threats for a variety of companies. Before eBay existed, the likelihood of a company in Chicago doing business with buyers around the United States and the world was quite slim. It was simply too expensive, too complicated, and not worth the effort to try to promote products to individuals scattered that widely around the globe. However, these businesses can now fully compete with companies in the backyards of their customers because eBay has created a central point of sale and distribution, providing opportunities for companies, but also threats (since their foreign competitors can now also sell to their local customers).

Previously I talked about how the Internet has provided new distribution channels for antiques, allowing local antiques dealers to reach a more global audience at a lower cost than ever before. However, the downside is that your competition can also access these channels, which means that the local antiques shop is suddenly competing against many other businesses. This channel can be just as strong an opportunity as it can be a threat to your business. If there's more information known about products and greater access to them, then the law of supply and demand comes into play. The greater the supply, the lower the price tends to be if demand for the product cannot be maintained. What might start off as an opportunity can quickly become a threat to a company that is not on top of the situation. Therefore, it is in your best interest to clearly understand the external opportunities and threats that you will find as you grow your business.

It's time to complete the SWOT worksheets and develop your external analysis of the opportunities and threats that you face. You should be drawing information from the data you researched to date. Before you complete your assessment, let's learn how Cecilia viewed *Ola Boston*'s opportunities and threats.

OPPORTUNITIES

1. Relatively little competition

2. Strong growth in the Latino community starting in the year 2000

3. Underserved Hispanic community

THREATS

1. Low entry barrier for this business, with a strong possibility that larger magazines and organizations in the industry will become interested in Boston's Latino community

2. Low switching cost for clients

3. Many powerful alternatives or substitutes (for example, the Internet)

Some of these threats present a major risk for *Ola Boston*. Cecilia must determine what she will do to take advantage of the opportunities while minimizing the threats. The only way she can do this is to use her core competencies as a business to determine the most logical marketing strategy to deploy. Like Cecilia, you need to determine how you will use the information to grow your business.

OLA BOSTON CASE STUDY

Strengths (S)

1. A knowledgeable team

2. A unique understanding of how to serve the Latino/Hispanic community

3. Flexibility to outsource the production process and other expensive aspects of the business

Opportunities (O)	Strategies to Use Strengths That Maximize Opportunities
1. Relatively little competition	1. Proprietary channel for the Latino/Hispanic community
2. Strong Latino growth in the Latino community starting in the year 2000	2. Unique presence to the Latino audience
3. Underserved Latino community	3. Connect Latinos with the right products and services
Threats (T)	Strategies to Use Strengths to Deal with External Threats
1. Low entry barrier for this business with a strong possibility that bigger magazines and organizations in the industry will become interested in Boston's Latino community	1. Create an affinity group among readers
2. Low switching cost for clients	2. Provide access to a Web site where the readers can obtain historical information about the Latino community
3. Many powerful alternatives or substitutes (for example, the Internet)	3. *Ola Boston* as a "total client solution": Integral P&S for readers (build the eBay for Latin community)
	4. Stimulate long-term contracts with sponsors

(Continued on next page.)

Weaknesses (W)

1. Lack of experience doing business in US

2. Limited expertise in financial planning

3. Lack of significant capital to fund business

Opportunities (O)	Strategies to Overcome Weaknesses to Ensure Maximization of Opportunities
1. Relatively little competition 2. Strong Latino growth in the Latino community starting in the year 2000 3. Underserved Latino community	1. Sign exclusive advertising contracts with journalists to provide editorial material relevant to the Latino community 2. Sign exclusive agreements with distribution channels 3. Hire experienced editor and finance manager
Threats (T)	Strategies to Overcome Weaknesses to Minimize Threats
1. Low entry barrier for this business with a strong possibility that bigger magazines and organizations in the industry will become interested in Boston's Latino community 2. Low switching cost for clients 3. Many powerful alternatives or substitutes (for example, the Internet)	1. Generate higher ROI for advertiser 2. Long-term partnerships with supply-chain actors 3. Target specific groups with specific messages and products, building relationships with individuals that last 4. Seek Angel / VC financial and strategic aid for a sustainable growth

The worksheets included in this chapter will help you determine your strengths, weaknesses, opportunities, and threats. These will be the basis for your action plan. In the next milestone, I'll begin the discussion of how you can seize opportunities and work with partners to further grow your business.

WORKSHEET 9.1

SWOT ANALYSIS

STRENGTHS/CORE COMPETENCIES

- What unique advantages does my company have in the marketplace or industry?

- What does my company do very well?

- What does my company do that surpasses our competitors?

- Is there access to resources or distribution channels or technology that is unique to my company?

- How do individuals within the organization contribute to our success?

- What expertise or unique experience do I or my employees have that will have a positive impact upon our business growth?

- What other strengths does my company have that provide it with a unique advantage in the market?

WORKSHEET 9.2

SWOT ANALYSIS

WEAKNESSES

■ Relative to our competitors, what areas are we simply not proficient at?

■ Do we lack experience in a vital area such as sales, or do we lack the ability to develop new products that will contribute to our growth?

■ Do we have a shortage of people with the right experience, skills, or expertise?

■ How much knowledge do we possess about certain markets or industry sectors that are relevant to our business?

■ Do we lack technical skills or need improvements in our ability to operate smoothly?

■ Are we experiencing production capacity problems because our systems are not working at peak performance?

■ Are our manufacturing/production costs too high, yet we are unable to lower them in the near future?

■ What other areas need improvement?

WORKSHEET 9.3

SWOT ANALYSIS

OPPORTUNITIES

- Is there strong customer demand in the market for our products or services and the value that we provide to our customers?

- Is there a lack of satisfaction with the products that are currently offered or available?

- Is our competition limited or weak in certain areas that we have not yet addressed or attacked with full effort?

- Is there a lack of competitors or substitute products or services that currently satisfy customers' needs?

- Are there readily available and/or easily accessed distribution channels (e.g., the Internet or the opening of a new trade channel) that we can take advantage of?

- Are there opportunities to easily enter a new or related market?

- What other opportunities are there in the market that will help me launch my business?

- Are switching costs (perceived or real) low?

WORKSHEET 9.4

SWOT ANALYSIS

THREATS

- Do barriers to entry, such as limited distribution channels or the closure of certain channels for importing or exporting products, affect my business?

- How much competition is there in the market?

- Are there a lot of substitute products, making it difficult for me to differentiate my value?

- Is my company affected by an increase in the price of supplies or lack of availability of certain supplies required to develop or deliver my product?

- Does inertia affect my business (i.e., people are "happy enough" with the present solution to their problem)?

- What regulations affect my business, now and in the future?

- Have there been any changes in customers' interest in my product or service?

WORKSHEET 9.5

STRATEGIC PLAN TO ADDRESS SWOT

STRENGTHS (S)

List your top three strengths or core competencies.

1.

2.

3.

In the left column, list the top three opportunities and threats that you encounter as a company. In the right column, list the strategies and strengths that you will deploy to maximize your opportunities and minimize your threats.

Opportunities (O)	Strategies to Use Strengths That Maximize Opportunities
1.	1.
2.	2.
3.	3.
Threats (T)	Strategies to Use Strengths to Deal with External Threats
1.	1.
2.	2.
3.	3.

(Worksheet continues on next page.)

WEAKNESSES (W)

List your top 3 weaknesses as a company.

1.

2.

3.

In the left column, list the top three opportunities and threats that you encounter as a company. In the right column, list the strategies that you will deploy to overcome weaknesses to maximize your opportunities and minimize your threats.

Opportunities (O)	Strategies to Overcome Weaknesses to Ensure Maximization of Opportunities
1.	1.
2.	2.
3.	3.
Threats (T)	Strategies to Overcome Weaknesses to Minimize Threats
1.	1.
2.	2.
3.	3.

MILESTONE 4

SEIZE THE OPPORTUNITIES

A marketing alliance with the right company can help you achieve your business and sales goals. Chapter 10 explores the questions you need to ask yourself and potential business partners to determine if there's a good match. It discusses the pros and cons of partnerships and alliances and helps you identify what would be the right fit for your business. Then it examines the steps you should take to develop a positive working relationship. Chapter 11 discusses how you can seize opportunities, expand into a new marketplace, and minimize the risk to your current business model. It describes a strategy that my company deployed to establish a specialized service focused on helping companies target the Hispanic market. The goal of this chapter is to help you understand that the decisions and issues that arise in launching a new business initiative within an established business are similar to the challenges of developing an entirely new business.

The worksheets included in Milestone 4 are:

■ Worksheet 10.1: Partner/Alliance Analysis and Strategy

■ Worksheet 10.2: Partnership Strategy

■ Worksheet 10.3: Partnership Checklist

■ Worksheet 11.1: Breaking New Ground

CHAPTER 10

IDENTIFYING PARTNERSHIP STRATEGIES

I not only use all the brains that I have,
but all that I can borrow.

—Woodrow Wilson

PLACELINKS

During the Internet boom in the late 1990s, I worked with an intriguing start-up called PlaceLinks. The founders, Christopher Sole and Jonathan Bachman, launched their business model with a proprietary software system that they designed to provide local search capabilities. Their original intent was to serve as an Internet portal (i.e., a destination Web site) like Yahoo or Google. Nowadays we're all familiar with search capabilities, but their system was, and remains, unique. They wanted to be *the* online site for finding very specific products in local markets. For example, if you are in desperate need of a pair of "pink Nike sneakers" and you are interested in buying them only in Hopkinton, Massachusetts, then you would go to Placelinks.com and type in the words "Nike + pink + sneakers" in the search area and "Hopkinton, MA" in the location button, and all the stores that offered that specific product in Hopkinton and the surrounding towns would be revealed. Sounds like a great service, doesn't it? Unfortunately, the founders failed to get enough funding for their idea, and they realized that they needed to reassess their situation and develop a strategy that wouldn't require a heavy level of capital. Their new strategy involved developing a series of partnerships with organizations that needed the technology they provided. The hitch was finding the right ones to partner and grow with them.

TIMING IS EVERYTHING

Let's consider this in terms of the timing of their business. When they began their company in the late 1990s, this level of local and relevant search was unheard of. Back then, if you searched for Nike, you would have been lucky if you found Nike's Web site, let alone a specific store in a local town selling a Nike brand. Of course, the reality is that if you type in Hopkinton and Nike now, you still will get a whole lot of unrelated gobbledygook.

But by the late 1990s, when PlaceLinks started its bid for venture capital funding, that funding for Internet start-ups was drying up, so PlaceLinks was a little too late and was unable to secure enough capital to grow the company into a true portal (the amount of money required to brand the company nationally was in the tens of millions and out of its reach). But these executives were true entrepreneurs who believed in the technology and their solution (yes, they had proven that there was a need for their product and that their product worked).

So, how did they proceed? They looked at the solutions available at the time for local searches and realized that the problem of "how to find specific items in a specific location" was currently being solved, albeit poorly, by customers using the Yellow Pages to locate retailers and using newspapers to obtain additional information about sales and products. They had access through third-party vendors to a basic Yellow Pages database, so they now needed to conquer the distribution network, the newspapers.

TRUE ENTREPRENEURIAL SPIRIT

Thinking like entrepreneurs, PlaceLinks's founders decided that the best way to offer their product was to make PlaceLinks an infrastructure company, meaning that they were interested in creating and supporting the infrastructure of the companies they sold their solution to. They recognized the fact that their software *was the value* the company offered. So, they decided to sell their software solution to the newspapers, which already had established consumers, advertisers, and Web site traffic, and allow the newspapers to deploy the PlaceLinks software on their Web sites. Makes sense, right? The newspapers had the customers, but they didn't have the technology to offer this service, and PlaceLinks had the technology but had few customers. Making the major newspapers their *partners* was the solution to growing their business.

The PlaceLinks founders proceeded to develop a marketing strategy targeting high-level newspaper executives and making their pitch: they would sell their software solution through a partnership relationship. It was a very logical decision that had all the makings of a success story. Unfortunately, their first attempt failed. Why? There were two reasons: (1) PlaceLinks was more invested in the strategy than the newspaper organizations were, and (2) the actual traffic that newspaper Web sites were seeing at the time was too small to provide significant revenue from the application. In hindsight, we now know that these kinds of applications would come to be used by over 30 percent of the population, but at the time, they were used by only 1 to 2 percent. They were clearly ahead of the curve.

Such a partnership would be a win for PlaceLinks, but it was not an obvious winning proposition for the newspapers. They liked the idea, but they saw the partnership as a "nice to have" rather than a "need to have" solution. The newspapers were also conflicted about embracing the new medium—they knew they were losing readership to the Web, and they didn't know how to operate in the new environment. Remember, they were still struggling with the competition the Internet provided to their paper-based versions of the news and had not yet determined how they would use the Web to be successful. Of course, it didn't help that after the Internet crash, most newspaper companies put their Internet investments on hold, because they were usually generating financial losses and no longer giving a boost to the newspapers' stock price.

The lesson in this is simple: the key to successful partnerships lies in having both parties equally invested in the success of the alliance, or it is simply too much work to maintain and will not be successful.

THE RIGHT PARTNERSHIP

The true challenge in establishing a winning partnership is figuring out which company or type of company would complement yours. To begin this process, you must first decide what you expect from a partner and how it will contribute to your company's growth and development.

Once you've completed your SWOT analysis, you should have an accurate understanding of your company's strengths and weaknesses. In choosing a partner, you need to find a company that is strong in areas in which your company is weak, and vice versa, so that you will both be able to grow. That's assuming, of course, that this company has similar customers and that you are able to develop a good working relationship.

A simple example of this type of win-win partnership is an alliance between a creative design firm and a public relations firm. Graphic designers typically don't provide any type of written marketing services, and most PR agents can't create visuals more sophisticated than a stick figure. However, their clients often need both services, so this type of alliance makes sense if the two firms

1. Offer complementary services.

2. Focus on adding value to similar types of organizations.

3. Do not compete with each other.

4. Work well together.

These criteria are all important in developing a partnership. A strong marketing alliance offers many benefits, including reducing risk, sharing costs, and improving time to market. How?

- *Reducing risk.* Risks arise in many ways for young companies. They include monetary risks and the risks associated with lacking manpower or people with the right expertise to do the work. By partnering with a company whose services support yours, such risks can be reduced.

- *Sharing costs.* By supporting each other as you grow, you can share many costs, including those associated with marketing, sales, and lead-generating activities. Perhaps your business has better contacts in a certain geographic location, while your partner has industry connections that you are interested in developing. By working together, you can develop co-marketing opportunities to offer both of your services as a package to prospective customers.

- *Improving time to market.* With access to your partner's prospects or customers, your growth curve and time to market might be significantly reduced. If you are carrying high fixed costs, like salaries or equipment, and you can gain customers faster, this can have a tremendously positive impact upon your ability to grow.

RISK-REWARD BALANCE

The key is that the risk-reward balance should be relatively equal for each organization. The long-term benefits must be greater than the effort required to develop the partnership. Otherwise the final result may not be worth the time and money spent on developing the partnership. This is what happened with PlaceLinks. The partner newspapers did not perceive the benefit to be valuable enough to make the effort required to fully develop the partnership. Therefore, it was not a win-win scenario, and PlaceLinks was not able to carry the partnership program alone.

PARTNERSHIP CRITERIA

How do you choose the right partner? This question has baffled businesspeople for decades. By determining your criteria early on, even before you begin your search, you should reduce the risk of choosing the wrong partner. Clearly, you will want to develop relationships with companies that meet your standards, but you first have to know what those standards are. Many companies haven't considered the value of developing a "wish list" noting the traits and values that a partner would ideally possess. You don't want to establish a partnership with a company or companies that don't meet your standards simply because you haven't determined what those standards are.

Let's develop your partnership standards by first reviewing your SWOT analysis. Think about your internal strengths and weaknesses. Consider the following questions:

■ How do your strengths and weaknesses help and/or hinder your business goals?

■ How can you minimize your weaknesses through the establishment of a partnership?

■ What types of companies can help you grow, keeping in mind the external threats and opportunities affecting your business?

■ What characteristics should these companies possess?

■ How many strong potential partners do you really have, and how many options are you truly likely to have?

CANINE PARTNERS

Let's say you run a dog-walking business in downtown Boston, and your major strength is your winning personality and your ability to interact with and gain the trust of your current customers (the paying ones, not the barking ones). However, your major weakness is that you are not comfortable with the sales process, so establishing new customers is a constant challenge. A partnership with a pet shop in your neighborhood might create the right balance. Assuming that the shop has a steady flow of customers and is willing to introduce them to you, this partnership could eliminate the "cold calling" that you dread. In turn, you would need to provide value to your partner. Perhaps you could give it a referral fee for each new client you gain, or you might have a reciprocal referral system in which you recommend the store to your own clients. But developing an alliance with a company that has the same core competencies (and weaknesses) as your business won't help either of you grow faster. Given the same dog-walking business scenario, you know that you are great at nurturing your customer relationships. If you establish an alliance with a company, such as a dog groomer, that is also good at nurturing relationships but very poor at developing new ones, your partnership won't nurture either of your businesses.

Finally, think about the threats and opportunities in the marketplace. Is competition in the dog-walking business in Boston growing fiercely? Then a partnership with key groomers and pet shops is even more essential, since you don't want your competitors establishing these relationships first, locking you out of important referral sources that would help you grow your business.

DEFINE KEY BUSINESS PRIORITIES

Your next step is to define your key business priorities to help you determine the types of companies that could be your best allies. Ask yourself:

- What are my top three business goals for the next one to three years?

- What type of companies can help me achieve those goals?

- Do I want to have exclusive relationships and, if yes, am I prepared to offer this as well as receive it? What are the pros and cons of exclusivity for my company?

- Will the partnerships be formal (contractual) or informal? How will I decide?

- Am I interested in expanding in a certain geographic location or within a key demographic market?

Make sure your partners already have established connections or are planning on focusing on these markets or your goals won't match.

BUSINESS VALUES

Partnerships work only if the parties share similar business values and principles. Make sure your philosophies of business relationships and customer relationships are aligned. You can have partners who seem ideal on paper, but if they simply don't treat their customers the same way you treat yours, the partnership won't work.

)) LET THE SEARCH BEGIN

Once you've established your standards, you're ready to begin your search. In the same way that you would prospect for potential customers, develop a list of the key companies that meet your standards and develop a plan to introduce yourself and begin a dialogue with them.

)) CREATING A WIN-WIN SCENARIO

It's a key question: will your partner benefit from this alliance? As could be seen from the PlaceLinks story, the partnership will be doomed if your partner doesn't see equal benefits from it. Therefore, while asking yourself what qualities you want a partner to have, make sure to ask those same questions of the other party. If you can't determine how your prospective partner will benefit from working with you and it can't verbalize its gain, then you both have an obligation to step back and carefully consider your next step. The level of work required to create a partnership is significant, and you don't want to enter into this process only to have it all fall apart in a few months.

)) IS THIS MATCH RIGHT?

Once you have identified a few strong matches, you should carefully and slowly begin to discuss ways that you can work together. Questions you need to ask include the following:

■ How do each of these potential partners' strengths and weaknesses fit with my company's core competencies?

- What is the potential market opportunity if we work together?

- What would the market potential be if I did not partner with this company?

- What advantages will I gain by working with this company?

- What advantages will the company gain if it partners with me?

- What are the risks on both sides if this fails?

- What happens when things change? How will we allow for the shift in power as knowledge changes or if the partnership becomes less valuable to one party?

- What are the opportunity costs (i.e., what opportunities might I lose by getting involved in this partnership or alliance)?

FURTHER INVESTIGATION REQUIRED

Once you have chosen one or two prospective partners, spend as much time as possible with the key decision makers within each organization to ensure that this is a good match. You may be thinking that you do not have the time, as you are a busy entrepreneur running a business. However, by investing this time up front, you will determine if your organizations have compatible values and thus will be able to succeed long term. Think of a partnership as a way of ideally developing many customer relationships at once. How much time would you spend developing 10, 20, or perhaps 50 customer accounts? That's how much time you should spend developing a partnership if it can provide you with the same number of customers.

YOU'VE GOT A GREEN LIGHT

Assuming that all signs are "go," you should move forward with the partnership. But a successful alliance requires a clear outline of the structure, duration, and management of the relationship, with focused goals that are measured frequently. Spell out what each of you is required to contribute. Keep the lines of communication open and work on the relationship to maximize your success rate.

SUCCESS FACTORS

What factors will help make your partnerships more successful?

- *Experience always helps.* The more experience you have in creating and managing partnerships or major accounts, the better your chances of success because you will understand up front how much work it takes to grow and nurture this relationship.

- *Internal champions are key.* There must be somebody at each organization who is responsible for the success of the program and acts as its champion to promote its growth.

- *Feedback system.* An efficient feedback system must be in place to deal with issues and opportunities as they arise.

The bottom line is that these relationships must be treated with as much care as you would give your largest customer account. The investment in energy and time may be significant, but the payoff can also be enormous.

A FINAL WORD ON PARTNERSHIP FAILURE

We've seen why PlaceLinks did not succeed in establishing its partnerships, which has some valuable take-home lessons. As a company, PlaceLinks continues to exist, continuing to focus on helping media and other companies aggregate their ad results and build network revenue and viewership through innovative searchable content. In establishing your partnerships, what other challenges do you need to be aware of?

- *Inability to meet demands.* Both companies entering into a partnership will have demands and expect certain needs to be met. Even if your intentions are good, if your company is growing and you are not able to meet these needs, then the possibility of success for the relationship can be severely hampered. Likewise, your partner may not be able to meet your demands or needs, so you must carefully investigate each other's ability to meet goals before entering into a partnership.

- *Time constraints.* You may not have the time to manage, nurture, and grow the partnership, since you are still growing, managing, and nurturing your own company.

- *Management.* You may not have the right people, or enough people, to manage the relationship. The reverse can also happen if your partner is not able to dedicate enough people to work with your company. This can lead to a great deal of resentment if you're working diligently to provide business leads for your partner company, but it is not reciprocating.

- *Excess reliance on partner.* You are taking a risk when you rely on your partner to perform its role, especially if you are relying on it to help fuel growth. If this doesn't happen and you have no control over your partner's actions, then the impact on your bottom line can be severe. You should never rely too heavily on any one relationship to grow your business. This rings true not only for partnerships but also for customers and major business accounts.

- *Scale and growth.* You don't know if your partner will be able to scale or grow with you or vice versa. What if you grow so rapidly that the partnership doesn't make sense, or your partner's growth leapfrogs your company's contribution to its bottom line? Like all of the other pitfalls, the best way to try to avoid this is to do your homework beforehand and find out as much about the organization as possible to ensure the greatest opportunity for success.

Here are some ideas to keep in mind in establishing your partnerships:

- Identify your strengths and weaknesses from the outset.
- Make sure the goals of the partnership are clearly outlined.
- Map out a clear process for working together.
- Measure and review your progress and problems on an ongoing basis.
- Ensure that your brand and reputation match those of your partner.
- Dedicate a champion at each organization, someone who will support the growth and development of the partnership.
- Communicate openly in both directions.
- Make sure that the projected outcome is a win-win for both organizations.

The next chapter will discuss the program that I created helping companies market more efficiently and effectively to the Hispanic market. You will learn how launching a new business model within an established company is very similar to developing an entirely new business.

(Worksheets start on next page.)

WORKSHEET 10.1

PARTNER/ALLIANCE ANALYSIS AND STRATEGY

List the strengths and abilities that are critical to success in your industry. Then, place a plus (+) in the "Your Company" column for the areas where your company is strong and a minus (–) where it is weak. To the best of your knowledge, do the same for two different potential partners.

Business Strengths and Abilities	Your Company	Partner A	Partner B
1.			
2.			
3.			
4.			
5.			
6.			
7.			
8.			
9.			

WORKSHEET 10.2

PARTNERSHIP STRATEGY

Think about several companies with which you'd like to develop a partnership. For each company, complete the worksheet. You may not be able to answer all, or even most, of the questions immediately, but you should know the answers before you launch into any type of formal agreement.

Possible Partner_____

Partner strengths:

Partner weaknesses:

How will the partner's strengths be leveraged to further grow your business?

How will you handle the partner's weaknesses?

What are the pros of the partnership strategy?

What are the cons of the partnership strategy?

What does your company offer your potential partner in terms of growth?

How can this company help you grow your business?

What costs can you share?

Do you share geographic territories or have other areas in common, such as contacts or industry relationships?

(Worksheet continues on next page.)

What values are important to you that your partner must share?

What is the potential market opportunity if you work together? If your partnership does not work, how will this affect your market opportunity?

Will the partnership include a formal contract, or will it be informal?

What are the risks on both sides if the partnership fails?

Can this partner meet the demands of your agreement, and vice versa?

Do you each have enough time to fulfill the demands of the partnership?

Who will manage the partnership and be its internal champion?

What's the risk of relying too heavily on this partnership?

Can this company scale its business as you grow, and vice versa?

Will the partnership be exclusive and, if yes, are you prepared to offer this as well as receive it? What are the pros and cons of exclusivity for your company?

WORKSHEET 10.3

PARTNERSHIP CHECKLIST

Checklist of critical factors influencing partnerships:

☐ You clearly understand your strengths and weaknesses from the outset.

☐ The goals of the partnership are clearly outlined.

☐ The process of working together is clear.

☐ Progress and problems are measured and reviewed on an ongoing basis.

☐ Your brand and reputation match those of your partners.

☐ There's a champion at each organization who is dedicated to supporting the growth and development of the partnership.

☐ Communication is flowing openly in both directions.

☐ The projected outcome is a win-win for both organizations in a relatively even manner.

CHAPTER 11

BREAKING NEW GROUND

*When one door closes another door opens; but we do often look
so long and so regretfully upon the closed door,
that we do not see the ones which open for us.*

—**Alexander Graham Bell**

Even if you've been in business for 20 or 30 years, the decision to change or expand your business model or change your company's strategic objective can be quite daunting. How do you seize opportunities to expand into a new marketplace while minimizing the risk to your current business model? While writing this book, I was approached by one of my financial clients to conduct a feasibility study to assess the opportunity for the client to develop services for the Hispanic market. This was a market that had always intrigued me. Unfortunately, my personal expertise was not broad enough to launch a specialized service focused on this area. However, my former student at Boston University, Cecilia Caferri (whose business model for the Hispanic magazine *Ola Boston* was reviewed in several previous chapters) had strong expertise and experience. She is from Argentina; she had previously been a regional marketing and communication manager in Argentina, Chile, Paraguay, Brazil, and Uruguay; and she was in the process of developing a business model to create a magazine for the Hispanic market. Some might say it was pure luck that Cecilia and I knew each other and were able to seize the opportunity. Louis Pasteur once said, "Chance favors only the prepared mind." In our case, we were both prepared for this opportunity, and we seized it.

Since Cecilia had the experience and knowledge of the Hispanic market, I gave her a contract to work on the client project with me. Together we created a feasibility study for my client. Not only were we able to provide the client with the knowledge it needed to make a decision about the feasibility of this market opportunity for it (which was a definite yes!), but I found myself overwhelmed by the growth opportunity in this market. I decided to offer Cecilia a job with my company while I developed the expertise and additional business partnerships (such as my partnership with the Hispanic News Press) required to develop this service for new clients. Our timing couldn't have been better, since she had just concluded that she was not going to proceed with the launch of her magazine *Ola Boston*.

In this chapter, I will share with you how we broke new ground and what processes we went through to determine if there was an opportunity to expand my firm's services without risking the current, successful business model.

CASE STUDY: CREATING A NEW SERVICE FOR CUSTOMERS: HISPANIC MARKET DEVELOPMENT SOLUTIONS

THE OPPORTUNITY

The numbers are overwhelming. According to the U.S. Census Bureau, Hispanic workers will account for more than 33 percent of total labor force growth in the United States by 2012, and Hispanics' economic clout will rise to $1,087 billion by 2010—accounting for 9.2 percent of all U.S. buying power. Larger than any other minority group, and with growing purchasing power, a high percentage of home ownership, and a young median age, the Hispanic market represents a tremendous opportunity to create a new niche area into which my clients could expand their own businesses. The question that I had to address was simple: Did these changing demographics solve a problem and/or create an opportunity for our current client base? If yes, how could we best capture this opportunity? If no, was there a large enough prospect base that we could target that was aligned with our present customer value proposition?

OUR FEASIBILITY STUDY

We needed to conduct our own feasibility study to determine whether the revenues generated by the potential opportunities were greater than the overall costs involved in the development of this new business practice. In other words, we had to ask ourselves:

- Was the effort going to generate adequate rewards and produce a profitable new business model without damaging an already successful business?

- Did we have the expertise and resources necessary to market and sell this service as a new solution for our customers?

- Would our customers want or need the service?

- What new target audiences did we need to approach to make the model work?

Basically, we had to determine if we could produce a business service that provided the research and tools that companies needed if they were to understand their own ability to capture business from the Hispanic market. With the addition of Cecilia—along with developing strong partnerships such as the Hispanic News Press as well as with an internationally focused design firm located in Buenos Aires, Argentina—allowed us to offer our customers the appropriate cultural expertise and competitive edge. In addition to assessing their "Hispanic readiness," we also offered an international perspective in creating the marketing program required to capture the market.

WHAT DID WE NEED?

I was confident that I had assembled a strong team of international talent, but I knew that I needed more than a team. I needed to offer real value to customers. Just because one client was interested in this service and was pleased with my company's ability to develop a feasibility study did not mean that there was a large enough need to create an entirely new service.

Therefore, before beginning to delineate a marketing strategy for the business, we had to review our customer base to see if there was indeed a good match. For a few clients in the financial field (banking and credit unions), there appeared to be a solid synergy between our expertise and the opportunities for our current customers. After carefully reviewing the prospective market pool, we concluded that there was a strong enough need in the market that we could uniquely fill and offer true value. We were convinced that our combined skills, experience, and expertise would create value and opportunities for our current and prospective client base. The decision was made to proceed.

DETERMINING OUR VALUE ADD

With a clear target audience, the next step involved determining what our unique value proposition was. For seven years, I'd been working closely with small to midsized organizations to determine their internal competencies and help them define their market opportunities and goals; I also worked with them on mapping out action plans to grow their businesses and helped them target various market segments. So we created the following value statement:

> The Hispanic market can provide real advantages to organizations if they can assess their readiness and develop a unique strategy to attract this target market to their company. Marketing Edge Consulting Group, LLC works with clients to first determine if their customer needs align with their business goals and values. If this synergy is present, we will assess their readiness and potential opportunity to target the Hispanic market and develop tactical marketing strategies for them to deploy. This solution is completed by an international team experienced in research, segmentation analysis, creative design, and marketing strategy.

POSITIONING THE BUSINESS

Now we had to decide how to position the business. Should we come up with another name for the company to demonstrate our international perspective? I was already incorporated as Marketing Edge Consulting Group, LLC. Should I become Marketing Edge Global? Would this name give me an advantage, and did it represent my company? Before we even decided if a name change was appropriate, I grabbed the URL (which was available, fortunately), and we began working on a logo and positioning statement describing the business. We came up with a variety of ideas (we even played with a few different logos and colors for the Global business). However, after careful consideration and discussions with a variety of marketing colleagues and brand experts, we concluded that since the current business name was recognized, there was no real advantage to changing it (see Figure 11.1). Nonetheless, we did decide that it was time for a new look for the logo and Web site. You've probably heard the fable about the cobblers' kids having no shoes; well, this marketing consultant had been so busy working on her clients' marketing programs and Web sites that her own site had not been updated in almost seven years. This was the ideal opportunity to correct that situation, since the expansion of the business meant more visitors to the Web site.

Figure 11.1 Rejected "Test" Logo for Marketing Edge Global

ORIGINAL STRATEGY

Until this point in my business, my sales and marketing approach had consisted almost entirely of networking. Prospects used my Web site to find out more about me and confirm my credibility after our initial personal introduction. But with a new solution, we needed to project the right message and image so that individuals could first find our Web site, then use that as the starting point to communicate with us. We were still going to use networking as a key strategy, but given the entirely new market opportunity, we now had more ground and industries to cover in a variety of channels. This changed the goal of the site because as well as serving as a credibility builder, it was now also going to have the additional role of introducing my company to prospective clients.

PROMOTING AND CREATING THE BRAND/IMAGE

We spent several weeks discussing our message and how we wanted to brand ourselves as a business. We chose words that we believed described our value to our customers, including

- Experience

- Globalization

- Innovative

- Credibility

- Creativity

- Expertise

- Integrity

- Passion

- Effectiveness

- Energy

Once we had agreed on the message and the value that we wanted to convey, we proceeded to redesign the logo with the goal of having it provide the sense of energy, passion, and global perspective that we offered (see Figure 11.2). We also decided that it was important to keep certain elements of the old logo in order to avoid losing the brand that I had already built.

Before   After

Figure 11.2 Logo Before Marketing Edge Expanded Services and Logo Design After New Services Launched

We then set out to explain our value on the Web site. After extensive review, we developed the following copy for the home page, written to show our experience, with the goal of demonstrating to potential clients that we're real people, truly interested in helping them obtain results.

HOW WELL DO YOU KNOW YOUR CUSTOMERS?

Understanding who your customers are and the value you provide to them is the key to successfully growing a business.

At *Marketing Edge* our philosophy is simple: *marketing begins with your customer, not your product.* Therefore, we partner with you to define your current and future customers' needs and build your sales and marketing strategy upon that knowledge.

We bring our passion, energy, integrity and expertise to every client engagement. We know what it takes to make a business succeed! Like you, we have been marketing directors, business managers, researchers, and creative directors.

Browse our Web site to discover firsthand how we have delivered solutions to dozens of clients in more than 30 industries throughout North America, Latin America, and Europe. Call us to learn how we can provide effective results that will *turn your business vision into reality.*

For a complimentary initial consultation e-mail Beth Goldstein directly or call 508.893.0976.

TRANSLATING THE SOLUTION FOR OUR PROSPECTS

Although our value statement was a good start, we knew that we still had important work to do if this new venture was to succeed. First we needed to educate our customers about the potential, and then we could begin to help them develop marketing programs to target the audience.

EDUCATING OUR PROSPECTS

Of course, we now needed to develop the Web site, create business cards, and, most important, determine how we would get our message and solution across to potential customers. Knowing that our target market was made up of the same types and sizes of businesses that we had already been working with, we knew that the market opportunity was not apparent to some of them. Therefore, our goal was twofold:

1. Provide proof of our knowledge and credibility.

2. Educate prospects about the potential of the market for their own business.

Our marketing program involved a variety of educationally focused activities, such as networking, developing partnerships with companies that were already visible in and integrated into the Hispanic market, conducting public speaking engagements, launching miniseminars, sending direct-mail campaigns to prospects, and creating research reports based on surveys we conducted to establish our credibility and expertise. Our belief was that once a need or opportunity was clearly established in the minds of our prospects, we could more easily open doors to offer our solution to help them grow. It was a win-win situation, if we did it right.

We took the best practice methodology that we were already deploying with current customers to help them market their businesses. We reworked the framework and entitled it Hispanic Market Development Solution. We also created a two-phase process called the Hispanic INSITE Market Assessment (see Figure 11.3), where we work with customers to evaluate the connection between the products and services that they offer and the Hispanic market's needs and interests. Once we determine a customer's *Hispanic Readiness* (that is, determine whether targeting the Hispanic market will provide a solid business and financial benefit for that company), we create and launch an integrated marketing program to grow its business.

Figure 11.3 Hispanic INSITE Market Assessment

While I was writing this book, we mailed our first direct-mail campaign to small to midsized financial institutions, including local and national banks and credit unions. We also began our market research report program to attract and educate potential new customers, with the goal of educating our prospects by demonstrating the power of targeting the Hispanic market. To learn more about the progress we made, visit the Web site (see Figure 11.4) at www.m-edge.com and you can see how the business has progressed since the book was finished.

Figure 11.4 Marketing Edge Web Site

POWER IS IN THE EXECUTION OF AN IDEA

One final thought: many individuals have asked me, "Why are you explaining your business strategy and approach in a book that is easily accessible to the public? Aren't you worried that somebody is going to steal your ideas and develop the business and compete with you?" Honestly, I am not worried about this because a good idea is only as strong as its execution. As the director of the Business Plan Competition at Boston University School of Management, I have the opportunity and the privilege to hear great ideas on a regular basis. Many times I hear the same wonderful idea from different students and alumni. There really aren't as many unique ideas as we'd like to believe. The success stories are those where teams can actually execute and carry out their plans.

Dreams of business success are realized only when a lot of sweat equity and hard work are invested in the business to make it happen. Therefore, anybody else who likes this idea can absolutely carry it forward if he or she is willing to invest the time, energy, and passion into it and possesses the expertise to make it happen. If you're out there and you like the idea, go for it. There's plenty of room for more than one company to carry out this type of idea. If you launch a similar business, congratulations! Please let us know how it's working for you.

In the next milestone, I begin to dig into the specific tactics that you are now ready to choose to grow your business. This includes your marketing and sales efforts, ranging from direct mail and advertising to networking and attending conferences.

(Worksheet starts on next page.)

WORKSHEET 11.1

BREAKING NEW GROUND

Questions to ask yourself include:

How would you describe the new opportunity for the business?

Will the new service or product produce a profitable business model without causing risk to your current business model?

Will the effort generate appropriate rewards?

Do you have the expertise and resources to market and sell this service as a new solution for your customers?

Do your customers want or need this service?

What new target audiences do you need to approach to make the model work?

PICK YOUR TOOLS:
THE MARKETING MIX

Milestone 5 covers the areas of marketing that most people think of when you say "marketing." These include strategies like brochures, Web sites, direct mail, and advertising. It begins with a discussion of the value of branding and includes an extensive review of the various marketing communication methods you can use to create, support, and enhance your brand and your message to the world. I wrap up the milestone with a discussion with two Web site development and branding experts and learn their perspectives on the critical factors to consider in online marketing.

The worksheets included in Milestone 5 are:

■ Worksheet 12.1: Communicating Your Message

■ Worksheet 12.2: Material Development Questionnaire

■ Worksheet 12.3: Logo Concept Questions

■ Worksheet 13.1: Promotional Marketing Piece Evaluation

■ Worksheet 13.2: Direct-Mail Checklist

■ Worksheet 14.1: Web Site Checklist

CHAPTER 12

BUILDING A BRAND: PERCEPTION IS REALITY

*The toughest thing about success is that
you've got to keep on being a success.*

—**Irving Berlin**

Branding is one of the hottest buzzwords associated with marketing these days. But what is branding, and why is it so important? Branding represents every touch point and every connection that you make when it comes to the customer. Therefore, seasoned marketers know that in order to brand an organization, they have to

- Define their customers' needs.

- Determine how they want to brand themselves in relation to their customers' needs.

- Define the message (or messages) that's most important to their customers.

- Ensure that they can meet their customers' needs in this defined area.

- Finally, integrate this message into every single touch point that they have with their customers, from sales and operations through to fulfillment and follow-up service.

Everything you do has to incorporate that branded message, because if you dilute the message in any way, you won't be sending a clear definition of what your company is and what value you provide to and for your customers. Therefore, branding is wrapped up not only in everything that you do but in how you are perceived. As the saying goes, "Perception is reality," so in order to ensure that your brand is strong, you need to make sure that your message is clear in every way.

HOW IMPORTANT IS PERCEPTION?

A few years ago, my family and I were in the midst of a major house renovation. We had decided to put new siding on the house, and our contractor, Bob, decided to begin the project in the middle of the winter (that's a story unto itself). We live in New England, and we tend to get quite a lot of snow here, so it was just our luck that a major storm was predicted right when we were launching the project. Our house is three stories high, and Bob covered the house with a big blue tarp running from the top of the roof to the front lawn so that when the snow fell he could continue working under the tarp. Our windows were covered, and all we could see from the inside was blue.

My son Ben, then three years old, asked, "Why do we have this blue thing outside the house, and why can't I see the front yard?" Two legitimate questions. So I responded that Bob was working, a big blizzard was coming, and Bob didn't want to get caught in the blizzard while he was working outside. Ben seemed okay with that explanation for a few hours, but when nightfall approached, he refused to sleep in his own bed. My husband and I had no idea what he was worried about, but we allowed him to sleep with us the first night. However, when he replayed this fear the next evening, and then the one after that, we were concerned and not so thrilled to have additional company in bed with us. I asked him to explain what exactly he was afraid of. Finally, he revealed, "I'm afraid of the lizard that is coming. I don't want it to eat me."

DON'T LET YOUR BRAND BECOME A LIZARD

So the moral of the story is: it doesn't matter how great a job you think you have done explaining something if the person on the other end has a totally different perception of what you're saying. If the other person isn't receiving the same information that you're sending, then you need to go back and try to understand who this person is and how he or she receives messages. You need to ensure that your message is clear and on target.

You might be talking to a three-year-old who doesn't know what a blizzard is and thinks that lizards are going to attack him, or, even worse, it might be your customer who perceives your value and benefit differently from the way you have attempted to explain it. To ensure that your message, your image, and the perception you want to convey are understood in the way that you want them to be accepted requires constant reinforcement of the message, along with feedback loops (such as surveys or a sales force) that provide continual updates regarding your image and perception with customers.

Many people associate marketing with brochures, Web design, and logos. Why? Because those are tangible items. It's harder to touch and feel market research and customer profiles. In reality, marketing collateral (direct mail, brochures, and business cards) is the icing on the proverbial cake. It's important and it completes the process, but depending on your preferences and the type of ingredients you already have in your cake, your icing and other toppings will vary (or you may not require them at all).

BRANDING

All the work that you've done to date to identify your customers and understand their needs serves as the building blocks for creating your public identity. Often people refer to that work as branding, but branding involves far more than simply the colors you choose for your logo or the tagline you design. Branding is the impression you leave with your customers through every written and verbal communication and other customer touch points. For example, if you tell the world that customers are your top priority, even the best literature and most customer-friendly design will not convince the world that this is true *if* your operations don't support a customer-oriented position. If you don't treat your customers royally, it won't matter that your pamphlets and your Web site say that your customer service is exceptional.

» YOUR MESSAGE TO THE WORLD

There are many ways that you can convey your message to your customers, prospects, potential business partners, employees, and the public at large. I'll discuss some of the strategies you can use to help promote and support your brand. But remember, branding is not just marketing's job. It involves operations, sales, product development, research, and anyone else in the company who interacts with customers.

Dale Bornstein, partner/director of global practices at Ketchum (www.ketchum.com), one of the largest global public relations firms in the world, shared her perspective on branding:

> In addition to ensuring consistency across all touch points, powerful brands have a clear sense of who they are and communicate that impactfully at every

touch point. Your brand is not just yours to manage. In today's world of consumer interactivity and consumer-generated media, your customer, client, employee, etc. comanages your brand with you. Authenticity at every touch point is critical to ensuring you are delivering on your brand promise and reinforcing what your brand stands for. Brands that win in the marketplace understand the importance of choosing communication and marketing tactics that are authentic for the brand and that further the brand's relationship with its audiences.

Branding, as a part of marketing a company, is dependent upon your customers. As Dale points out, you cannot brand yourself without your customers' supporting and reinforcing your message. If you cannot deliver on the message, then the brand that you are trying to create will be lost.

Let's review the myriad types of material that you can use to promote and support your brand and business image. Among them are the following:

- Sales literature

- Image/logo design

- Direct mail

- Conference and exhibition material

- Public relations

- Advertising

- Online and e-mail marketing

- Partnership material

The next two chapters will discuss these, and a variety of in-person activities will be explored in the next milestone, including personal selling techniques, networking, and developing an elevator pitch.

WHAT'S IN A NAME?

How important is your business name?

Clearly you want people to remember who you are and to be able to recall what you do. The more your business name explains your business, the more often that will occur. However, the name is not a critical factor if you otherwise do a great job of branding your company.

Plenty of companies, including Monster (the career services site), Google, and, of course, Yahoo, have created enduring brand names. On the other hand, if you don't have an enormous budget to brand yourself, then doing what Staples (the office supply superstore) or Priceline (a company that competes on price) did and using your name to describe your business works very well. It lets customers and prospects know what to expect. For example, Staples was a perfect name for a business that offers every type of "staple" or supply needed for office or personal use. Another example is hair-cutting salons, which have been known to have clever, memorable names like "Curl Up and Dye," which is a great (although perhaps somewhat morbid) twist on words. The bottom line is, you might gain some advantages when you use a name that's equated with your value and business model, but it's not essential to your success.

DETERMINE WHAT WORKS FOR YOUR BUSINESS

Now I'll explore how these marketing tools can benefit your business. Clearly you probably won't be able to afford all of these tactics on an entrepreneur's budget. But except for Coca-Cola, Microsoft, Nike, and other massive organizations that attract customers from almost every demographic sector around the world, many companies don't require all of these options, anyway.

SALES LITERATURE

Sales literature can be a brochure, fact sheets, trifolds, or even simple folders filled with printouts. Knowing what will work best for you begins with understanding your customers. Are they engineers who really want a lot of detail before they can comfortably make a purchasing decision, or is simple, basic material enough to intrigue them? Do they even need to read about you or your company? It's easy to convince yourself that you have to have a brochure, when in reality people may be more interested in meeting with you and perhaps seeing examples of your work. If you're an interior designer, seeing a portfolio that contains examples of homes that you've redesigned is likely to be more convincing to a client than a fancy brochure that talks about what you can do but that doesn't demonstrate your skill and abilities.

SPENDING TOO LITTLE MONEY OR EFFORT

Being able to put your best foot forward during your first encounter with a prospect can make or break your opportunity to impress your prospect. If you decide that you need a brochure, make sure it's professional. Nowadays it's pretty easy to go to a local office supply store like Staples or Office Max and, using a preprinted trifold paper, create a professional-looking brochure. That's perfectly acceptable, but make sure that your brochure is well written, explains who you are, and promotes the image that you want to project.

I've seen professionals do this on their own. In some cases they've done it very well, but other times they've used fuzzy pictures because their printer was running out of magenta ink. Even worse, they didn't proofread, and their copy was littered with typos. Don't let this happen, because your brochure is your face to the world and the impression that you will leave with prospects.

This also holds true for business cards. This is part of your initial introduction to a prospect. If the edges are perforated and the card looks sloppy and unprofessional, customers will feel less confident about working with you. Think about it. Would you want to hire somebody who couldn't afford to spend $100 on a clean, professional business card? What statement and message does that create about this person's business?

OVERSPENDING

As easy as it is to spend too little time or money, you also can err on the other side and overspend. It's critical to recognize the point where you've spent enough to have a professional look but have not gone into overkill with a brochure that's so fancy that it either misses the message or kills your marketing budget.

My first job out of college was working in marketing for a health-care organization. It was the mid-1980s, when health-care companies did not advertise and spent little money promoting their services. My employer was ahead of the curve and created a brochure that was quite sleek and sophisticated. But unfortunately it had the opposite impact from the one the company intended it to have: it gave customers the impression that the company was spending more money on brochures and marketing than on patient care. This couldn't have been further from the truth. But in this case, perception was reality, and the brochure prompted negative feelings from the company's customers. As somebody fresh out of college, I learned a valuable lesson: marketing must match your customers' needs and interests in every respect, or it will fail.

)) ALIGN YOUR BUDGET WITH YOUR EFFORT

Remember that your marketing budget includes more than your brochures, so don't create material that is so expensive that it prevents you from doing any other sales and/or marketing activities. There's a point of no return in every marketing venue, and it's important to learn when spending more won't generate you any more revenue. Learning this will help you maximize your ROI (return on investment) in all areas.

)) DO YOU REALLY NEED A BROCHURE?

So, what questions do you need to ask yourself to determine whether you need a brochure? It's important to consider the following questions:

- Who will read the material?

- What will they do with the information they learn?

- What do you want them to do with the material (i.e., what is your call to action)?

- Is your current material professional-looking, and does it present you in the best light?

- Is it easy to understand?

- Is it well written, and does it describe important information that your customers need in order to make decisions to buy from you?

- Is it targeted toward your audiences, addressing their needs, their concerns, and the benefits they get from working with you or purchasing from you?

- Do customers use the material to make purchasing decisions, or are there alternative sources of information (like your Web site or your product) that might be more valuable?

- How clear is your current message?

- Would somebody outside of the industry understand what you've written, or is it full of industry jargon that prospects might not know?

IS NEW LITERATURE WORTH THE INVESTMENT?

My rule of thumb has always been that you should make sure you'll get at least 18 months' use out of the material, because if you're going to spend a lot of money creating and printing new or redesigned material, you don't want the message to be obsolete in the first six months. So don't spend money on a fancy brochure if you think your message, price, or product will change dramatically in the next few months. When information that is time-sensitive (like price) must be included in the literature, it might be more cost effective to spend money on nice folders and print professional fact sheets with the same information. The cost savings are tremendous, and it's just as professional.

DO YOU NEED A DESIGNER?

Does your design make a solid, professional statement? Don't try to be your own designer or save money by hiring an amateur. If you do, you will be throwing away money on something that simply doesn't look professional, is too trendy or dated, or simply doesn't work. Make sure that whatever you create works, both online and offline. It's worth the money to invest in a designer who can be creative with your money and guide you through the process.

WHAT ELSE DO YOU NEED TO THINK ABOUT?

One question you should ask yourself is: would I benefit from material other than brochures, like a white paper? If you're in the high-tech market or your key customers are members of the scientific community, writing a white paper might be more of a credibility builder than writing a brochure. Think about how you want to spend not only your money but also your time. Hiring a technical writer to assist you might be a better investment than hiring an individual who specializes in writing marketing material.

DESIGN TIPS

How important is your choice of logo in determining the promotion of your brand? Good design should be clean, professional, and representative of who you are. There's rarely a "right" or a "wrong" logo. It just must match your message and image. Tina Pfeiffer of CP Designs (www.cp-designs.de), an international designer based in Germany, suggests that you ask yourself and your team the following questions before hiring a designer to create a logo that supports your brand and business image:

- What is the purpose of the logo?

- What role does it play?

- Does it need to be versatile in terms of its use?

- Will it appear on the following: paper, Web site, brochure, letterhead, merchandise, vehicles, other material?

- Should it make a statement or be a subtle branding element?

Finally, ask yourself, can you live with it for years to come? Clients will identify you with it, and the brand will be built around it. It should reflect and support who your company is, now and in the future.

This chapter has covered a variety of types of support material that you can develop to promote and support your message. The next chapter will review the material that is used more actively, such as e-mail marketing, direct mail, PR, and advertising. These elements continue the critical role of promoting your value and your benefits to your customers. However, this promotion doesn't stop with marketing material. It's essential that your message is reinforced internally so that every person who has an impact on your customers can ensure that your brand is supported and your value is continually understood in the light in which you want it to be seen.

WORKSHEET 12.1

COMMUNICATING YOUR MESSAGE

Does your business name clearly represent what you do?

If you have a tagline, how does it convey your value to your customers?

If you don't have a tagline or it doesn't convey your value, what sentence would clearly explain your company's benefits to your most important customers?

Think about the following material that you use to explain your value to your customers. Evaluate its importance in terms of communicating your message on a scale of 1 to 5 (with 1 being not very important and 5 being very important).

Collateral	Importance				
Brochure	1	2	3	4	5
Fact sheets	1	2	3	4	5
Image/logo design	1	2	3	4	5
Direct mail	1	2	3	4	5
Conference and exhibition materials	1	2	3	4	5
Public relations	1	2	3	4	5
Advertising	1	2	3	4	5
Web site	1	2	3	4	5
Tagline	1	2	3	4	5
Online and e-mail marketing	1	2	3	4	5
Partnership material	1	2	3	4	5
Other:					
Other:					

WORKSHEET 12.2

MATERIAL DEVELOPMENT QUESTIONNAIRE

Considering your audience, ask yourself:

- What do you want readers to do with the information they learn from your material (i.e., is there a call to action)?

- Is/does your current material

  - Professional and easy to understand?

  - Present you in the best light?

  - Well written?

  - Describe important information that your customers need in order to make the decision to buy from you?

  - Targeted toward your audiences, addressing their needs, their concerns, and the benefits they get from working with you or purchasing from you?

- Do customers use the material to make purchasing decisions, or are there alternative sources of information (like your Web site or your product) that might be more valuable?

- How clear is your current message?

- Would somebody outside of the industry understand what you've written?

- Would your reader benefit from material other than brochures, like a white paper?

WORKSHEET 12.3

LOGO CONCEPT QUESTIONS

- Whom are you targeting in terms of demographics?

- What is the purpose of the logo?

- What role does the logo play in your business strategy?

- Does it need to be versatile in terms of its use?

- Will it appear on the following: paper, Web site, brochure, letterhead, merchandise, vehicles, or other materials?

- Should it make a statement or be a subtle branding element?

- Can you live with it for years to come? Clients will identify you with it, and the brand will be built around it. It should reflect and support who your company is, now and in the future.

CHAPTER 13

MARKETING IN ACTION

To sit back and let fate play its hand out, and never influence it,
is not the way man was meant to operate.

—**John Glenn, former astronaut and U.S. senator**

DIRECT MAIL

Does direct mail work? This is a question that I am frequently asked, and my response is one that is best delivered by a politician: it depends. Yes, it can definitely work if you align the message and the call to action with hot prospects who want or need your product. Getting all of those forces to work together, however, is a challenge, which is why direct-mail responses tend to hover around 1 to 2 percent. Plus, you have to be quite clever these days to get businesses and individuals to actually open your mail. Like sales literature, direct-mail pieces come in a variety of shapes, sizes, and forms. Some businesses choose to send letters in plain envelopes, while others may use postcards or send interesting pamphlets enclosed in fancy, colorful envelopes to try to increase their chances of getting their customers to open the mail.

THE LIST

The key to creating a great direct-mail piece, or really any piece that is being sent to an unknown audience, begins with purchasing the right list. Getting your message to the *right* audience is of the utmost importance. Even the best campaigns will fail if you don't reach your target audience. If you're using an in-house list, then you should know who these individuals are and have a sense of their relationship with your company.

NAMES FOR HIRE

If you're renting a list, it's critical that you know the source that you are purchasing or renting the list from in order to ensure that the names are qualified and verifiable. Many companies buy lists from magazines or associations that can provide important demographic information (like income, location, titles, and gender). After using your customer profile to identify key demographic features of prospects to approach, you are ready to begin to think about where you can find these people. For example, if you're in the business of creating products for horses, think about how horse owners learn about products, which magazines they read, and which groups they belong to. Then you'll be able to narrow down your search. If women make the purchasing decision, ask the list owner if you can purchase only the female names on the list, or perhaps individuals within a certain geographic area or age group.

Some other ideas to keep in mind when renting names include:

■ How will you use this list? Are you going to be using the list for traditional mailing only, or will you want to e-mail or call the people on the list?

■ If you want to call or e-mail these individuals, additional permission is required for these activities (along with additional details about each prospect). This usually costs more and has its own restrictions.

■ Find out how many times you can use the list. Most publications rent for one-time use, with additional fees for future mailings. However, don't assume that this is the case for every list. You need to ask because some lists can be purchased for multiple or unlimited uses.

■ Of course, once an individual on the list responds to your message and agrees to correspond with you (whether as a result of a mailing, an e-mail, or a phone call), you officially own that person's name (meaning that you can correspond with that person as often as you like because he or she is part of your database).

■ Make sure you're following ethical and legal guidelines for business telemarketing. This begins with working with a reputable list source, but it is also your responsibility to make sure that you understand the laws and rules that are in place. This also holds true for e-mail marketing—you certainly don't want to "spam" prospects unless you are willing and ready to spend time defending your company's ethical procedures to your prospects.

Answering these questions will help you figure out how much you will need to spend on each list, how often you will correspond with the prospects, how you will correspond with them, and whether you need to rent the names more than once.

THE MESSAGE

Next, make sure that your message is on target. This begins with understanding your audience and relying on your customer profiles to address needs and values. If you have several different audiences and your message is different for each, don't try to send all of these audiences the same campaign. It will fail. The message has to match the audience in order to succeed in any sales effort.

Here are a few other direct-mail tips:

- If you're using an envelope, be sure there's teaser copy on it if you want it opened. An example of teaser copy is: "Open by Jan. 1 for a limited, free trial offer!"

- If you can afford it, mail at least two or three times to increase your response rate.

- Make sure you have several methods for the customer to contact you, including phone, e-mail, Web site, and fax.

- Try telemarketing to improve your results. You can call beforehand to let people know that the offer is coming or afterward to gauge response to an offer.

- Make sure there's a call to action, and, whenever possible, have the response options available include phone, e-mail, and online. A call to action means that there's something that you want people to do by a specific date, such as, "Call us by April 15 to get a free three-month supply of dog biscuits."

- Be sure you can measure the results, or you've wasted your money and time.

TEST, TEST, TEST, TEST

I can't emphasize enough the importance of testing. I recently worked with a local university to help it fine-tune its admissions marketing efforts and increase the number of applications it received from top-ranked students. We created a three-part series involving a "bird" that was part of a research project at the university. We decided to test the campaigns with sophomores and juniors in high school (the university's target audience).

What we discovered after conducting one-on-one interviews and several small focus groups was that the first campaign did not provide enough information about the university. It wasn't going to achieve its goal of getting prestigious students interested in the school. We also discovered that the images on the brochure were so beautiful and the message was so intriguing that the students were motivated to read the brochure, so its physical qualities achieved an important part of the call to action of getting them excited about the university.

With some tweaks to the campaign, we were able to inexpensively develop an improved campaign with greater impact. The only cost for this market research was the snacks we provided to the students while they were waiting to provide us with feedback about the campaigns. Excluding consulting fees, the research cost the university about $20—affordable on any entrepreneur's budget.

⟩⟩ READERS TAKE ACTION

One of the most important aspects of any direct-mail campaign is the call to action. Don't just send people information without giving them some type of response mechanism. That could be a bounce-back card for them to complete to get more information about your product or service, or it could be something that drives them to your Web site for a continued dialogue. Without this, you won't be able to measure the success of your campaign, and you will be missing a major sales/relationship development opportunity. Whatever your offer or call to action is, some key pointers include the following:

- You are speaking directly to your target audience.

- You have ensured that there is a simple way for the recipient to reach you. Don't make the call to action so complicated or hidden that it has no effect.

- There is a deadline associated with your call to action. This is as important as the call to action, since it will help you deal with a problem that has been discussed before: inertia. You want to get people off the fence and ensure that they act. A deadline will help achieve this goal, because we all know that tomorrow never comes.

So what types of responses work best? Clearly your offer depends entirely on your audience and your message. You might want to consider these things:

■ *Coupons.* Give people a discount on your services or products for a limited time.

■ *Membership.* If you offer a service like a spa or health club, you can offer them a complimentary membership or a trial membership. Make sure you assign a dollar value to this offer to show its importance.

■ *Referral.* Ask them to refer a friend, with both receiving a discount or something else of value.

■ *Raffle.* If you ask them to participate in a survey or give their opinion on something, you can offer an opportunity to win something valuable (e.g., an iPod or digital camera) to elicit a stronger response rate. Offering a limited quantity of items to the first individuals who respond (say, the first 25) usually works well. This not only boosts response rates, but lets you know early on how many responses you can anticipate. If the number is strong at the beginning, you might be able to avoid a second or third mailing.

■ *Renewals.* If your business provides a service that is renewable, then offer this early in your relationship. Magazines do this all the time. They ask you to renew almost immediately after you begin your subscription. It's money in their wallets early on, so this might be an option for your business, depending on what value you offer.

■ *Rebates and warranties.* Many software firms use this technique so that they can get access to their customers. Think about the times you've purchased an item from a major electronics or retail store like Best Buy, Wal-Mart, or Circuit City. The product manufacturer doesn't know who you are. Often its only or largest distribution channel is one of these major retailers. By offering a rebate or a warranty on a product, the manufacturer has the opportunity to ask you, the customer, to give them your name and mailing address, the reason for your purchase, and something about your interests. In addition to giving the company insight into why you made the purchase, this opens the door for the manufacturer to develop a dialogue with you, an option that wouldn't have been available without the rebate or warranty information. This provides an opportunity to cross-sell and upsell later on in the business relationship, which can be a win-win for the consumer and the manufacturer.

- *Sweepstakes.* If you rent a list and want to be able to correspond with the individuals on the list without continuing to pay for it, then you'll need to get the people on the list to contact you directly. Sometimes offering a sweepstakes with an appealing giveaway can accomplish this goal. However, make sure the giveaway is a good match with your prospective customers. For example, don't give away iPods if your audience is women over 80—it's probably not a good match and wouldn't be appealing (unless a lot of these people have grandchildren—then it might work if you positioned your message the right way).

- *Free articles or other giveaways.* If you're in the information business (perhaps you write newsletters or are in research or academia), then giving knowledge might be more valuable or appropriate for your audience than giving a digital camera. When I worked in the newsletter industry, we would provide our customers and prospects with survey results and industry analysis, since these were things that we knew would be important and useful to them.

- *Trials.* Trials are a great way to get prospective clients to try something before they purchase it. This is a low- or no-risk option for them and can sometimes be the only force that gets them past inertia. Once they're vested to some degree with your product or service, they may be more willing to go the distance and make the commitment to buy it.

The bottom line: the better you understand your audience and their needs, the better you will be able to target them and market to them.

CASE STUDY: PLACELINKS CAMPAIGNS

Remember the challenge PlaceLinks (www.placelinks.com) had developing partnership strategies in Chapter 10? The company had a lot more success with a customized mail campaign that we ran. Here's the situation.

Challenge: PlaceLinks provided a sophisticated technology solution for newspaper organizations. The technology allowed newspapers to improve their readers' search capabilities and give them greater access to local advertisers (stores, restaurants, movies, etc.). The benefit of this software to the newspaper organization was that it gave the newspaper an additional revenue stream because it could charge its advertisers an additional fee for this service.

)) PLACELINKS DIRECT-MAIL CAMPAIGN 1

PlaceLinks launched a direct-mail campaign to the newspapers to promote this service. This campaign consisted of a postcard mailed to 5,000 executives. Unfortunately, there was minimal response, so the company was not able to access decision makers within the newspaper industry. The cost to create and mail each piece was $2.50 per prospect, so the entire 5,000-piece mailing cost $12,500.

)) PLACELINKS DIRECT-MAIL CAMPAIGN 2

PlaceLinks Campaign 2: Pushing the Envelope

We decided to try a more sophisticated approach. The Gold Ceramic Envelope campaign was launched with phenomenal success. We sent custom-designed envelopes, depicted above, to 50 executives in the newspaper industry, with their names and their organizations' names printed on the front of a ceramic envelope filled with gold Godiva coins. The envelopes were beautifully gift wrapped and overnighted with the following letter:

Dear John Smith:

There really is gold in new Web site products, and I'd like to tell you how PlaceLinks *pushes the envelope* of online advertising technology to bring profits to companies like yours.

We offer a zoned, revenue-generating promotions and advertising directory that can be added to your company's Web site, without the effort and expense of creating and maintaining your own in-house system.

Plugging our Directory into your Web site allows you to:

1. Gain advertising revenue from new online markets using our directory, promotion, and coupon applications,

2. Increase the "stickiness" of your site,

3. Expand your online reach with e-mail advertising services, and

4. Decrease Web site production costs by releasing Internet teams to work on other projects.

Our Directory is the only one of its kind that has a built-in e-mail promotions system. This revenue-generating application allows you to send advertiser-driven e-mail news or Shopper news directly to your online subscriber base. With opt-in e-mail growing at over 40 percent annually, we provide you with one more opportunity to reach your online revenue goal.

I welcome the opportunity to show you how PlaceLinks can contribute to «COMPANY»'s 2001 growth strategy. I'll call you in the next few days to share with you why I am so enthusiastic about our solution. Of course, you're welcome to contact me directly at 781-xxx-xxxx or via e-mail at jxxxxx@placelinks.com. You can also "check out" our company at www.placelinks.com.

I look forward to speaking with you!

Sincerely,

Executive VP

www.placelinks.com

P.S.: To discover how you can mine *gold from your Web site,* please take a brief telephone call from PlaceLinks!

PlaceLinks' executives connected with almost 80 percent of these media executives (most of whom thanked them for the unique gift). They secured in-person appointments with approximately 15 percent of the individuals with whom they spoke.

COMPARING THE TWO CAMPAIGNS

How did the two campaigns compare? The first campaign used a general list of individuals working at newspaper organizations and was sent by regular postal mail at a cost of $2.50 per prospect. There were 5,000 pieces mailed, so the total cost was $12,500. Campaign 2 was clearly more expensive per prospect, coming in at $50 per executive. However, this campaign was targeted to the top 50 decision makers, was mailed with priority packaging (adding to the perception of value), and had a final cost of $2,500 and an 80 percent access rate. This resulted in 40 conversations with key executives and led to business for PlaceLinks. Which would you pick as the winning campaign?

PUBLIC RELATIONS

PR activities vary widely, from managing media or analyst relationships to helping companies with trade show support, running focus groups, and the one type of service you don't want to use, managing crisis communications. Yes, sometimes you need a great PR person to protect and defend your reputation so that you can build and maintain your company's image.

As with all marketing activities, the more focused you are on your goals, the more successful your PR strategy will be. It's important that you work closely with your PR agent so that the agent can identify appropriate media for you to use to reach key influencers and your core audience in your market. You may want to be in the *Wall Street Journal*, but the reality is that a trade journal may be more likely to get you in front of the decision makers and customers in your industry.

ADVICE FROM A PROFESSIONAL

According to PR expert Jon Boroshok, owner of TechMarcom (www.techmarcom.com), a marketing communications firm located outside of Boston, there are some real challenges involved in hiring the right public relations firm:

A start-up or early-stage company that has a strategic or technological edge but a thin PR budget can communicate effectively if its agency is innovative, resourceful, tech savvy, and not wasteful. Unfortunately, many companies and investors haven't been quite sure how to select such an agency. Using a rationale that paralleled the old adage, *"nobody ever got fired for picking IBM,"* some companies have been advised by VCs and investors to retain a large, "brand name" PR agency with an important downtown address. They often wound up paying for the name of a CEO who didn't work directly on their account and typically hadn't contacted a reporter in years.

Jon's advice for companies looking for a PR agency is as follows:

- Make sure that your agency has a conceptual understanding of your company, the technology, and your marketplace, but don't look for a clone of yourself. Can the agency communicate effectively with your target audiences? The account team's business acumen and life experience should complement your pedigree.

- Location, location, location is out! Are you paying for the view from your agency CEO's office instead of for results? A prestigious address does not make an agency do better work or increase the chances of media coverage.

- Agencies love to drop names of contacts, but these may not be the right reporters, editors, and analysts for your company. With downsizing and media mergers, journalists change jobs and beats frequently. Experienced pros develop new relationships as needed.

- Look at the agency's clip book but don't be too impressed, especially by clips for big-name clients. See what it's accomplished for clients that are about your size and budget. The people showing you past results should be the same people who will do the actual work on your account.

- Make sure you have complete access to the agency CEO. Your day-to-day contact should be on at least the same level that you are. For example, if you are a VP, your direct contact should be at least a VP too. Watch out for agencies that artificially elevate the titles of inexperienced staffers.

- Big agencies pay big money for top business development specialists that you may see only until you sign the contract. Once a small or midsize client is signed, that client will be paying part of the overhead, but none of those specialists will work on the account. Before signing, meet the entire account team and ensure that the agency won't use bait-and-switch tactics by including the roster in the contract.

■ Your needs and budget may vary from month to month. Your agency should be able to work with a flexible budget. Most agencies and out-sources will require prepayment of monthly or project fees.

■ You can find marcom alternatives through networking, referrals, or online searches (use key words such as PR, tech PR, outsourced PR, marcom, etc.), or by looking at press releases from similar-sized companies in industries related to yours. Agencies that advertise or attend trade association meetings will recoup those costs in their fees.

■ Chemistry counts. You'll have regular contact with your agency. Nobody will ever provide a bad reference, so trust your gut instinct. Marketing communications is an investment. Selecting a source that matches your company's culture and personality is likely to give you the best return.

■ Outsourced providers are a limited resource, often working for several clients simultaneously. Make sure they have the bandwidth to take on additional work for your account and can meet your deadlines.

)) PR ON YOUR OWN

Here are some inexpensive ideas to consider when your budget is very tight, and you'd like to attempt some of these public relations activities on your own:

■ If you're putting on a seminar, speaking at a conference (in person or even a Webinar), or announcing a contest winner, create a press release and send it to the media channels that your customers pay attention to.

■ Conduct a survey. This is a great opportunity to report the "findings" and establish yourself as an expert. Unable to find great research conducted about the Hispanic market in New England, my business partner, the Hispanic News Press, and my company partnered and launched our own survey. This gave us the ability to establish an additional foothold in the market and be the experts reporting the findings and latest trends.

- Write an article for a trade journal or paper to generate interest in your company.

- Announce partnerships or joint activities if the affiliation is prestigious and will be beneficial to your company.

ADVERTISING

Advertising takes many forms including newspapers and magazines, radio, cable and networking TV as well as outdoor billiards. Many of these are growing in popularity. Given the cost of advertising, and the fact that readers often need to see an ad multiple times before they act, buying ads may not offer the best return on your investment. For example, it is believed that when somebody reads a magazine, that reader will notice each ad only one out of every seven times he or she looks through the publication. Since it takes a reader approximately three "notices" to act on your message, you'd need to advertise 21 times to capture the reader's attention and brand your company. Given the prices for an ad in most publications, this might not be your best method of reaching your customers.

On the other hand, if your customers rely on newspapers to get information about the types of products or services that you offer, then you must consider this as part of your marketing mix. For example, when my consulting firm conducted research for a client who was targeting the Hispanic community in a small town in New England, we determined that the community relied on a few key Spanish-language publications as well as radio stations to learn about products and services. Therefore, it made sense to create Spanish-language print and radio ads. However, this isn't always the case. Ask yourself:

- Do I have the funds it takes to use advertising as a real marketing tool for my company?

- Can I be creative enough with my advertising dollars to really capture the attention of my customers in a short period of time and ensure that I get up to speed rapidly?

Use advertising if it is part of an integrated strategic marketing and sales effort, and if you can afford to spend the money on an ad campaign without seeing any measurable return on your investment in the short term.

Mompreneur (mom entrepreneur) Alyssa Dver started a business called Wander Wear® (www.wander-wear.com) in 2003. While attending a Red Sox baseball game with her three-year-old son, she realized that there was no practical way to locate him if he wandered off (his communication skills were still limited at the time). She quickly recognized a strong and very real need for an affordable product that would help keep children safe in public places. She launched Wander Wear with a product called Parent Locator Tags. These tags are $2\frac{1}{2}$ inches in diameter and are made of plastic. They have nonremovable durable plastic loops and give parents and caregivers the ability to write cell phone numbers on the back using a pen.

Having a small budget, Alyssa used her marketing background to creatively gain exposure and free PR for her business, while supporting the work of local charities. She began working with charities and other nonprofit organizations to offer her products as a fund-raising item for their database of contributors and supporters. This was a winning proposition for the charities, which rely on their members to financially support their efforts, and it also gave Wander Wear positive exposure and goodwill as a result of its efforts and its affiliation with important causes:

It's critical that your product is valued by the members of the charity and they can feel honorable about offering it," Alyssa points out. They may even do their own press releases and Web site promotions to help sell as much of the product as possible. You can also use this opportunity to demonstrate your support for the charity by writing a press release or creating other communication to your own database informing them of the program. The charity will quite likely appreciate your added PR efforts to help drive purchases that in turn generate more money to them.

One recommendation: make sure you use an order code or time limit in the release and in the other marketing programs affiliated with this so that you can track and manage what goes to the charity and what does not. If you do wind up contributing a fair amount of money to the charity as a result of the program, be sure to do a follow-up press release and communication out to your contacts!

This chapter has covered a variety of marketing tactics that you can use to brand your company and get the message out to your prospective customers. The next chapter continues the discussion by turning to online and Web marketing experts.

WORKSHEET 13.1

PROMOTIONAL MARKETING PIECE EVALUATION

This exercise is designed to challenge your current thinking about what makes a promotional marketing piece effective. Choose a piece that your company has done or one that appeals to you and then answer the questions below. Think about how or whether the message corresponds to the needs of its target audience. Recommend changes (if any) that would allow the company using this marketing tool to better communicate its message to its audience.

There is no limitation on the types of media that can be reviewed (direct mail, advertisement, e-mail promotion, brochure, radio commercial, and so on). Try this with a few different types.

Rank this DM piece or ad on a scale of 1 to 5 (where 1 is ineffective and 5 achieves the goal). Please discuss why you gave the piece the rating that you did.

	Ineffective			Effective	
Visually appealing	1	2	3	4	5
Easy to read	1	2	3	4	5
Offers enough information	1	2	3	4	5
Clearly communicates the product's or service's benefits	1	2	3	4	5
How do you rate the overall effectiveness of the ad or direct-mail piece?	1	2	3	4	5

(Worksheet continues on next page.)

Can you tell from the marketing piece who the target audience is?

Does the message in the marketing piece correspond to the needs of its target audience?

What changes (if any) does this piece need in order to better communicate the company's message to its audience?

WORKSHEET 13.2

DIRECT-MAIL CHECKLIST

☐ If you're using an envelope, be sure there's teaser copy on it if you want it opened. An example of teaser copy is: "Open by Jan 1 for a limited, free trial offer!"

☐ If you can afford it, mail at least two or three times to increase your response rate.

☐ Make sure you have several methods for the customer to contact you, including phone, e-mail, Web site, and fax.

☐ Try telemarketing to improve your results. You can call beforehand to let people know that the offer is coming or afterwards to gauge response to an offer.

☐ Make sure there's a call to action, and, whenever possible, have the response options available include phone, e-mail, and online. A call to action means that there's something that you want people to do by a specific date, such as, "Call us by April 15 to get a free phone." Examples include

- Coupons

- Refer a friend

- Raffle

- Renewal

- Rebates and warranties

- Sweepstakes

- Free article or other giveaway

- Trial

☐ Be sure you can measure the results, or you've wasted your money and time.

☐ Are you speaking directly to your target audience?

CHAPTER 14

THE POWER OF THE WEB

*Anyone who has lost track of time when using a computer
knows the propensity to dream, the urge to make dreams come true
and the tendency to miss lunch.*

—Tim Berners-Lee, inventor of the World Wide Web

THE WEB AS THE HOLY GRAIL

When the Web was first commercialized, individuals and companies flocked to it as if it were the Holy Grail. The Internet became the message and was not seen as simply another distribution or communication channel to support a sales effort. Now that we've lived with the Web, and it's become a part of most of our everyday lives, the excitement has settled down. It's seen as just another way of reaching our customers.

It's a *part* of a marketing program instead of the entire marketing program; its importance is relevant to customers' needs and decision-making options. For some organizations, it may not even rank among the top five marketing tools needed to grow their businesses. Like every other strategy that I've discussed, it all depends on your company, your strengths, and, most important, your customers. If your customers are online and are using the Web to learn about products and services similar to yours, then you need to be there. If they aren't, then you need to figure out how much of your marketing budget and time should be devoted to this channel and communication tool.

THE POWER OF THE WEB

Online strategies include both push (e-mail marketing that you send/push to prospects) and pull strategies (having a Web site that you can pull individuals to so that they can learn about your business). Some businesses have a Web site because, like having a business card, it conveys a message to the market that this is a legitimate company and gives prospects additional information to help them decide if doing business with that company is something they would like to pursue. If you do decide to invest in a Web site, remember that it should be a part of your overall strategy and not your only strategy.

VIRTUAL PUSH STRATEGIES

E-mail marketing has some powerful capabilities compared to more traditional push methods like direct mail. It is fast to create and deliver, and it's relatively low cost. With e-mail, you can create a message and not have to worry about printing, production, or postal delays of any type. Of course, the ease of delivery and creation can create a false sense of casualness and have a negative impact if you're simply shooting off a message to prospects and don't think about the importance of the message, its timing, or your customers' interests and needs. Some major advantages of e-mail marketing include the following:

■ *Time.* You'll receive responses to your outreach effort in hours as opposed to weeks with traditional postal mail. As a matter of fact, if you don't hear from your customers or prospects in the first few days of the campaign, you can pretty much assume that you won't hear from them.

■ *Testing.* E-mail allows you to test various copy options quite easily and determine if one message is more powerful than another. For example, you can split your list into several groups and mail each of them different messages. Studying the response you get from these groups can help you determine which message to send to the next groups.

■ *Engaging.* The interactivity of e-mail allows you to embed links to your Web site to get prospects more engaged with your company and, if you're targeting them appropriately, even begin a dialogue. This level of relationship building can be effective and helps you measure the success or failure of your campaign quite rapidly.

■ *Personalization.* E-mail allows for a high degree of personalization and a unique, one-on-one experience with your customer. If you have knowledge about customers' past purchases or interests, you can use this to your advantage and mention information relevant to their specific needs in your e-mail. For example, when I go on the Amazon Web site, it immediately recognizes me, welcomes me to the site, and then suggests books to buy based on other books that I have purchased. The company even sends me e-mails when books come out that cover topics relevant to publications I've already purchased and suggests that I might consider buying these new releases. That can be more powerful than a friend or colleague suggesting a book on a topic that she knows I'm interested in. My business and personal library will confirm that this definitely works as a revenue-generating strategy for Amazon. It also helps build loyalty and customer satisfaction. Even though I intellectually recognize the fact that it's computer-generated, it still creates the sense that Amazon cares about my needs and interests.

E-MAIL: THE DOWNSIDE

Spam, a word no longer associated exclusively with processed meat, has cost organizations billions of dollars in lost productivity and computer and power resources. None of us wants to spam our customers or prospects, but if you aren't careful in your e-mail marketing approach, the perception can be that you're flooding individuals with useless, unwanted information. That can sully your and your company's image and alienate customers. Be very careful in creating and launching your e-mail campaigns. When you purchase any list, make sure you can trust the agency or company from which you acquired that list, since you want to be certain that you are working with a reputable organization. Even more powerful, work with a trusted organization whose member list might be interested in your product and have it e-mail your information as a recommendation to its members.

MAXIMIZING E-MAIL EFFICIENCY

What can you do to increase your chances of making your e-mail message effective?

- Make sure that your message is on target and appropriate for the respondent.

- Introduce yourself, and your company, right away.

- Be clear and concise.

- Tell the respondent what you are offering.

- Make it easy for him to respond.

- Engage him immediately.

As with all good marketing, you must be able to measure the results of your campaigns or it's simply not worth doing them. What do you need to measure? When it comes to e-mail marketing, it's important to know how many of your messages were

- Sent.

- Opened.

- Read.

- Responded to (i.e., the recipient followed the call to action).

- Forwarded.

- Bounced back and why.

Do your research when it comes to e-mail vendors. Many of them can and should provide you with vital statistics reflecting the results of your campaign. Constant Contact (www.constantcontact.com) is a great and relatively inexpensive provider of e-mail services designed with the needs of small business owners in mind. E-mail marketing is relatively inexpensive compared to creating brochures and direct-mail campaigns. However, if it is perceived as spam or undesirable mail, the negative impact of this perception can cost you a lot in terms of your reputation and the growth of your business.

THE BANNER PUSH AND OTHER ONLINE ADVERTISING METHODS

There are many types of online advertising and promotion. You're no longer limited to just placing a banner ad and paying for click-through traffic. Banner ads are basically embedded advertisements on a Web site whose goal is to drive traffic to the Web site they are promoting. Other online methods you might consider include the following:

- *Blogs.* A blog is a Web-based journal that provides commentary and/or news about a specific topic. It usually has links to other Web sites and media related to the blog topic.

- *Webinars.* A Webinar is a Web-based seminar run by a company or group where participants can all view the same screen run by the presenter. It is a live conference, and it typically has archiving capabilities for individuals who miss the live session.

- *Search engine optimization/marketing.* This allows users to improve the ranking of their Web site in search engine listings by purchasing higher rankings or placement.

- *Podcasts.* This is a way to distribute multimedia shows about a specific topic in audio or video format.

- *Online social networks (e.g., YouTube, MySpace, LinkedIn, Friendster).* These online sites help connect individuals with similar interests. One popular business social network that entrepreneurs might find valuable is LinkedIn, a network that connects businesses by industry, functions, geography, and areas of interest and helps members identify jobs, people, and business opportunities.

When choosing sites and methods to use, it's critical that you understand who is on a particular site and what they're looking for, as well as ensuring that the organization's customer base is well suited for your business.

BUILD THE WEB SITE AND THEY WILL COME—NOT

Simply creating a site won't ensure that you will have traffic. Creating a Web site is really no different from creating a brochure. You have to think about your customers, what information they seek and need to know, and how quickly they want to know it, and then focus your message on your customers, not your product. This is how you will differentiate yourself and engage your customers so that they continue returning to your site or decide to engage in a business relationship with you.

I met with the brand and marketing communications firm RainCastle Communications (www.raincastle.com), based outside of Boston, to discuss various strategies it suggested for online marketing effectiveness. Paul Regensburg, president, and John Canestraro, vice president of interactive technology, provided me with a wealth of knowledge. "We estimate that 35 to 70 percent of buyers want to contact a company through its Web site. Think about your own buyers. They want to build a relationship with you even while you are not there, since they can visit you any time and e-mail your Web site address to others." Given this high percentage (which of course depends on your prospects and customers), RainCastle developed a nine-step approach to Web development and effective online marketing, which the company shared with us:

1. *Understand the business effect of a Web site.* What do you want your site to do for your business? Without establishing clear expectations and objectives up front, you cannot gauge how well your site is working for you. Ask yourself the following questions:

   a. What impression do you want your site to give visitors?

   b. What do you want your visitors to do after they've been to your site?

   c. Are you educating your visitors appropriately about your company?

   d. What value do you provide on your site, and how well does it help you connect with your buyers?

   e. Are you making a lasting first impression?

   f. Does your site give visitors an accurate impression of your level of quality, innovation, and sophistication?

2. *Have realistic expectations.* You must understand that a site, no matter how well designed, can't accomplish everything for your business. Here is what a site can and cannot do:

   a. It cannot single-handedly build a brand, but it can reinforce your brand identity with strong first impressions and stronger ongoing impressions.

   b. It cannot close sales on expensive products or services, but it can shorten the sales cycle by providing detailed product and service information, demos, and innovative messages that are available 24/7.

   c. It cannot replace live events and face-to-face connections with customers, but it can make it easier for customers to register for live events, provide online events and connections, and enable ongoing interaction with event attendees.

d. It cannot qualify prospects, but it can help prospects qualify themselves through specific content, tools, and other resources that make it easier for them to contact you when they need your products or services.

e. It cannot build personal relationships, but it can create a sense of community, affinity, and loyalty among your prospects, customers, and partners.

f. It cannot replace all of your marketing efforts, but it can provide a multiplying effort for your other marketing efforts in generating leads from existing customers and prospects who visit your site.

g. It cannot drive visitors on its own, but it can drive traffic with a lot of work and effort on your part to make this happen.

3. *Know what your audience is seeking.* On the Web, this presents new challenges because you need to understand not only what types of information or content your audience wants, but how it wants this information presented. Together, these two factors make up the Web experience. According to a study conducted by the Media Management Center (Northwestern University's Media Research and Education Center), experiences that people say drive their Web site usage include the following:

a. "Connects me with others."

b. "Entertains and absorbs me."

c. "Makes me smarter."

d. "A credible, safe place."

e. "There are features that I regularly follow."

f. "It usually has something that surprises me."

4. *Combine brand and response marketing.* Getting customers, prospects, and partners more engaged with your brand is one of the things that the Web has the potential to do effectively. A good Web site can nurture leads and customer relationships while reinforcing brand values in a way that no other medium can.

5. *Integrate online and offline marketing efforts.* It's important that you magnify the impact of your marketing efforts. Making sure that your online marketing efforts are working together with your offline efforts is one of the most critical tactical steps you can take. These efforts must be aligned and properly coordinated to multiply your results.

6. *Integrate your Web site with your sales strategy and activities.* Personal contact remains crucial to your sales, and your Web site can be a powerful tool for supporting the efforts of your sales force. Web-savvy organizations are using their sites as "field sales assistants" to strengthen their sales arsenals. A properly developed Web site gives a salesperson the ability to provide prospects with the information they need, on the fly. Online demos and other engaging, dynamic content—not possible with static printed content—can add an even more compelling dimension to a sales presentation. The Web also dramatically simplifies the task of pushing out new sales support content to your sales force. This can give your sales force a powerful and flexible tool for closing more sales while building affinity with customers and prospects.

7. *To drive results, drive visits.* You must take a proactive approach to driving the right prospects and customers to your Web site. Different strategies that you can use include these:

   a. E-mail marketing

   b. E-newsletters

   c. Online, print, and TV ads

   d. Articles in trade journals

   e. Direct mail

   f. Public relations

   g. Trade shows, seminars, and speaking engagements

   Create effective integrated marketing campaigns, linking all customer touch points with your Web site. In addition, make sure that search engines find your Web site. This should be an important part of your Web success strategy.

8. *Test, measure, and improve.* Measuring the effectiveness of your Web site is the key to continuous improvement. Carefully tracking and ana-

lyzing Web site trends to measure success, then finding ways to improve your success, is a continuous feedback loop that is crucial to getting the most from your site. Questions to consider include the following:

a. Are you driving prospects to your site effectively?

b. Once there, are visitors finding what they came for, or are they getting frustrated?

c. Are you inspiring action?

d. Are you taking advantage of these leads?

9. *Stay a step ahead with new technologies.* The tools and technologies that are available to enhance the capabilities of your Web strategy are changing continually. Keeping pace with emerging technologies is an important way to keep your online edge. Some examples of new technologies are these:

a. Automated personalization that enables one-to-one marketing integrated across print and online

b. Technology that enables you to track and assess results in real time, letting you hone your online marketing efforts faster and more effectively

c. Content management tools that will streamline and automate the process of keeping your Web site content fresh, up-to-date, and relevant

d. Streaming video technologies that make it possible to deliver high-quality video efficiently and cost-effectively via your Web site to provide demos, event invitations, and risk-free trials

The next milestone moves from tactical marketing programs to more personal, one-on-one strategies involving sales and networking to grow your business.

WORKSHEET 14.1

WEB SITE CHECKLIST

Based on RainCastle's nine-step approach to getting the most from your Web site.

Who is your audience? Consider the following:

☐ Current customers   ☐ Prospects

☐ Partners   ☐ Competitors

☐ Vendors and suppliers   ☐ Salespeople

☐ Distributors   ☐ Employees

☐ Prospective employees   ☐ Investors and analysts

☐ Trade press

Which of the following are strategic goals for your Web site, and how will you achieve them using your Web site?

Web Goal	Y/N	How Will You Achieve This?
Attract new customers		
Retain current customers		
Cross-sell current customers		
Increase inquiries and conversions		
Reduce cost of converting prospects to customers		
Educate and inform		
Deliver corporate news and updates		
Generate direct sales		
Personalize the customer's experience		
Other:		
Other:		

(Worksheet continues on next page.)

What impression do you want your site to give visitors?

What do you want visitors to do after they've been to your site?

Are you educating your visitors appropriately about your company?

What value do you provide on your site, and how does it help you connect with your buyers?

Are you making a lasting first impression? How?

Does your site give visitors an accurate impression of your level of quality, innovation, and sophistication?

Are you driving prospects to your site effectively? How?

Once there, are visitors finding what they came for, or are they getting frustrated?

Are you inspiring action? How?

Are you taking advantage of leads generated by your site?

How can your site integrate with your other efforts?

	How It Will Integrate with These Efforts
Sales team	
Direct marketing	
Event marketing	
Product launches	
Public relations efforts	
Advertising	
Collateral	

When developing your Web site and focusing on how it can reinforce your brand and position, consider the following:

☐ Consistency of message

☐ Clarity of message

☐ Positive experience

☐ Quality

☐ Conciseness of message

☐ Freshness of content

☐ Strong representation of your brand

MILESTONE 6

WHY ENTREPRENEURS MUST KNOW HOW TO SELL

Many entrepreneurs are already comfortable and familiar with the sales process. However, for those who dread networking or see self-promotion as beneath them, this section of the book is a must read. Selling is not about forcing a service or solution upon somebody who doesn't want or need it. It's about actively listening to your prospective customers, identifying their key needs, and determining how you can meet those needs. It's an essential part of a marketing program. This milestone covers the sales process, from networking and planning sales calls to how to cultivate relationships. The final chapter covers the importance of elevator pitches and how to develop a strong pitch for your company.

The worksheets included in Milestone 6 are:

- Worksheet 15.1: Sales Checklist

- Worksheet 15.2: Customer Needs Checklist

- Worksheet 16.1: Networking Aptitude Self-Assessment

- Worksheet 16.2: Getting Comfortable with Small Talk

- Worksheet 16.3: Conference Preplanning Checklist

- Worksheet 16.4: Networking Event Planner

- Worksheet 17.1: Elevator Pitch

- Worksheet 17.2: Elevator Pitch Delivery Checklist

CHAPTER 15

PERSONAL SELLING SKILLS

I have never worked a day in my life without selling.
If I believe in something, I sell it, and I sell it hard.

—Estée Lauder

SALES IS NOT A DIRTY WORD

Why does the word *sales* so often conjure up an impression of doing something malevolent or evil? When I worked for a health-care organization in the 1980s, we *never* used the word *sales* to describe the professionals who worked for the company who were, yes, selling our services. They were associates who spent their time in the field (their territory) providing information to individuals who needed the neurologic services we offered. Basically, they sold. But the thinking was that if we called them salespeople, few people would have been willing to speak to them. Well, in the 1980s, selling and health-care services did not mix. Nowadays it's commonplace to see medical offices advertise and promote their services, but the stigma associated with selling still lingers in some people's minds.

So why does sales make *you* think of unethical practices? Have all of those "used car salesmen" ruined it for the rest of us salespeople who not only need to sell our services but also enjoy the process? I hope not, but I have had numerous clients tell me that they really don't sell anything; their approach is more professional (meaning that they don't think sales is a professional endeavor). Then they describe what they do, and it sounds a lot like selling to me: they meet with potential customers to better define and understand their needs and then help them explore solutions that will address those needs. If they can offer solutions, terrific. If not, then hopefully they will point these potential customers in the direction of somebody who can solve their problems.

There's nothing wrong with that, right? Well, from their perspective, this is not selling but exploring opportunities. But trust me, it's "Sales 101," and regardless of the word they use to describe the process, it's important for them and their businesses. Many of them are actually quite good at it as long as they don't view themselves as salespeople.

DISPELLING MYTHS

In this chapter, I hope to dispel the myth that sales is about convincing people to buy your product or service, even if they don't need it, don't want it, or perhaps can't afford it. Sure, we all know people who will sell anything to make money, but that's not the technique I'm advocating. We will review how you approach individuals who have an interest in and need for your service and how you show them the value you provide so that they can decide if they want to conduct business with you. It's about creating a win-win situation: you win a new customer, and your customer wins a solution to a problem or accesses a new opportunity.

THE GOOD, THE BAD, THE UGLY

We've all had our share of negative sales experiences. These experiences go beyond the stereotypical pushy used car salesperson who has no interest in understanding your needs and simply wants to sell you the car that will earn him the largest commission. I have never purchased a used car, and I often wondered if this "used car salesperson" really exists or is just a myth.

My question was answered a few years ago when I was attending a sales meeting in the Midwest (U.S.) with a group of colleagues. We were working for the health-care organization that I mentioned previously, and we were discussing our sales strategy (although we called it a marketing strategy because we were still in denial over what we did). We were in a hotel meeting room while next door a "motivational" sales meeting was being held for what we presumed was a local used car dealership. How did we know it was a used car dealership? Well, it wasn't from the sign on the outside of the door. We could hear the very loud, booming speeches coming from the adjacent room where the "top" sales managers were trying to rally the troops and get them motivated to sell cars. We could hear the methods that they suggested to intimidate their customers into buying these cars and what they needed to do to make more and more sales and basically rip off their customers as much as possible.

It was clear from the "strategy" the sales managers were presenting that *repeat business* and *customer satisfaction* were not phrases in their sales lexicon. They were interested in immediate, bottom-line sales results. Their bottom line reflected results for the current month, not the current year or any other longer period of time. Repeat business was not an objective for these folks; they just wanted to get as much up-front money from their customers as possible, and they didn't care about customer needs or long-term relationships. They were the epitome of bad salespeople, the type you don't want to have to deal with because they are centered on meeting *their* own needs and *not yours*. But they'd be happy to try to convince you that their needs are your needs. This is clearly not the type of strategy you want to emulate.

TRUST AND SALES

Of course, not all car salespeople operate this way. When I was in my midtwenties, I had my heart set on buying a two-door Saab 900S. I knew what amenities I wanted, and I went to a dealership recommended by a friend. As I was test-driving the car (and falling madly in love with it), I told the salesman (whose name I still remember almost 20 years later) that I had always wanted to drive a manual/stick shift but had never learned. He asked me, "If you knew how to drive one, would you prefer that to an automatic?" and I responded, "Absolutely." "Great," he stated. "Then I will teach you how to drive one and ensure that you are safe and comfortable before you leave the dealership." Not only did he get me a great price on the car, but he also kept his promise and taught me how to drive it. He did such a great job teaching me that on my ride home through downtown Boston I didn't stall once, even after getting caught in baseball traffic driving through Kenmore Square (the heart of Red Sox nation). I was so thrilled with that buying experience that when I was ready to buy a Volvo 14 years later, I went back to the dealership and asked for the same salesman. He had left, but the salesperson I worked with was just as responsive to my needs as my Saab salesman had been many years prior, and I purchased my next Swedish car from the same dealership.

That's the type of salesperson you want to be. You want people to want to work with you and to remember your name 20 years later (in a positive light). You want them to trust that their interests are your interests (and this should be the truth) and that your goal is to provide them with solutions to their problems or challenges. This is how I have developed my consulting practice, and this should be how you develop your own business.

SALES SKILLS

Many of you have probably already sold, even if you didn't recognize the activity as sales. What skills do you need in order to sell?

- Strong communication and listening skills

- Analytical skills

- Organizational skills

- Time management and discipline

- Keen interest in learning

- Passion for the value you provide

)) STRONG COMMUNICATION AND LISTENING SKILLS

Number one on the list is communication skills. What does it mean to have good communication skills? Does it mean that you must be able to talk for 20 minutes nonstop about all the features of your product or service? No, although being able to express yourself well is an important part of being a strong communicator. The key to being a good communicator is knowing when to speak and when to listen. A good salesperson is one who knows how to ask key questions, who then sits back and actively listens to his prospective customer, and who then asks a few more questions and listens again for the customer's response. If the salesperson is doing all the talking, then it's impossible for him to understand your needs. As a rule of thumb, try to speak no more than 20 percent of the time; instead, spend your time *actively* listening to what your prospect is telling you. That person is giving you clues to the mystery of how you can solve her needs; if you don't listen, you'll miss the clues and lose the opportunity to present information and solutions that could help you develop a new customer.

)) ANALYTICAL SKILLS

What does it mean to be analytical? Do you have to have an engineering degree to be able to succeed in this category? Of course not. Having strong analytical skills means being able to see, hear, and understand the information that your prospective customer gives you; analyze the clues; and turn those data into a discussion of how you can provide a solution for the customer. Let's revisit my Saab purchase. If my dealer had not been paying attention to what I had said about wanting to drive a manual-transmission car, then he might not have offered to teach me how to drive a stick shift. He did not know this, but I had been to three other dealers who had offered me comparable price quotes on the manual-transmission car, and I was ready to buy it from another dealer. However, being taught to drive the car using a stick shift really *sealed the deal* for me. This was not a high-level analytical process, but the salesman had to think about what I had said, assess my needs and the situation based on actively listening to me, and then determine how he could fulfill my needs and win my business.

)) ORGANIZATIONAL SKILLS

Why is being organized important in selling? Sales can be a very complicated process. You must have some type of system to help you keep track of your customers and prospects, and their identified needs. Otherwise, the chances are that after your first or second meeting, you'll have a hard time remembering the specifics of each customer's needs and thus will be unable to meet those needs. You also need to be able to organize your process so that you work effectively and efficiently and don't waste customers' time. Fortunately, the field of customer relationship management has grown by leaps and bounds over the past 20 years and makes the process easier.

These customer software systems work even for individuals who aren't directly responsible for sales but who still need to manage multiple relationships with lots of required follow-up and activities. There are dozens of tools on the market that are inexpensive and easily customized to meet your needs. Many of my clients have used basic software programs like ACT, Filemaker, and Goldmine, while others have used proprietary software or enterprise management software tools that are specific to their industries. Some use Microsoft Access, Outlook, or even an Excel file to track information about their customers. You need to evaluate what works best for you and your company. Regardless of the tool that you choose, make sure you learn it and use it to help you organize your time and activities to your best advantage. Chapter 19 further discusses what to look for in a system to ensure your greatest opportunities for success.

» TIME MANAGEMENT AND DISCIPLINE

Time management goes hand in hand with being organized. Great salespeople don't simply have a system for managing their time; they manage their time to *their* best advantage. What does that mean? They understand which prospects have the greatest propensity to buy so that they can determine how much time they will spend with each category of prospects. Prospects who fall into the A category—perhaps defined as those who are likely to buy within the next 30 days—should get more attention than those in the C category, who might be viewed as being unlikely to buy in the next year. Great salespeople don't have more time on their hands than the average person; they just know how to use their time to their advantage.

Why do salespeople need to be disciplined? This skill is required to make the calls—every day or however many hours a week are required to make your sales objectives. Discipline is also required to follow up or follow through with everything that you promised to your prospective customers. Nothing leaves a worse impression than promising something and not delivering on your promise. Part of your time management process should involve defining and categorizing your most important leads. Do you spend the majority of your time working the leads that will generate the greatest revenue or business for your company, or do you work all your leads at the same pace? If you don't focus on the most promising leads, you need to begin doing so immediately. Start by reviewing your time schedule and trying to understand how you are currently allocating your limited resource of work hours. If you conclude that you are not using your time to your best advantage (not spending the most time with your A prospects), then you need to figure out a better way to allocate your time to start generating revenue quickly for your business. It's not rocket science, but it is truly a function of being organized and methodical enough to achieve your personal and business goals. Remember how Dan, the computer networking expert, refocused his time and it had an immediate and positive impact on the bottom line of his business.

Consider the prospects in your system. Which are the top candidates for business in the next month? What about the next six months or one year? Now you can begin to determine how much time you need to spend with each to develop a relationship and gain their trust and business.

KEEN INTEREST IN LEARNING

Even before you begin working with your customers, understanding and defining their needs, you have to know your product inside and out. This begins with the features of the product that you are selling, but it expands well beyond that into understanding the benefits that your products provide to your customers. These benefits will vary greatly depending on the customer, but you have to know each one of them so that when you are listening to your customers, you can explain the specific benefits that will hold the greatest appeal for each target customer.

PASSION FOR THE VALUE YOU PROVIDE

How many times have you purchased a product or service from somebody who was wishy-washy or lackluster about its value? Even if you were really excited about the product, if the salesperson didn't seem to care, that could easily deflate your interest level. On the other hand, when people have been passionate about what they were selling and convinced me that they really believed in it, this could easily sway me from my own wishy-washy position and be enough to get me over the proverbial fence to make the purchase. That's why business owners are typically the best salespeople for their companies: because it's rare that they don't feel passionately about what they're selling. If you're hiring individuals to sell for you, keep this idea in mind, because you want your salespeople to have the same enthusiasm and zeal that you have for your products or services.

DON'T SPILL THE BEANS

I spend a lot of time in the field coaching clients on their sales skills. I occasionally witness the common mistake of their telling the prospect *everything* they can possibly think of about the product or service they are presenting, regardless of its value or relevance to the prospect. This often overwhelms the prospect and may even turn her off from doing business with them. It's critical that you customize your presentation to address the customer's needs and concerns. Talking about product features and benefits that are irrelevant is simply a waste of the customer's time— and yours.

I hate to beat a dead horse by discussing my car-buying experiences again, but my purchase of a Volvo SUV (XC90) serves as an ideal example of why understanding benefits and customer needs is critical to the sales process. I like to shop around before I purchase a car. After deciding that the Volvo XC90 was the car I wanted, I visited three car dealerships before making a buying decision. You already know which dealership I chose (the same one where I bought my Saab), but you don't know the experiences I had in the two other dealerships. The first dealership I went to was in the suburbs, and I visited it on a Saturday afternoon with my two rambunctious kids (my son was 9 and my daughter 11 at the time). I wanted my children to be involved in the purchasing decision. Well, the truth is, I didn't want them heavily involved, but I did want them to support my decision, since I believed that if they liked the car, they would be more vested in helping maintain its cleanliness. (For those parents out there reading this, you know that I was under an illusion.) Nonetheless, I took them with me and allowed them to check out the cars in the dealership.

Their definition of checking out a car meant testing every funky feature, from how easily the back seats can disappear and enlarge the trunk space to hearing how loud the horns are on various models. After 10 minutes in the dealership, I had a strong desire to sneak out the back door, leaving them on their own. Unfortunately, the manager didn't allow me to get away with that; he came to my side to show me the features of the SUV. He pointed out every safety feature known to man or to future Volvo owners. Volvo is clearly known for safety, but the hoard of information that I heard about safety, children, and Volvos was unbelievable. Clearly, this manager honed in on features and benefits that he believed (accurately, I will state) are important to a mother of two children.

A week later, I entered my second Volvo dealership in a rather classy suburb west of Boston. Accompanied by nobody under the age of 12, I had a business suit on and was on my way to a client meeting. The benefits that were pointed out to me included the sleeker, sexier options available on the car, such as the interior design, color options, and music system.

So what's the point of the story? Basically, each well-trained salesperson was able to learn enough about me to decide what he believed were the important features and benefits for me to know about the car. But each missed the key factor that was going to pull me over the fence to make the purchase: price. If the first dealer had spent the entire time telling me about the cool options available and never mentioned the safety features that are so important to parents, then his ability to close the deal would have been minimized dramatically. But if he had determined that price was the bottom line for me, he might have closed the deal. Likewise, the second dealer did not believe that safety was an important issue for me, since I told him that this car was for my business. Each salesperson had a menu of benefits in his head that he could offer me. But first he had to learn about my needs to decide which benefits to present from the list. He had to listen *actively* and assess my needs as either a mother or a businesswoman, since discussing every single benefit (as so many of us are tempted to do) would not have been the best way to win my business. In the end, each of them tried to sell me the car but failed to fully understand the one critical factor that would finalize the deal—the best price.

PREPARING FOR YOUR PROSPECT COMMUNICATION

Clearly, these stories highlight the importance of actively listening to your customers. Before you meet with any prospects, you must know the benefits of the products that you offer and know which of those benefits match the needs of different customers. Review your customer profiles, determine which customers need which benefits, and think about this before *each* communication with a prospective new customer. Answering the following questions will allow you to service prospects better and show them how your product helps solve their problems.

- What are their needs?

- What are their habits and behaviors that influence their decision-making processes?

- Why do they value my products and/or services?

- What questions do I need to ask to uncover their needs?

- Based on what I already know about each customer, what benefits are likely to be the most important?

INDUSTRY KNOWLEDGE IS ALSO KEY

Why do good salespeople need to know about industry-related issues? Well, if you're involved in an industry that's changing in some way, either in decline or growing, you have to understand how that affects your sales projections and goals. For example, if you sell cars that are gas guzzlers and increases in gas prices have decreased demand for your type of car significantly, then this information is enormously valuable in your strategy. Your car may still be a great product and provide lots of value for your customers, but you need to understand how to position the benefits to highlight the other features of the car while downplaying the negative attributes. That doesn't mean lying or hiding information, but you need to address the concerns up front and understand how they will affect your sales. The better prepared you are, the better the chances that you can respond to customer concerns about poor gas mileage with information demonstrating other strong features and benefits or by making comparisons with similar cars.

COMPETITION

Finally, understanding your competition is critical in every sales activity. You need to have a solid knowledge of how your product or service compares to that of your competitors or substitutes. As with industry knowledge, the better the data you have about all the forces that affect your solution, the better prepared you will be to combat any questions prospects have and to be able to focus on the value you offer relative to your competitors. Remember, your competition is not only those companies providing identical or similar services, but also those companies providing a substitute solution that rivals yours. So, if you sell healthy, expensive dog food, your competition includes all types of dog food (even the really unhealthy kind), since any dog food can be a substitute product that satisfies a problem for prospects: feeding a hungry canine.

You also have to listen to your customers to understand what is important to them. If getting their dogs fed on a daily basis is *all* they care about and they are price sensitive, then they might not be good prospects for your business. However, if you can determine that nutrition is important to your customers and that they're willing to spend more on your product, then you know that your focus should be on explaining all of the benefits associated with your product as it relates to the health of their dogs.

The next chapter discusses the value of networking to increase your prospect list.

(Worksheets start on next page.)

WORKSHEET 15.1

SALES CHECKLIST

Evaluate your sales skills and determine where you might need additional support. Rank your skills on a scale of 1 through 5 (with 1 meaning that you need a lot of support and training and 5 meaning that you're quite proficient). For any skills ranked less than a 3, write down strategies or training that you will seek to improve these.

	Rank Your Skills	Strategies to Improve Skills
Strong communication and listening skills • Ask the right questions • Good listening skills • Present relevant benefits	1 2 3 4 5	
Analytical • Process information • Show direct client benefit	1 2 3 4 5	
Organizational skills • System to track information • Good follow-up	1 2 3 4 5	
Time management skills • Use time to your advantage • Categorize prospects to maximize time	1 2 3 4 5	
Keen interest in learning • Enjoy learning about customer needs • Understand features and the benefits they offer	1 2 3 4 5	
Passion for the value you provide • Enthusiasm and zeal for the company's value to the customer	1 2 3 4 5	
Preparation • Identify customer needs before meeting • Research industry • Research competition	1 2 3 4 5	

WORKSHEET 15.2

CUSTOMER NEEDS CHECKLIST

Use the checklist below to prepare for each customer meeting

☐ Company information

☐ Industry and competitive factors that affect this customer

Below identify the specific customer needs that you will address in the meeting, along with the benefits offered by your product's or service's features.

Customer Needs	Benefits Your Product or Service Provides	Features (how the benefits are offered)

CHAPTER 16

NETWORKING

Every time you win, it diminishes the fear a little bit.
You never really cancel the fear of losing; you keep challenging it.

—**Arthur Ashe, tennis player**

Networking is one of the most useful and cost-effective methods of jump-starting a business. What do I mean by networking? It's more than collecting business cards—it's creating give-and-take relationships. Think of networking as formal socializing *with a twist*. Your goal in business networking is not to establish friendships but to meet as many individuals as possible who have the ability to help you grow your business and vice versa. That can mean seeking out people who will refer business to you or even someone who knows someone who can send customers your way.

IT'S NOT ABOUT MAKING FRIENDS

If you develop new friendships in the process of networking, terrific. But that is not your objective! If you are currently attending networking events and you have found some great new buddies, but they are not giving you referrals or introductions to individuals who can help you grow your business, you're not performing the networking task correctly. You have to set clear objectives for the results you hope to achieve through networking and make sure that you are asking for these leads and also reciprocating.

Networking is a two-way street. You have to help others establish or grow their businesses, just as they help you with yours. When I began my consulting practice in the late 1990s, I wasn't sure where my clients would come from. I didn't have a marketing budget for fancy brochures or advertising. I also knew that the types of individuals and companies with which I was interested in working were not going to make the decision to hire a consultant because I had some cool brochures or direct mail. So instead of pouring money and time into these items, I joined a formal networking group called BNI (Business Network International, www.BNI.com) and spent a lot of time attending industry networking events and meetings. I figured out where my potential clients would be and where people who had connections with those clients were, and that's where I spent my time.

BUSINESS NETWORK INTERNATIONAL

BNI has an interesting business model that is worth investigating for many entrepreneurs and small business owners. This group is set up to help individuals meet, discuss their businesses, and identify leads for one another. You spend time in weekly meetings networking with a purpose and a clear goal: to grow your business. This is a very formal and structured business networking group. Friendship development is optional; lead development is mandatory. In fact, not providing leads to other members can result in expulsion from the group. This may sound extreme, but this group is dedicated to helping people grow their businesses. For some entrepreneurs or business owners, BNI also serves a second purpose: it's a way to hone your elevator pitch. Elevator pitches are discussed in the next chapter.

ASKING FOR REFERRALS

The most important skill I gained from BNI was how to ask for advice, input, and, of utmost importance, referrals. The key is being specific about the type of contacts that you need. If you're looking for an introduction, don't ask, "Do you know any marketing directors?" Instead, be very precise and ask, "Can you introduce me to the marketing director at XYZ Corporation?" If the person you are talking to knows the person you want to be introduced to, make sure you get as much information as possible about that individual. In addition, the best lead is an actual introduction, so ask the person you're talking to if he would be willing to call the other person or send her an e-mail formally introducing you and explaining why the two of you should connect. But make sure you reciprocate or leads won't keep coming to you.

Not all networking groups and activities are designed as tightly as BNI is. Make sure you understand the dynamics and the unstated policies of the group or event before you attend. In many cases, industry events give you the opportunity to personally meet as many people as possible, but they are not set up for heavy-duty business conversation. What happens after these events is the key to successful networking. Remember, you cannot establish a relationship in one session. Relationships take time, so how you communicate afterward is the key to building strong relationships that will grow your business.

DISTINGUISH YOURSELF

Paul Horn of Paul Horn & Associates (www.paulhorn.com) is a communications and networking expert located in Boston. He has helped a number of my customers and students improve their networking and presentation skills. He shared four key strategies that he has found to be quite effective. They are the following:

1. *Meet with people face to face.* To grow a business, you have to be out there meeting with customers and with new prospects. You can't rely on ads, letters, word of mouth, or having an attractive building and convenient evening hours.

2. *Use a personal touch.* Many businesses offer services and products that are not that different from those provided by their competitors. In such cases, consumers often decide who to conduct business with based on personal relationships. Therefore, entrepreneurs can gain a competitive edge by taking the time to really understand what is important to the person with whom they are trying to establish a relationship. As the old saying goes, "People don't care what we know until they know that we care."

3. *Smooth out your rough edges. How* you talk with your customers and prospects is as important as *what* you say to them—sometimes even more important. You may need to develop or polish your public speaking or presentation skills.

4. *Keep practicing and working on your networking skills.* For some people, networking comes easily, but for many others, it doesn't. If you're in the latter category, don't worry—as with other skills, these can be honed with practice and coaching.

GOLDEN RULES OF NETWORKING

Paul follows two golden rules when it comes to networking, as explained on the next page.

RULE 1: NETWORKING IS RECIPROCAL

Networking is effective only when it's a give-and-take process. You should be looking for ways to help others even as you ask them for help. That, of course, is more than a business strategy; it's a philosophy or approach to life! "What goes around, comes around," as they say. That golden rule applies here. How do *you* want to be treated? With just a sales pitch? No, of course not. You want to believe that someone is listening to you and wants to understand your needs and goals.

Networking is often used in a job search context. For example, you want a job in banking, but you don't know any bankers, so you ask the people you know if they can make some referrals to the bankers they know, and schedule some "informational interviews." There is nothing wrong with that. That's part of what is meant by networking. If you've developed good relationships with friends or acquaintances, they're usually happy to do you a favor, especially if they know you well and sense that you would be willing to reciprocate at the appropriate time. It's critical that you think of networking as a give-and-take process of building relationships with people to develop win-win situations.

WARNING: NO STALKERS, PLEASE

You shouldn't feel that you have to "work the room" as though you were some sort of hungry predator. You can be purposeful in your approach without pouncing on or cornering people. If you're focused on learning about other people—their goals, their challenges, their interests, and how you might help them, not just yourself—you will not come off as selfish, and you will probably feel more comfortable with networking, too.

》## RULE 2: OPPORTUNITIES ARE UNLIMITED

If networking is defined in a broad sense—as a give-and-take process for building relationships—then it's obvious that the opportunities for networking are everywhere. Virtually any encounter you have, whether at work or during leisure time, can offer you a chance to create or strengthen a relationship. So networking can take place not just at formal networking events, but in the supermarket aisle, at your kids' Little League games, or while conversing with a fellow passenger on a plane.

In fact, it's often in these chance encounters that the most effective networking takes place—because no one feels there's an ulterior motive at work. There's simply room to develop a degree of familiarity and trust that may open the door to a business conversation later on. If you've had a nice chat with a fellow passenger about the book you noticed he was reading and the conversation rolls around to what you each do for work, you might offer your card, ask for his, and send him a note later on. If the conversation has been mutually enjoyable, then he is likely to respond to that later outreach—or maybe even refer someone else to you.

While networking with individuals, some things to keep in mind include the following:

- Make sure your approach is friendly and open.

- Try to put the other person at ease.

- Introduce yourself with a smile and a handshake.

- Ask for and use the other person's name.

- Ask questions about the other person's business or industry.

- If appropriate, extend some kind of offer or invitation (for an appointment, to receive some articles that the other person might be interested in).

Paul also points out that networking can take many forms, in addition to actual conversations. These include

- Sending articles of interest to people you've just met, especially if the topic came up during your exchange with them.

- Inviting people to events as your guest.

- Creating relationships with nonprofit organizations and attending and/or helping out with their events.

- Developing and practicing your elevator pitch so that it sounds casual and natural. This technique is discussed at length in the next chapter.

- Looking for opportunities to introduce other people at events.

To gauge your networking skills and your comfort level with networking, I've included several valuable worksheets in this chapter. These will help you assess your skills and ability and give you ideas and strategies to increase your comfort level.

CONFERENCES

Attending or exhibiting at conferences gives you an opportunity to network by exposing you to as many people as possible in a short period of time. It can also give you the chance to do the following:

- Check out the competition.

- Learn the latest trends in the industry.

- Identify new customers.

- Identify new partners.

However, conferences can be overwhelming, like trying to drink water from a fire hose. You're thirsty and you want a drink, but it's too much at once, so you end up dry and parched. This won't happen if you have a game plan. In advance of attending a conference, you should do these things:

- Before the conference begins, find out who's going to be there and who could be potential prospects, partners, competitors, or important networkers or relationship builders (people who know people you want to get to know).

- Decide upon the people you'd like to meet with and learn more about them (research their businesses online).

- Prioritize this list and make sure you approach the most important people on it first (in case you run out of time).

- Develop a plan to meet these people.

  - Will you introduce yourself right away, or will you try to network at various events?

  - What will you say to introduce yourself?

- Prepare a list of opening statements that will make you more comfortable approaching these people.

- Prepare a list of frequently asked questions (and responses) about your products so that you're not caught off guard without a response.

- Prepare a list of general small-talk topics that you might use to begin a conversation.

- Prepare a list of key benefits and perhaps new information about your company that you can share.

In order to network efficiently, make sure that you have your business cards on hand at all times and that you get business cards from the individuals you meet. On the back of each card, write information about the person and rank how important she or he is to your business. (Don't make this complicated. A simple ABC method of ranking people is more than sufficient.) This will help you tremendously when you get home and enter all the names into your database. This information will also help you develop your follow-up strategy and personalize your message to each person when you contact her (e.g., "When we met last week, I recall that you were interested in . . .")

SEMINARS AND WEBINARS

In addition to attending conferences, you can also hold your own seminar or Webinar (Web-based seminar). This allows you to feature your business and even yourself as the expert on a topic. You can invite individuals whom you are interested in getting to know better to hear your presentation or the presentations by your colleagues or partners. You should definitely sell this as a learning opportunity, since it's rare that somebody will want to attend an event just to hear about you and your company. If you choose a topic that is important and valuable for people to learn about, your attendance rates will increase. If you hold a live seminar, then it's best to conduct it during hours that are convenient for your audience (before or after work) or during an event where these people are already going to be listening to presentations. For example, if there's a conference for dog walkers in your local city and you see from the agenda that there are gaps when the audience won't be attending any prescheduled meetings, then you might want to contact the conference planner and see if you can offer a free miniseminar on a topic that would provide additional educational value.

Here are some ideas that will increase the odds that your seminar will be successful:

- Make sure it's educational and valuable for attendees.

- Have plenty of literature on hand, both about your company and about the topic.

- Hold breakfast events or cocktail parties.

- Follow up with all attendees, even those who did not sign up for your event but who were on your mailing list.

- Follow up with no-shows, since these busy folks may very well be your best prospects.

The final chapter in this milestone covers the critical skills required to develop and deliver an elevator pitch for your business.

(Worksheets start on next page.)

WORKSHEET 16.1

NETWORKING APTITUDE SELF-ASSESSMENT

(Developed in conjunction with Paul Horn of Paul Horn & Associates.)

ARE YOU A CAVE DWELLER OR A CAVE NETWORKER?

Answer these questions as *honestly* as possible to determine your networking aptitude.

	Hardly Ever	Some-times	Almost Always
1. If I'm walking and I see a group of people trying to figure out a map, I'll ask them if I can help.			
2. When I sit down at a table of strangers at a business event, I introduce myself to everyone.			
3. On behalf of my company, I invite customers or acquaintances to a few sponsored events each year.			
4. When someone I know joins my circle of conversation, I introduce that person to others.			
5. I am comfortable offering a handshake to men and women when meeting them for the first time.			
6. I keep an eye out for articles that might interest a friend or colleague, and if I see something, I'll send the person a copy or tell him about it.			
7. I send a thank-you note within a few days after I've met with a new prospect or been treated to a meal.			
8. While waiting in a long line, I am comfortable striking up conversations with strangers.			
9. I know and use the names of business colleagues' secretaries and administrative assistants.			
10. I remember people's names after I've been introduced to them.			

	Hardly Ever	Some-times	Almost Always
11. If I notice the keynote speaker—someone whose work I admire—standing alone at a business event and apparently not occupied, I'll introduce myself and strike up a conversation.			
12. I have a 10- to 30-second "elevator speech" that sums up what I do for my customers.			
13. I do regular volunteer or pro bono work for a charity or nonprofit organization.			
14. I return all phone calls within 48 hours.			
15. I can comfortably enter or leave a group conversation with people I've just met.			
16. If I learn that a friend of a friend is moving to my area, I'll offer to help her out.			
17. If I notice that a new family has moved in across the street, I'll make a point of introducing myself.			
18. When I send out holiday cards to customers, I add a short, personal note.			
19. I'm on the board or chair a committee in at least one local business or service organization.			
20. I give a talk to some business or nonprofit group at least once a quarter.			

CALCULATE YOUR NETWORKING SCORE AND PROFILE

NETWORKING SCORE

Number of *Hardly Ever* answers: _____ x 1 = _____

Number of *Sometimes* answers: _____ x 3 = _____

Number of *Almost Always* answers: _____ x 5 = _____

TOTAL POINTS: _____

(Worksheet continues on next page.)

NETWORKING PROFILE: INTERPRETING YOUR SCORE

Less than 25 points: You are a Cave Dweller. You should get out more.

Between 25 and 50 points: You are a Cave Guard; you are on the lookout for approaching parties but wary of engaging with them.

Between 50 and 75 points: You are a Cave Scout; you are curious about the outside world and ready to approach individual travelers when you feel it's safe, but you are reluctant to visit other caves.

Between 75 and 100 points: You are a Cave Networker; you are comfortable visiting other caves and eager to invite new acquaintances back to yours.

WORKSHEET 16.2

GETTING COMFORTABLE WITH SMALL TALK

(Developed in conjunction with Paul Horn of Paul Horn & Associates.)

Write down some questions you might ask or an experience you might share with someone about any of the following topics (or make up some of your own).

Topic	Question to Introduce Yourself	Experience
Foreign travel		
Raising kids		
Airlines/flying		
Traffic/commuting		
Summer vacation spots		
Computers/PDAs		
Sports		
Health and fitness		
Pets		
Other_____		
Other_____		

(Worksheet continues on next page.)

Write down some questions you might ask somebody specifically related to business that will allow you to better identify that person's needs and qualify his or her ability to do business with you.

Benefit You Want to Discuss or Want to Identify	Question to Introduce This Benefit

WORKSHEET 16.3

CONFERENCE PREPLANNING CHECKLIST

☐ Before the conference begins, find out who's going to be there and who could be potential prospects, partners, competitors, or important networkers or relationship builders (people who know people you want to get to know).

☐ Decide upon the people you'd like to meet with and learn more about them (research their businesses online).

☐ Prioritize this list and make sure you approach the most important people on it first (in case you run out of time).

☐ Develop a plan to meet these people.

- Will you introduce yourself right away, or will you try to network at various events?

- What will you say to introduce yourself?

☐ Prepare a list of opening statements that will make you more comfortable approaching these people.

☐ Prepare a list of frequently asked questions (and responses) about your products so that you're not caught off guard without a response.

☐ Prepare a list of general small-talk topics that you might use to begin a conversation.

☐ Prepare a list of key benefits and perhaps new information about your company that you can share.

(Worksheet continues on next page.)

Write down the 10 most frequently asked questions about your business, product, or service. Along with each question, include your short response.

1.

2.

3.

4.

5.

6.

7.

8.

9.

10.

WORKSHEET 16.4

NETWORKING EVENT PLANNER

(Developed in conjunction with Paul Horn of Paul Horn & Associates.)

Networking Event	Date/Time	Invited Audience or Participants	Individuals to Meet	Follow-up

CHAPTER 17

THE ELEVATOR PITCH

*It usually takes me more than three weeks
to prepare a good impromptu speech.*

—**Mark Twain**

You are probably familiar with an "elevator pitch," even if you have not directly referred to it by that name. An elevator pitch is a prepared, concise mini-speech that highlights your business's benefits to somebody in the proverbial elevator. How many of you have had the experience of walking into a business luncheon or getting on that elevator and realizing that Mr. VIP was standing in front of you? Perhaps it was a potential customer or an important financial partner whom you really wanted to meet but didn't expect to encounter any time in the near future. Somehow you found yourself unprepared and tongue-tied. Or, worse, you were so nervous that you blathered on and on about your business, never quite finding the right words to accurately or concisely describe what you do or to give this person any hint as to why she should be interested in you or your business. Did you send her running out the door once an escape was in view? Did you promise yourself that you wouldn't let this happen again?

Even if this scenario hasn't happened to you, chances are that you'll be thrown into a similar situation at some point if you aren't fully prepared. An effective, appealing introduction is the first and usually the most lasting impression that you leave with somebody. If the person or group listening to your pitch can help you succeed, you want this time in front of that audience to count. (Elevator pitches also help in a variety of social situations, but that's another book entirely.)

STIMULATE INTEREST

Elevator pitches have a few goals. The most immediate is to stimulate enough interest to give you the opportunity to explain and "sell" your business in more detail at another time. You're looking for an invitation to follow up with this person. The long-term goal can vary from obtaining funding to turning prospects into customers or even hiring employees. As a result, many individuals develop several targeted pitches, one for each objective. Let's start with one pitch for now, but as you improve, you'll probably develop an arsenal of ways to present yourself and your business. Keep in mind the fact that the "elevator" part of the term should not be taken literally. These opportunities occur everyplace, from the soccer field to the local grocery store or a dinner party at your best friend's house.

THE "SO WHAT" FACTOR

Whenever my students or clients practice their first elevator pitch, I say, "So what?" Many of them are taken aback, until they see that I'm smiling and don't mean to offend. Still, I do expect an answer. While some of them can tell me why it's important for the prospect to know this information, many cannot and stumble through their responses. I urge everyone to go through this exercise while putting together his or her first pitch. It's harder than it might seem.

Let's say you're a computer saleswoman, and you develop an elevator pitch for a group of nontechnical prospects that highlights some of the features of the newest computer on the market. One of those features is the computer's great memory bandwidth, and you tell them that the computer has a memory bandwidth of 667 MHz with 8.5 GB/s with dual channels. You've probably put them to sleep. Save that conversation for the engineers.

A good salesperson would say something like, "The solid memory bandwidth will improve your performance significantly, meaning that your computer programs will run faster and smoother, allowing you to get your job done more rapidly." Your customers will clearly be more impressed with that information, since it addresses the benefits that are important to them: speed and efficiency. They don't care about the mechanics of the computer design—they care about getting their job done more quickly.

That's the "so what" factor. *It's what it means to your customer.* The features alone are not enough. You need to connect the features with an essential customer need—in this case, speed and efficiency. Therefore, in crafting your initial elevator pitch, this is an important concept to keep in mind. When you're done with the pitch, ask yourself, "So what will this mean to the person I am speaking with?" If you can comfortably answer that question, then you're heading in the right direction. If not, go back and try again.

ARE YOU REALLY PREPARED?

Having a fully polished pitch, one that will lead to an invitation for a longer meeting, requires you to ask yourself other questions, as well. These include the following:

- What might intrigue this person about my business?

- What is important to him or her?

- How does this person make decisions relevant to my company's product or service?

- Why would this person want to buy from my company or work with me?

- What impression do I want to leave with this individual?

- *So what* will this mean to the person I am speaking with?

Notice how similar these questions are to the ones you use to profile your customers. You should now be quite proficient at answering questions about individuals who affect your business's growth.

Here are some guidelines and tips I developed with my business partner, Paul Horn, to help you craft and deliver your elevator pitch.

)) CONTENT AND ORGANIZATION

- Begin your pitch by clearly defining who the target audience is (i.e., who's standing in the elevator with you).

- Remember, you need to deliver this message in two minutes or less, so choose your words and thoughts carefully.

- Once you have answered the questions described earlier about the person, you can begin to script your pitch.

- Remember, there are no perfect elevator pitches. You must deliver a pitch that feels natural to you. It should incorporate your own expressions and phrasings. Otherwise it will sound fake and rehearsed.

- Finally, once you've developed your pitch, there are three important steps to take: (1) practice, (2) practice, and (3) practice.

PRACTICE SOME MORE

Some people like to practice in front of the mirror, while others prefer to rehearse in front of friends and family. I personally like to practice in front of Biscotti, my hyper 80-pound dog. So, a trick I've learned is to position him with a sit command and deliver the pitch directly to him. He's a bit fidgety, so if I can keep his attention for two minutes without his walking away to look for a comfortable bed to curl up in, I know that my tone and inflection are probably engaging enough for human beings.

ELEMENTS OF THE PITCH

In general, your elevator pitch should include the following elements:

- Your company name and your role in the organization

- A clear, concise description of your product or service and the benefit(s) it provides

- The current or potential demand for this product or service

- A statement about what makes your product or service unique or sets it apart from competing products or services

- A brief but compelling statement about your product's or service's value as it relates to this person (e.g., increasing market share or doubling revenue in less than 12 months)

- Your organizational and/or technical capacity to implement that strategy

- Your personal energy and passion for making this business succeed

However, not all of these elements are appropriate for every audience. Therefore, you must customize your pitch to ensure that you're addressing the interests of the person listening. Once you've gotten past the first pitch, it might be a good idea to develop a few more that will work with the variety of individuals with whom you interact on a regular basis.

DELIVERY

Appropriate, well-organized content is obviously important. But your elevator pitch will also be judged—consciously or unconsciously—on how well you deliver it. Paul always reminds me of the old saying, "The audience doesn't separate the dancer from the dance." In other words, human beings respond not only to what is being said but also to how it is being said, so you yourself are an important part of the pitch. Paul emphasizes that you therefore need to be aware of the following areas:

- Your voice

- Eye contact

- Facial expressions

- Gestures, posture, and body language

These all influence how effective your words are and how you are received.

)) VOICE

Be conscious of the following points related to your voice:

- You need to pace yourself. Don't rush through the speech, or it will sound rehearsed or garbled.

- Your inflection of certain words to provide meaning or emphasis is important.

- Make sure you're speaking at an appropriate volume. If you're in a quiet space, your volume will be different from what it will be if you're in the bleachers watching your son's baseball game.

- Speaking at a tone that keeps others' attention is of critical importance, or they'll be fidgeting, wondering when they can make their exit.

)) EYE CONTACT

Your ability to maintain eye contact has a strong impact on your perceived credibility. I'm not suggesting a staring contest, but looking someone in the eye will convey confidence. If you're staring at the ceiling, or if your eyes are darting around, you'll make the other person feel uncomfortable, and you might lose your shot at getting a second meeting.

While eye contact is important for American business exchanges, remember that sustained eye contact may not be as appropriate in other cultures and societies, particularly outside of the West.

FACIAL EXPRESSIONS

Facial expressions also are important.

- Make sure you show your excitement and sincerity.

- Don't be stone-faced and unapproachable.

- The best way to judge your facial expressions is to videotape yourself presenting your pitch. If this option is not available to you, then ask a trusted friend or colleague to critique you or simply watch yourself in the mirror.

GESTURES, POSTURE, AND BODY LANGUAGE

Even if you have the space, you don't necessarily have to strut across the stage (and if you're really in an elevator, this won't be an option).

- Appropriate gestures can help you explain an idea, demonstrate your passion, and channel nervous energy.

- Guard against defensive body language, such as arms folded across the chest, or distracting habits like hands playing with change in your pocket.

- Stand with confidence and ease. This is your opportunity to tell your story.

ELEVATOR PITCH TEMPLATE

The following is the general template you will use to develop your elevator pitch:

Target Audience_____

Hello, thank you for asking about my company. I'm _____
(your name), and_____ (Company name) provides
_____ (product or service) for _____
(target market). We offer _____ (competitive advantage)
to the _____ (target customer) to meet or satisfy the
_____ (target customers' major
want or need that your company fulfills). Our business is important because
_____ (i.e., your passion, skills, and technical expertise).
If this is of interest to you, I'd love to provide you with a little more detail.
Can we set up a time to speak about this further?

YOUR "SO WHAT" WRAPPED UP IN A PHRASE

It can be helpful to think of a catchy phrase (almost a tagline) that customers can remember about your business. It doesn't have to be anything flashy—just a few simple words that help you stand out from the crowd. This is your "so what" wrapped up into one memorable phrase. A few good examples are these:

- Allstate: "You're in Good Hands"

- Avis: "We Try Harder"

- BMW: "The Ultimate Driving Machine"

- Campbell's Soup: "M'm! M'm! Good!"

- Club Med: "The Antidote for Civilization"

- GE: "Imagination at Work"

- Microsoft: "Where Would You Like to Go Today?"

- The *New York Times*: "All the News That's Fit to Print"

- Nike: "Just Do It"

- Timex: "It Takes a Licking and Keeps On Ticking"

- VISA: "It's Everywhere You Want to Be"

- Wheaties: "The Breakfast of Champions"

Although my business is nowhere near the size of these companies, I created a tagline: "Turning Business Vision into Reality." My goal is to make a statement about the value that I provide for my customers. If you create a statement, remember that it should help drive home the vision and passion of your company and should be customer focused. Plus, it should be easy to remember. See if you can think of a catchy phrase for your business. If you can't, don't worry. As long as you have a strong understanding of your customers and how you meet their needs, a tagline is not critical to your success.

WORKSHEET 17.1

ELEVATOR PITCH

First define your target audience (who's standing in the elevator with you), and then complete the information below, remembering that you need to deliver this message in two minutes or less.

Target Audience_____

What are three things that might intrigue this target group or person about my business?

1.

2.

3.

What is important to this person as it relates to my business? (This is the "so what" factor.)

How does this person makes decisions relevant to my goals?

Why would this person want to buy from my company or work with me?

What impression do I want to leave with this individual?

In seven words or less, what is my value to my customers?

(Worksheet continues on next page.)

Now, begin crafting your script. Remember, you do not need to use these exact words. As a matter of fact, you should not use these precise words because this template wouldn't be natural for most people. This is provided as a guideline to use in creating your pitch. It's more important to be natural and honest than to develop a script that sounds stilted and insincere.

In general, your elevator pitch should include the following:

- Your company name and your role in the organization

- A clear, concise description of your product or service and the benefit(s) it provides

- The current or potential demand for this product or service

- A statement about what makes your product or service unique or sets it apart from competing products or services

- A brief but compelling statement about your product's or service's value as it relates to this person (e.g., increasing market share or doubling revenue in less than 12 months)

- Your organizational and/or technical capacity to implement that strategy

- Your personal energy and passion for making this business succeed

Here is the general template you will use to develop your elevator pitch:

Target Audience_____

Hello, thank you for asking about my company. I'm _____ (your name), and _____ (Company name) provides _____ (product or service) for _____ (target market). We offer _____ (competitive advantage) to the _____ (target customer) to meet or satisfy the _____ (target customers' major want or need that your company fulfills). Our business is important because _____ (i.e., your passion, skills, and technical expertise). If this is of interest to you, I'd love to provide you with a little more detail. Can we set up a time to speak about this further?

WORKSHEET 17.2

ELEVATOR PITCH DELIVERY CHECKLIST

(Developed in conjunction with Paul Horn of Paul Horn & Associates.)

DELIVERY

- ☐ Make strong eye contact.
- ☐ Use only appropriate gestures.
- ☐ Watch your body posture and body language.
- ☐ Be aware of your facial expressions.
- ☐ Appropriate gestures can help you explain an idea, demonstrate your passion, and channel nervous energy.
- ☐ Guard against defensive body language, such as arms folded across the chest, or distracting habits like hands playing with change in your pocket.
- ☐ Stand with confidence and ease.

VOICE

- ☐ Pace yourself. Don't rush, or it will sound rehearsed.
- ☐ Use inflection to provide meaning or emphasis.
- ☐ Be clear and articulate.
- ☐ Speak at an appropriate volume.
- ☐ Speak in a tone that keeps the other person's attention.

FACIAL EXPRESSIONS

- ☐ Make sure your excitement and sincerity show.
- ☐ Don't be stone-faced and unapproachable.
- ☐ Videotape yourself presenting your pitch, ask a trusted friend or colleague to critique you, or watch yourself in a mirror

MILESTONE 7

RELATIONSHIP MANAGEMENT

The sales process is critical in building relationships. This milestone discusses the various stages of this process, such as phone call preparation, in-person appointments, and follow-up and servicing meetings. It covers the tips and strategies you can use to increase your success, and highlights specific methods to manage the sales cycle, including sales analysis worksheets that will help you plan your time more efficiently.

The worksheets included in Milestone 7 are:

- Worksheet 18.1: Sales Stages Checklist

- Worksheet 18.2: Sales Tips

- Worksheet 19.1: Sales Conversion Worksheet

- Worksheet 19.2: Sales Time Analysis Worksheet

- Worksheet 19.3: Sales Conversion Calculation

CHAPTER 18

THE SALES PROCESS: TIPS AND STRATEGIES FOR SUCCESS

My motto was always to keep swinging. Whether I was in a slump
or feeling badly or having trouble off the field,
the only thing to do was keep swinging.

—**Hank Aaron**

SALES STRATEGIES

You're now ready to think about specific strategies that you can use during various stages of the sales cycle. This information should be seen as a guide to help you determine how you can sell your products or solutions using a customer-focused model. However, it's important for you to develop your own personal sales style and to be comfortable with the process in order to grow your business. If you're not comfortable with selling, then I strongly advocate that you attend a sales training program to improve your skills and confidence and enhance your relationships with prospects and customers.

There are five key stages in the sales process:

1. Preparing for the call

2. The actual phone call

3. Preparing for the in-person appointment

4. The actual meeting

5. Follow-up and servicing of account needs

STAGE 1: PREPARING FOR THE CALL

Cold calling is an activity that almost everyone—even highly skilled sales-people—loathes. Ideally, you will have warm leads (where you have met the person or somebody has suggested that you call) so that you don't need to make a lot of completely cold calls (with no introduction and no knowledge of the person). But for many business owners, cold calling is required at some stage of their business for growth.

I have actually gained a few customers through cold calls, but it's usually more of a fluke than a typical result for a consulting practice. In one case, I "cold-faxed" (basically the same as a cold call but using the fax machine instead of a telephone) the CEO of a software business after reading an article about his company. He actually called me back about 30 minutes after I sent the fax. I was stunned by this fast response, but I saw it as the exception, not the rule. Obviously it is much more desirable to make calls when you have some mutual acquaintance or some other connection in common.

What should your approach be when you are preparing to call a prospect? Many salespeople begin this activity by reviewing their database, choosing which prospects to call, and determining the order to call them in. Important strategies for success include the following:

- *Have an organized contact list.* Make sure the names of your prospects are in one central location, such as a customer relationship database like Goldmine or ACT or even an Excel spreadsheet. (An important note: spreadsheets are not ideal for tracking customer information, because once you begin to track meeting dates and important details about a customer's business, it will be more difficult to access this information quickly and use it.)

- *Determine prospect status/ID.* Once you have all of the names in your system, review your list carefully and try to determine the status of each person. Status/ID refers to the person's role as it relates to your company. Some general categories are these:

  - *Customer.* A person or organization you currently do business with. You might even have a separate ID for "Former Customers."

  - *Key account.* This is a very important customer that generates a lot of business for your company.

  - *Partner.* For marketing purposes, this usually refers to a company or individual with access to multiple prospects.

  - *Prospect.* A person or organization with whom you'd like to conduct business with.

- *Competitor.* A company that provides similar services or satisfies the needs of your current customers or prospects.

■ *Determine the prospects' rank.* Once you have determined each contact's status, it's important to now rank the potential of each prospect (A, hot; B, lukewarm; C, cold lead). Your criteria will be strictly related to your business. Some ideas to begin the ranking process are noted here:

  - Present or past relationship with your company (people who might not be ready to buy, but are not cold leads)

  - Potential business revenue or volume they can generate

  - Expressed interest in a specific product

  - Known purchaser of similar products sold by your competition

  - Other factors that affect sales potential such as demographic or psychographic matches

■ *Prioritize your list by rank.* Prioritize the A, B, and C prospects in your database so that you can easily begin by making calls to A prospects, then B, and maybe C. You might want to use your B list to practice making calls. The hardest folks to call are your C list of cold leads. However, make sure you have a polished presentation before you speak with people on your A list.

■ *Set a phone schedule.* It's important to create a schedule for phone calls as well as for meeting times. This is critical because if you don't set aside certain times of the day and specific days to make these calls, then the calls very likely won't happen (something else will always get in the way).

■ *Set a call minimum.* Schedule a minimum number of hours that you will devote to making calls. If this is going to be 10 to 15 percent of your time, then you may dedicate five hours a week to making calls. Pick a schedule that works for you *and* one that you will stick to. I have found that making calls on Monday morning and Friday afternoon is not very effective for my business because my prospects are simply not available during those times. But this criterion varies depending on your customers and your business. You might need to try various times before you make your own determination. Here are a few different schedules to consider:

- Tuesday through Friday, 9:00 to 10:15

- Tuesday and Friday, 9:15 to 10:30; Wednesday and Thursday, 1:15 to 2:30

- Tuesday and Thursday, 8:30 to 11:00

■ *Predetermine your potential meeting schedule.* Schedule a minimum number of hours a week to go on appointments, but allow for flexibility based on prospects' needs. You may decide that you are going to spend the same number of hours going on in-person calls as making telephone calls until business picks up, and then you will spend more time out with prospects. Perhaps include one morning and one afternoon each week. For example, you might decide that Wednesday mornings and Thursday afternoons are the times you would ideally like to go out to meet with prospects, but hold Friday mornings as a possibility. This will help when you schedule appointments because you can state, "Are you available on Thursday at 1 p.m., since I'll be in your area visiting other customers?"

》 STAGE 2: THE ACTUAL PHONE CALL

This sounds obvious, but it's worth emphasizing: the phone call is critical to your success, so plan it out carefully. A sample script that you can use as a guideline for developing your own is given here. The important aspect of a script is to have ownership of it. What does that mean? Your script should reflect your own ideas and should be in your own words and your own conversational style. If it appears that you are reading a script or have memorized something that you're saying to your prospects, you'll sound insincere, and you probably won't land an in-person appointment.

SCRIPT TEMPLATE

Introduction. Good morning, _____ (the prospect's name). I am the _____ (title) for _____ (your company name). My name is _____ (your name).

Reason for the call. The reason I am calling is because we have a new business service designed to allow owners like you to _____ (benefit, benefit).

Seek more information/actively listen. _____ (The prospect's name), I'm wondering what you or _____ (the prospect's company name) is currently doing in terms of xxx services? {The prospect's response.} Are you satisfied with the services you are receiving?

Request for the appointment. _____ (The prospect's name), from what you've told me, I really think we'd both have something to gain by sitting down for 15 minutes. I'm going to be visiting _____ (another business) next Wednesday morning. I'd like to stop by to briefly discuss our services with you. Does 11 a.m. work for you, or would after lunch be better?

Close. Thank you! I look forward to seeing you next week. If you need to reach me beforehand, please call/e-mail me at xxxx@xxx.xxx or xxx-xxx-xxxx.

There are many factors that increase your success with phone calls:

- Know your value proposition and benefits as they relate to each prospect.

- Listen carefully.

- Practice and tape-record your pitch to see how you sound. If your prospect is OK with this, you can tape your phone conversations so that you can listen to how you sound and critique and improve yourself. However, remember that you have to inform the person with whom you're speaking that you are recording the conversation. If you think that might make the other person uncomfortable, don't do it. Another option is to role-play with colleagues, friends, and family and have them critique you. Remember, the more you practice, the better and more confident you will be.

- Have a rehearsed script that you are comfortable following, but be prepared to improvise as you uncover more information about your prospect.

- Be professional.

- Be confident.

STAGE 3: PREPARING FOR THE IN-PERSON APPOINTMENT

Assuming that you were successful and have landed an in-person appointment, how should you prepare for that meeting? Here are some steps and guidelines to follow.

PREPLANNING SESSION

■ Update your database with information about the prospect that you learned from the phone call.

■ Determine the goals of your meeting based on your phone conversation. Did you learn anything new about the prospect and her needs during the call? If so, make sure you address these needs, and prepare your presentation based on this knowledge.

- What do you expect or want to occur as a result of this appointment?

- Do you want to close the deal, or is your goal to get a presentation with other key decision makers at the organization?

- Be realistic in determining your goals as you prepare for success.

■ Research the organization or company online or through contacts and use this information to demonstrate to the prospect that you have taken the time to learn about her business and are seriously interested in working with her.

■ Imagine your meeting and your conversation. This may sound very New Age, but imagining a conversation can be very empowering, forcing you to think through the opening, closing, and goals of the meeting.

■ Practicing what you're going to say in front of the mirror will help prepare you and help you to develop confidence in what you're going to say and how you're going to say it.

》 STAGE 4: THE ACTUAL MEETING

Now you're ready for your meeting. Here is a sample outline of how the conversation might unfold. This is just a guide. The key is to be prepared and actively listen, so you don't need a prepared speech. However, you should have questions that will help you better identify the prospect's needs. This will allow you to have a focused meeting in which you can discuss those benefits that you think will be of highest value to the prospect.

1. *Small talk/introduction.* Many meetings begin with small talk, which should be limited to a few minutes, to allow you to get to know the person better and understand his personal and business goals. Some topics for small talk include recent events, sports, weather, and kids

(if you notice pictures of the prospect's children on his desk).
However, don't get too personal or political. This is simply a warm-up
for the real dialogue to follow. This is not a personal visit, and you
really want to get down to business. If you spend too much time on
personal information such as talking about the prospect's kids or
his community activities, then you might not get to your real goals
(especially if time is a factor).

- If small talk allows you to uncover critical information as it relates
  to your product, then it's OK to explore it further.

- Remember, this prospect agreed to meet with you for a specific
  amount of time. It's critical that you respect that limit.

2. *Acknowledge the reason for your visit.*

- Demonstrate your knowledge of the prospect's business.

- Confirm the amount of time allotted for the meeting. You can say
  something like, "I mentioned in our phone call that this wouldn't
  take more than 15 minutes of your time. I want to be sure that still
  works with your schedule."

- Conversation/exchange stage. Ask probing questions to discover
  more about the prospect's business or personal needs as they relate
  to your product or service.

- Please note: Prospects should speak approximately 80 percent of the
  time. This is only a guideline and there's no scientifically "correct"
  amount of time, but if you use 80 percent as a benchmark, it will help
  you think about the amount of listening time you should allocate.

- Determine in your mind the solutions that will best meet the
  prospect's needs. Now you have entered into the solution selling
  stage of the conversation.

3. *Solution selling stage.* Now that you understand the prospect's needs
   and have thought about a solution for those needs, you should do the
   following:

- Confirm these needs and present your solutions.

- Check for understanding and acceptance. You should make a statement that ensures that you're both in sync about the customer's

needs, such as, "It appears that texture and taste are critical factors in deciding which new pies to purchase for your restaurant. Based on the taste test we just completed, do the pies you've tested meet or exceed your needs and expectations?"

4. *Closing stage.* Finally, you should close the conversation by

- Asking for the next step, which should be the goal of your meeting. This does not necessarily need to be asking for the sale if it's not appropriate at this stage.

- An example of a good next step could be to suggest that the next meeting be with the prospect's business partner (so that you can close the deal), or perhaps suggest that there should be a meeting next Wednesday at 9 a.m. to review specific customized products or to sign paperwork. The following is not a request for a next step: "I''d love to get together again to discuss your needs. Give me a call when you're ready." It does not necessarily lead to any activity related to the purchase of your product, and it takes you out of the driver's seat. You want to be in control and move forward.

STAGE 5: FOLLOW-UP AND SERVICING OF ACCOUNT NEEDS

The initial follow-up to a meeting is just as critical as the actual meeting. You've come all this way with a prospect; don't blow the opportunity because you simply didn't bother to follow up. When you return to your office, remember to

- Update your database with

  - Notes of your conversation and important information about the prospect.

  - The ranking of the account (if it's changed from a B to an A—hopefully not vice versa).

  - Next steps and dates.

- Send a thank-you to the prospect. This can be an e-mail or a letter (with a letter being more impressive and memorable these days). You should include the following elements:

  - Thank him for his time.

- Restate his needs.

- Restate the benefits you discussed.

- List promised action items.

- Include additional ideas or research that you conducted after the meeting related to the topics discussed or questions raised.

Once you've updated your system, make sure you set aside the time to complete the follow-up steps, which may include other action items agreed to during the meeting or perhaps more research.

ADDITIONAL SALES TIPS

Here are some ideas and tips to keep in mind throughout the relationship-building process.

)) CALL TIMES

To increase your chances of speaking directly with the decision maker (and avoiding the secretary or administrative assistant who screens calls), try calling at these off hours:

- 7 a.m. to 9 a.m.

- Lunchtime

- 5 p.m. to 7 p.m.

Typically, the higher up in the company a prospect is, the better this strategy works, since C-level individuals (CEO, CFO, CIO) tend to get in early and/or stay late. However, keep in mind the fact that in larger organizations, C-level individuals are very difficult to reach, and it may require additional creative thinking on your part to locate them and speak to them.

)) HOT BUTTONS

All decision makers have a series of "hot buttons," issues that can keep them up at night. If you discuss one of their hot buttons and show how your product or service will address this issue, you will be able to connect with the prospects. Here are some typical big-picture issues that may help you:

- Quality

- Service

- Price

- Competition

- Industry changes

- Regulations or tax implications

OPEN-ENDED VERSUS CLOSED-ENDED QUESTIONING TECHNIQUES

You can use both open- and closed-ended probes. An open-ended question is one in which you give the person the opportunity to speak on a topic at length. Here are some examples:

- During our phone call, we talked about xxx; how is this affecting your business?

- Given today's economy, what business issues keep you up at night?

- Where do you see your business two years from now?

A closed-ended question is one that seeks a short yes or no response and is used to get commitment. Examples of closed-ended questions are these:

- Have I given you enough information to allow you to set up our next meeting with your boss (identified critical decision maker)?

- Can you meet next Wednesday at 3 p.m. to discuss this further?

- Based on the information that we have discussed, can I write up an order for our product?

The final chapter in this discussion of sales covers sales as a process. I'll discuss various methods to manage the cycle so as to grow your business efficiently.

(Worksheets start on next page.)

WORKSHEET 18.1

SALES STAGES CHECKLIST

1. Preparing for the call

☐ Make sure your contacts are in a central, easily accessible location.

☐ Review the status/ID of various prospect groups.

☐ Rank your prospect groups by potential to purchase.

☐ Prioritize your list for calling.

☐ Set a phone schedule.

☐ Set a minimum number of hours for calls.

☐ Predetermine potential meeting times.

2. The actual phone call

☐ Develop a script that includes the following stages:

- Introduction
- Reason for call
- Seeking more information/active listening
- Request for appointment
- Close

☐ Speak with confidence.

☐ Know your value to the prospect.

☐ Listen carefully.

☐ Ask relevant questions.

☐ Update your database with information learned during the call.

3. Preparing for the in-person appointment

☐ Review database/CRM system with contact information.

☐ Determine the goals of the meeting.

☐ Research company information if needed.

☐ Imagine the conversation.

☐ Practice, practice, practice.

4. The actual meeting

☐ Remember to actively listen.

☐ The meeting flow might follow this pattern, but make it natural:

   1. Small talk/introduction

   2. Acknowledge the reason for your visit

   3. Confirm the amount of time available

   4. Begin asking probing, open-ended questions

   5. Confirm need

   6. Check for acceptance/agreement

   7. Present solutions

   8. Close to get to meeting goal

   9. Agree on next step

5. Follow-up and servicing of account needs

☐ Update your database with notes, ranking, and next steps.

☐ Send a thank-you that includes these things:

   • Appreciation for the meeting

   • Restatement of needs

   • Restatement of benefits discussed

   • List of promised action items

   • Additional ideas or research that you conducted after the meeting related to the topics discussed or questions raised

☐ Complete all follow-up activities.

WORKSHEET 18.2

SALES TIPS

Call during times when the prospect is more likely to answer his or her own phone (i.e., before 9 a.m., at lunchtime, or after 5 p.m.).

"Hot buttons" to get the prospect engaged in a dialogue about pain might include these:

- Quality
- Service
- Price
- Competition
- Industry changes
- Regulations or tax implications
- Other_____
- Other_____

Open-ended questions encourage the prospect to speak. Examples include:

- During our phone call, we talked about xxx; how is this affecting your business?
- Given today's economy, what business issues keep you up at night?
- Where do you see your business two years from now?
- Other_____
- Other_____

Closed-ended questions seek a yes or no response and are used to get commitment. Some examples are:

- Have I given you enough information to allow you to set up our next meeting with your boss (identified critical decision maker)?

- Can you meet next Wednesday at 3 p.m. to discuss this further?

- Based on the information that we have discussed, can I write up an order for our product?

- Other_____

- Other_____

CHAPTER 19

MANAGING YOUR SALES CYCLE

You don't have to see the top of the staircase to take the first step.

—**Martin Luther King**

Most business owners would say that their customers are their number one priority. So why do so many of them stumble when it comes to customer relations? It's simple: treating your customers as your top priority requires significant effort and important tools, and many companies haven't taken those steps.

One tool that I highly recommend is a customer relationship management (CRM) system. Don't panic. Such a system need not cost a lot of money, and it does not require a major overhaul of your computer system. It is, however, a more sophisticated system than an Excel spreadsheet. Systems like ACT, Goldmine, and Filemaker, to name a few, are designed with the individual and the small business owner in mind.

What are the bottom-line benefits of implementing a CRM system? They can include the following:

- Improvements in customer retention and loyalty because you're better able to serve your customers' needs.

- Increased market share through the use of cross-selling and upselling.

- The ability to provide more customized levels of customer service.

- Increased efficiency and effectiveness for you and your team because the system helps you manage your time and activities.

- Increased competitive advantages because you have solid access to data about your customers, which you can use to strengthen your relationships with them.

- Knowledge is power. Having the ability to use the data stored in a CRM system will enable you to turn raw material into knowledge, which in turn will allow you to better serve your customers' needs.

How do you figure out which is the best system to use for your business? Some important features include

■ An easy-to-use interface that encourages customer communication. If you're running a small business, you should not need an IT department to help you run the system.

■ A system that is customizable and easy to integrate with your current software, whether that's Outlook or Access. If there's a standard CRM system that's used in your industry, this should be carefully assessed, since it will very likely include important fields of information customized to meet your business and customer needs.

■ Customer data available on demand, in real time. This means that the data are not buried and you are able to "pull up" or access customer details easily.

■ The ability to capture and integrate customer demographic data that you either purchase or have in another program. If you are able to use all the data you have about customers and prospects, you can better customize and target your markets. This allows your marketing team to run campaigns that are targeted to specific audiences (e.g., women over 65 within 15 miles of your office).

■ The ability to help with your time management challenges by offering to-do lists, action items, callback times, alerts, and schedule overviews.

■ The ability to create and track the results of mailings (letter, fax, and e-mail) to individuals and target groups.

■ The ability to create phone calling lists to individuals and target groups based on specific demographics or their status/ID.

■ The ability to share information across internal groups, departments, and branches so that marketing and sales can work with operations, production, and anybody else who needs access to the data.

■ Reporting and analytical capabilities that simplify the process of reviewing your pipeline and assessing your leads, and that help you forecast future sales. This is a great tool that also will enable sales managers to track how their employees are doing so that they can better support their efforts.

From a business perspective, some of the benefits that can be achieved through the deployment of a CRM system include these:

- Increased conversion of prospects to customers

- Customers increasing their knowledge about your products and services

- Increased opportunities to customize and develop new and improved products and solutions because your awareness of customers and prospects' needs has increased and is more focused

- The ability to gather data about customers' needs more efficiently

- Decrease in lost customers and the return of those previously lost

- Increased or improved personalized/customized service

CRM HELPS YOU MANAGE AND CREATE KNOWLEDGE

The CRM system that you use should be viewed as a knowledge center. Therefore, from a management perspective, you should be able to generate reports that

- Show your pipeline of prospects, which will help you predict future sales and determine if new campaigns or outreach strategies are needed.

- Indicate how many and what type of calls have resulted in sales (increasing ROI).

- Identify which lists work best if you are renting names.

- Help you determine which target groups (based on status, demographics, or industry type) bring the greatest return on your marketing investment.

- Calculate how much time and money you spend converting each prospect into a customer.

- Determine the most—and least—effective salespeople, allowing you to support those who need more assistance and eliminate those who are in the wrong job.

- Break down the revenue per call, in addition to the number of calls or contacts reached.

- Simplify the follow-up and fulfillment of marketing material requests.

MANAGING YOUR INDIVIDUAL SALES CYCLE

Now that I've discussed the overall benefits of deploying a CRM system in a company, I'll review the personal benefits of using the data to help you manage individual sales cycles and numbers. Whether you are a small business owner or work in a small business, you need to sell. Once you have spent a few months wearing your "sales" shoes, you will begin to see patterns and cycles emerging. How do you manage your sales cycle to ensure that you achieve the greatest amount of success in the most efficient and cost-effective manner possible?

You begin managing your sales cycle by understanding how long it takes to go from prospect to purchase and defining the steps in between. For example, turning a cold prospect into a purchase may involve moving from a warm lead (an expression of interest) to a hot lead (an expression of strong interest), to a commitment to sign a contract, and finally, to a sale. That process may take a week for smaller sales (a household product costing under $100) or more than a year for larger engagements, such as the purchase of a new technology system with a six-figure price tag.

MUFFIN'S MAGNIFICENT BISCUIT FACTORY

Let's discuss a company called Muffin's Magnificent Biscuit Factory. The company sells gourmet, nutritious, and wholesome dog biscuits through small boutique pet shops and supermarkets, including specialty markets and mainstream supermarkets with a natural foods section in the store. In order to grow, the company wants to land a major account like Whole Foods, which has hundreds of stores in North America specializing in natural and organic food. However, the owner realizes that this is an ambitious goal and, even if the company is successful, it may take a long time to land that account. Therefore, he decides to diversify the company's sales approach and target a variety of pet stores and small retail boutiques where it wants to sell its product.

Let's say you're a new salesperson working at Muffin's Magnificent Biscuit Factory. You don't have a lot of data on the sales statistics for this business, but you have been given a goal of landing 15 sales (new accounts) for the month. You've heard that sales conversions for other people in your business run around 6 percent. How many prospects do you need to have in order to make those sales numbers, and how much time will it take to achieve success?

You should start by calculating how many prospects you need in order to meet your sales goal. Keep in mind that the prospects you're contacting should be those you identified as having the greatest customer lifetime value for your business. You'll have to guess at some of the information because you don't know all of the statistics, but you've been in sales before and have solid industry knowledge, so this is a strong educated guess:

A. Number of new business customers required in the next month:

$A = 15$

B. What percentage of phone calls result in a conversation? You think it's 20 percent.

$B = 20\%$

C. What percentage of conversations result in an in-person appointment? You think it's 50 percent.

$C = 50\%$

D. What percentage of in-person appointments result in a sale? You think it's 50 percent.

$D = 50\%$

Now perform the following calculation to figure out how many prospects you need in order to achieve your goal:

E. Number of prospects in pipeline required for success:

$$E = \frac{A}{B \times C \times D}$$

$$E = \frac{15}{20\% \times 50\% \times 50\% = 5\%}$$

$$E = 300$$

You now know that you need *300 prospects* in order to gain *15 clients* and meet your goals. That's assuming, of course, that your conversion assumptions are accurate. If you can convert phone calls to actual conversations at a higher rate or turn more in-person appointments into sales, then you won't need 300 prospects. But it's better to err on the conservative side because there's rarely harm done by exceeding your goals.

Now you need to figure out how much time you need to spend to achieve this goal. Begin by multiplying the number of prospects needed times the percentage of phone calls that result in a conversation.

F. The number of completed calls you will have:

$$F = E \times B = 300 \times 20\% = 60 \text{ calls}$$

Then calculate the number of in-person appointments by multiplying the number of phone calls times the percentage of calls that result in an in-person meeting:

G. Number of in-person appointments:

$$G = F \times C = 60 \times 50\% = 30 \text{ meetings}$$

You already know the following:

▪ Each phone attempt takes 1 minute on average.

▪ Each live phone conversation with a prospect lasts 10 minutes.

▪ Each in-person appointment lasts 30 minutes.

▪ You have to meet with a prospect only one time to close a sale.

Now you can figure out how much time it will take to meet your sales goal:

H. Minutes spent on an incomplete call: 1 minute per phone call

$$H = 1 \text{ minute}$$

I. Minutes spent on a complete conversation: 10 minutes per live call

$$I = 10 \text{ minutes}$$

J. Minutes spent meeting with a prospect in person: 30 minutes per meeting

$$J = 30 \text{ minutes}$$

K. Time spent on incomplete calls:

$$K = H \times (E - F) = 1 \text{ minute} \times (300 - 60) = 240 \text{ minutes}$$

L. Time spent on complete calls:

   L = I x F = 10 minutes x 60 calls = 600 minutes

M. Time spent on in-person appointments:

   M = J x G = 30 minutes x 30 appointments = 900 minutes

N. Total minutes spent acquiring customers:

   N = K + L + M = 240 + 600 + 900 = 1,740 minutes = 29 hours

O. Total minutes spent per customer acquisition:

   O = N ÷ A = 1,740/15 = 116 minutes

P. Hours spent per customer acquisition:

   P = O ÷ 60 minutes = 116/60 = 1.9 hours

Now you know that in the next month you need to spend *29 hours* prospecting to land *15 new client accounts* and meet your goal.

Finally, consider how long the sales cycle takes. If it takes three months to close a sale and you don't have enough prospects in your pipeline to achieve your goals, you should refine your technique and develop more prospects to achieve your sales objective. In this case, you need 300 prospects to meet your goal, but based on the original information, you had only 60 in your database. This is a perfect example of how sales and marketing need to work together to ensure that goals are met. If you realize that you need more prospects, now is the time to discuss with marketing how you're going to get more of them into the system. Perhaps marketing needs to develop a specific marketing campaign or rent some lists to support your sales effort. Whatever the outcome, make sure you align your goals for success.

ALIGNING SALES AND MARKETING

Prior to becoming a consultant, I spent my career shifting roles between those two estranged cousins: sales and marketing. In the process, I discovered that when sales and marketing teams don't communicate or understand each other's unique perspectives, the business almost always is destined to fail. This applies to both small companies and larger established organizations in a range of industries.

As a consultant, I found managing alienated sales and marketing staffs to be an especially profound challenge. Salespeople complain that the marketing folks simply don't "get it," and they often ask, "Why don't they spend some time in the field with us so they can see what it's really like to work with customers and then produce material that helps us sell?" Likewise, the marketing folks can be heard grumbling about how the salespeople are never satisfied with the literature they produce and ask, "Why can't they just go out there and sell? They have all the tools they need!"

WHY DON'T THESE GROUPS GET ALONG?

How does the disconnect begin? Think of your typical salesperson, out on the road, meeting with customers and motivated to achieve and exceed sales goals. This person is usually gregarious, a good public speaker and active listener, and in touch with customers and prospects on a daily basis. On the other hand, the marketing gurus are in their offices, crunching numbers and reviewing the data from the field. If they communicate with customers, it tends to be one step removed, in the form of a survey or other response vehicle. If sales and marketing don't each respect the other group's understanding of the customer's needs and how each plays an important role in meeting customers' demands, the animosity and resentment begins.

So how do you create a harmonious working relationship between sales and marketing? It isn't rocket science, but it does require hard work, effort, and incentives. Goals should be aligned, and each group should have the opportunity to experience life on the other side, so that both groups grasp firsthand the value that each plays in growing the business. Once they see how the other group contributes to improving the customer's experience, they will better appreciate the other group's role and also be better at performing their own job.

Many books have been written about the disconnect between sales and marketing. If your organization has two separate areas responsible for these functions, then it's critical to have each group think of the other as its internal customer. With this goal in mind, they can learn to better understand the needs and values of their internal customers, and the entire organization will benefit.

Now you are ready to turn your business vision into reality. Let's proceed to the final milestone, making it happen.

(Worksheets start on next page.)

WORKSHEET 19.1

SALES CONVERSION WORKSHEET

Begin the sales calculation by answering the following questions about your business to the best of your ability. If you don't know, take an educated guess. You will need these numbers for the next worksheets, so be careful in completing your calculations.

A. Number of new business customers required:

A = _____

B. What percentage of phone calls result in a conversation?

B = _____%

C. What percentage of conversations result in an in-person appointment?

C = _____%

D. What percentage of in-person appointments result in a sale?

D = _____%

Now perform the following calculation to figure out how many prospects you need in order to achieve your goal:

E. Number of prospects in pipeline required for success:

$$E = \frac{A}{B \times C \times D}$$

Now you need to figure out how much time you need to spend to achieve these goals. You begin by multiplying the number of prospects you need times the percentage of phone calls that result in a conversation:

F. The number of completed calls you will have:

E = (E) x (B) = _____

Then you calculate the number of in-person appointments by multiplying the number of phone calls times the percentage of calls that result in an in-person meeting:

G. Number of in-person appointments:

G = (C) x (F) = _____

WORKSHEET 19.2

SALES TIME ANALYSIS WORKSHEET

Now, complete a time analysis to understand how much time you will spend prospecting. Please make sure you use the numbers you calculated in the previous worksheet to complete your time analysis.

SALES TIME ANALYSIS

H. Minutes spent on an incomplete call:

H = _____

I. Minutes spent on a complete conversation:

I = _____

J. Minutes spent meeting with a prospect in person:

J _____

K. Time spent on incomplete calls:

K = H x (E - F) = _____

L. Time spent on complete calls:

L = I x F = _____

M. Time spent on in-person appointments:

M = J x G = _____

N. Total minutes spent acquiring customers:

N = K + L + M = _____

O. Total minutes spent per customer acquisition:

O = N ÷ A = _____

(Worksheet continues on next page.)

P. Hours spent per customer acquisition:

P = O ÷ 60 minutes = _____

Q. Sales cycle (how long it takes to close a sale) in days:

Q = _____

If your sales cycle is 90 days from cold-calling a prospect to closing the deal, and you don't have any prospects in your pipeline, or not enough to achieve your goals, you need to take action immediately to increase the number of prospects you have.

WORKSHEET 19.3

SALES CONVERSION CALCULATION

Use the formula below to determine how many prospects you need based on your ability to convert prospects into new customers.

A. Number of new business customers required = _____

B. What percentage of prospects become qualified leads? _____%

C. What percentage of qualified leads become hot leads? _____%

D. What percentage of hot leads become sales? _____%

Number of prospects required in your pipeline is:

E. Prospects _____ = $\dfrac{\text{new clients required} \underline{\hspace{1.5cm}}}{\text{B} \underline{\hspace{0.8cm}} \text{x C} \underline{\hspace{1.2cm}} \text{x D} \underline{\hspace{1.2cm}}}$

How long does this cycle take? _____months.

If you don't have any prospects in your system now and it takes three months to convert a prospect into a sale, you will need more prospects to meet your goals.

Compare E (the number of prospects in the pipeline required for success) to Q (sales cycle in days) and develop a strategy to ensure that you meet your goals.

E. Number of prospects in pipeline required for success = _____

Q. Sales cycle in days = _____(There's no formula here. You need to review your open and close dates to determine this number.)

MILESTONE 8

TURNING YOUR BUSINESS VISION INTO REALITY

There are no secrets to success. It is the result of preparation,
hard work, and learning from failure.

—Colin Powell

Milestone 8 is about execution—the most important step in this process. Now that you have identified your customers' needs, understand your own strengths and weaknesses, and fully grasp the market challenges, you need to act on this knowledge, with passion and commitment. Chapter 20 reviews how to create the foundation for a solid marketing plan; Chapter 21 explores the pros and cons of passion as a business strategy. The milestone concludes with a discussion of putting together a marketing execution strategy. This is the final phase of turning your business vision into reality.

The worksheets included in Milestone 8 are:

- Worksheet 20.1: Marketing Plan Outline and Milestones for Completion

- Worksheet 20.2: Marketing Budget Worksheet

- Worksheet 21.1: Advisor List

- Worksheet 21.2: Marketing Execution Strategy

- Worksheet 21.3: Passion as a Strategy

CHAPTER 20

LAYING THE FOUNDATION
FOR A MARKETING PLAN

*Our goals can only be reached through a vehicle
of a plan, in which we must fervently believe,
and upon which we must vigorously act.
There is no other route to success.*

—**Pablo Picasso**

In his best-seller, *Winning,* former General Electric CEO Jack Welch discusses strategy as resource allocation. Welch points out that a company has finite resources and that how a leader chooses to allocate those resources will influence the success of the business. How do you use a company's finite resources to develop a winning business proposition? Resources take several different forms: money, equipment, and people. Assessing your priorities wisely and then assigning resources accordingly can have a critical effect on a business's success.

AN OLD-FASHIONED EXAMPLE

Even the success of classic mom-and-pop shops depends on appropriate resource allocation. Imagine that you are the owner of Ben's Ice Cream Shoppe on Main Street in the center of a small town in the Midwest. There is one other ice cream shop in town. Can you both survive and thrive? Absolutely, if each shop offers a unique value to customers.

Let's say your ice cream is tasty, but the real value you offer to customers is that you have a friendly business. When customers (kids and adults alike) walk through your doors, you and your employees greet each person by name and know his or her favorite ice cream flavor and toppings. Your prices are reasonable (not too expensive, but not cheap), but since your customers tend to be price-sensitive, you also offer lots of promotional discounts, enticing them with items such as buy-one-get-one-free coupons. You also focus on training your staff to provide superior customer service. It's not about the product for your customers; it's about the experience. What you are truly selling is your central location and the friendly family atmosphere.

Meanwhile, on East End Road, the less traveled side of town, is Hillary's Heavenly Ice Cream Parlour. There's not a lot of foot traffic in this area. The staff is cordial, but the employees don't remember customers' names, let alone their preferences for sprinkles or hot fudge. However, the ice cream is "to die for." It's imported from Italy, and it's not available anywhere else within a 100-mile radius. Hillary's value to its customers, then, is the quality of its product. Its staff members don't need to memorize customer orders because that's not the *need* they are satisfying. This ice cream shop allocates its resources by focusing its time and effort on keeping the high quality of its product by bringing in new flavors from Italy and serving only the finest gourmet toppings (which are more expensive than those sold by your shop). This shop spends little time on training staff about customer service and even less on promotions and discounts because it is confident that customers will visit because of the superior product.

ALLOCATING YOUR RESOURCES TO SUCCEED

Can you both remain profitable? Yes, because each business understands its value and develops its entire business strategy, including resource allocation, to meet the goals and needs of its customers. You may even share some customers, since your warm atmosphere might be what customers seek when they're having ice cream with their toddlers, while the superior flavor at Hillary's Ice Cream Parlour is worth the trip and extra cost when they want a really special ice cream treat.

The point is, when you develop your marketing plan, you must start by focusing on your value to your customers and then allocate the resources that will help you meet and even exceed your customers' expectations. Every organization has finite resources, so you must prioritize based on your target market. Define your customers' most important interests and needs, and determine which of them you can satisfy, given your own resources, capabilities, and strengths. Be realistic about your resources. You can have the loftiest goals, but without the resources to support them, they are just ideas that sound good.

THE MAKING OF A MARKETING PLAN

So what are the components of an effective marketing plan? As you create your plan, remember that it must be realistic and consistent with your available resources. Goals without the resources to support them are like responsibility without any power: it sounds good in principle, but it can't be executed. Moreover, resources within any organization are finite, so you need to prioritize based on your target markets. Define your customers' most important interests and needs, and determine which of them you can satisfy given your own resources, capabilities, and strengths. The following is an outline of the information that should be included in your marketing plan, which, as noted, reflects the chapters and milestones in this book:

MARKETING PLAN OUTLINE

I. Executive Summary

    1.1 Business vision

    1.2 Growth opportunities

    1.3 Goals of the business

II. Client Profile

    2.1 Customer demographics

    2.2 Client needs

    2.3 Segmentation of target markets

III. Market Opportunity and Challenges

    3.1 Industry profile

    3.2 Demand analysis

    3.3 Market penetration

IV. Competitive Assessment

    4.1 Competitors and substitutes

    4.2 Competitive advantage

V. Marketing Channels and Mix

   5.1 Collateral development

   5.2 Image, logo, and ID package development

   5.3 Advertising, radio, and TV

   5.4 PR efforts

   5.5 Direct mail

   5.6 Web strategy and online marketing efforts

   5.7 Conference attendance and networking opportunities

   5.8 Business partnerships and alliances

VI. Sales Planning Process and Analysis

   6.1 Breakeven analysis

   6.2 Lifetime value of a client

   6.3 Referral patterns

   6.4 Sales cycles

VII. Infrastructure and Support System

VIII. Timetable for Implementation and Milestones

IX. Budget

X.   Methodologies to Measure Success

XI. Management Team

XII. Appendix/Supporting Documents

A WINNING EXAMPLE

While talking in generalities about marketing plans can be helpful, I've found that it's even more valuable to read an actual marketing plan so that you can see how the material reflects, supports, and highlights how the business will satisfy customers' needs. This should be a living document, one that you use and refer to on an ongoing basis rather than something that simply sits on your desk collecting dust.

Let's say you want to create a gourmet coffeehouse and café. Think Starbucks, but without the "chain" atmosphere. What would your marketing plan look like? A few years ago, Edward Urquhart and two other business school students in my Entrepreneurial Marketing class at Boston University School of Management set out on this mission. Here is the plan they created to determine the need for and feasibility of launching the café, which they dubbed BeanTown Coffee.

As you read the highlights of their plan, along with my comments, you will see how they researched the issues and created a plan for a business that addressed the customer base and its need for this service. Their experience and expertise was critical to the launching of the business, and they allocated their scarce resources based on achieving the highest level of customer satisfaction. While this is an abbreviated version of their plan, it will give you a sense of what a well-designed plan should include. One final note: these students were given the challenge of launching the business with a $25,000 marketing budget, so they had to use true entrepreneurial bootstrapping techniques and allocate resources carefully.

BEANTOWN COFFEE MARKETING PLAN

1.0 Executive Summary

1.1 Business Vision

BeanTown Coffee is Charlestown's number one gourmet café and upscale meeting place. BeanTown Coffee roasts and grinds premium coffee beans on the premises and sells assorted coffee beverages, along with exotic teas and premium fresh juices. BeanTown also offers homemade pastries, cakes, and confections exclusively from Montilio's, recognized as Boston's finest bakery. Additionally, BeanTown sells coffee-related accessories and equipment. A picturesque view of the Boston waterfront skyline accents a comfortable, clean, and relaxing lounge, laid out in three zones with distinct accoutrements and feel. The high-quality products and warm, inviting atmosphere are complemented by fast, friendly, and knowledgeable service; impeccably clean surroundings; and a convenient location for residents, commuters, and tourists.

1.2 Growth Opportunities

BeanTown will benefit from word-of-mouth advertising, continued commercial expansion of the Boston Harbor Waterfront, and improved access to Charlestown courtesy of the "The Big Dig." In addition, marketing programs will build a sense of community around the café. Because of the size of and the limited access to the community, growth opportunities for the Charlestown location are limited. Sales are expected to grow from $740,000 in 2003 to $800,000 in 2005. However, expansion to other locations in the Boston area is a very real growth possibility and is the ultimate goal of the business.

1.3 Business Goals

BeanTown Coffee will be profitable within one quarter and will achieve at least a 10 percent net profit margin in the first year of operation. BeanTown will become a brand name associated with high quality standards and consistent service. The long-term business plan includes the opening of additional cafés in the Boston area.

Comment: The goal of the executive summary is to allow anybody to pick up your plan and easily understand your business goals and objectives, including your unique opportunity to develop the plan and your value proposition. Think of this as teaser copy to pique the interest of prospective readers so that they continue reading your plan, whether they do this to make an investment decision, work for your company, or become business partners. You need to show your passion for the business as well as your vision if you are to grow.

2.0 Client Profile

2.1 Customer Demographics

BeanTown Coffee will target "coffee connoisseurs" with disposable income, a taste for high-quality coffee, and a desire to be treated with courteous, prompt, and informed service. BeanTown will seek a narrow segment of the coffee-drinking market, those who are willing to pay for premium products.

BeanTown's core target market is the working residents of Charlestown. Charlestown's population is increasingly young, urban professionals with disposable income. More than 70 percent of these 14,775 residents commute to work outside Charlestown.

(Continued on next page.)

BeanTown's location will be strategically selected in order to access resident pedestrians as well as commuters, representing another 2,800 potential customers. Because Charlestown is only 1.3 square miles in area, a well-positioned store is accessible by a large majority of the pedestrian population. Many of Charlestown's residents walk and ride bicycles through the neighborhoods, making stops at BeanTown Coffee convenient. BeanTown will be located on the waterfront, near City Square, Olive's Restaurant, and Bread & Circus, all of which draw a similar target consumer audience.

More than 6,000 people are employed by Charlestown's 700+ businesses. Many of these employees commute into Charlestown, including a large number employed by the Charlestown Navy Yard. BeanTown Coffee will also target these nonresident professionals.

In 2001, there were an estimated 12.6 million domestic and international visitors to Boston, with a total economic impact of $7.5 billion for the Greater Boston region. Charlestown receives a share of these tourists, who will appreciate a warm cup of coffee and a soft couch to fall into after visiting the Bunker Hill Museum.

2.2 Client Needs

BeanTown Coffee's value proposition is "quality coffee, espresso, and pastries, consistently prepared and promptly served in a comfortable environment, conveniently accessible to Charlestown's residents and visitors." Repeat customers will become accustomed to unparalleled product quality and service in a relaxing atmosphere with the historic Boston waterfront as a picturesque backdrop.

Comment: The goal of the client profile is to identify your target market and how members of the audience value your business's products or services. This section must clearly outline who your customers are, what their needs are, and how your value proposition will satisfy those unique needs. This was clearly articulated by BeanTown as "quality coffee, espresso, and pastries, consistently prepared and promptly served in a comfortable environment, conveniently accessible to Charlestown's residents and visitors."

3.0 Market Opportunity and Challenges

Charlestown is shaped like a triangle, surrounded by water on two sides and cut off from Boston proper on the remaining side by Interstate 93 (see Exhibit 1). There are two major routes into and out of Charlestown, the

Charlestown Bridge on the east side and the Bunker Hill Bridge on the west side. More than 70 percent of the 15,000 residents commute to work outside Charlestown. This "commuter population" represents BeanTown Coffee's core target market segment.

Charlestown has been revitalized in the past five years, in part because of the construction efforts of the Boston Redevelopment Authority. Charlestown has become one of the neighborhoods of choice in Boston, and many young, affluent professionals have made it their home. Landlocked and isolated, Charlestown's 1.3 square miles of neighborhoods come alive with foot traffic during the evening and weekend hours. This "resident pedestrian population" is another target market segment.

Charlestown is home to a major commercial shipping terminal, employing thousands while attracting truck, railroad, and shipping traffic. In addition, the Charlestown Navy Yard and 700 other businesses employ thousands of professionals, many of whom commute into Charlestown. The "commercial traffic" associated with these businesses represents another target market segment.

Charlestown was founded in 1629 and is Boston's oldest neighborhood. Much of Charlestown burned to the ground during the Battle of Bunker Hill in 1775 and was subsequently rebuilt. The Bunker Hill Monument was built to commemorate this famous battle and is a popular tourist destination. The U.S.S. *Constitution* ("Old Ironsides"), the oldest commissioned ship in the United States Navy, is another popular tourist destination. Charlestown draws an estimated 500,000 tourists per year. This "nonresident tourist population" is another target market segment.

Specialty coffee is a $5 + billion per year market, growing at a rate of more than 20 percent per year in the past five years. Starbucks successfully borrowed the cultural "experience" of the corner café from Italy and used it to penetrate, educate, and grow the U.S. market. As a result, consumers in the United States now expect good coffee and a warm, inviting atmosphere and are willing to pay a premium for it.

Charlestown's population is expected to remain constant because existing dwellings have exhausted the available land, as shown in Exhibit 2. Commercial traffic and clients visiting any of the 700 businesses in Charlestown are also expected to remain constant. Tourism should

(Continued on next page.)

increase upon completion of "The Big Dig," but this growth will be discounted. Exhibit 3 reveals approximately 15,000 potential consumers per day, assuming that the Bunker Hill Bridge commuter traffic will not detour to visit BeanTown. A 2000 National Coffee Association survey reported that 53 percent of adults drink gourmet coffee beverages, up from 35 percent in 1997. The study also reports that this number increases substantially within higher income brackets, a positive influence given Charlestown's high-income status. Exhibit 4 estimates market penetration resulting in approximately 500 actual customers per day.

Comment: BeanTown clearly understands the Charlestown population and can define its target market. A common mistake in business plans is overstating the target audience for your business. That can lead to a loss of credibility and possibly cast doubt on the entire plan. The individuals developing this plan did not make that mistake. They explained who the audience would be and provided justification for that audience's interest in their product.

4.0 Competitive Assessment

Charlestown currently has two coffee shops: a Dunkin' Donuts located near the Bunker Hill Bridge and Sorelle's, a small high-end coffee shop located on Main Street. Sorelle's is well positioned to capture resident pedestrian traffic, but poorly positioned to capture commuter traffic, and it has no on-premises parking. Dunkin' Donuts is well positioned to capture commuter traffic using the Bunker Hill Bridge, but it is poorly positioned to capture pedestrian traffic and commuter traffic using the Charlestown Bridge. BeanTown Coffee's strategic location positions it to capture both pedestrian traffic and commuter traffic crossing the Charlestown Bridge. Therefore, BeanTown's primary competitor will be Sorelle's, not Dunkin' Donuts.

Dunkin' Donuts has strict franchising requirements, including a traffic and population survey from which revenues are predicted. Dunkin' Donuts requires a factor of safety in revenue predictions to ensure that the addition of another competitor (normally assumed to be a Starbucks) will not result in business failure. McDonald's and Burger King have similar standards. Therefore, the existence of the Dunkin' Donuts leads to an assumption that Dunkin' Donuts believes that there is room for an additional competitor. Because of Charlestown's small size, it is unlikely that further competitors will enter once BeanTown is established.

Exhibit 5 provides a comparative assessment of the three businesses. BeanTown's competitive advantage will be a combination of a strategic location, high-quality coffee and pastries, and fast, friendly service. Dunkin' Donuts has a great location and fast service, but its store environment is neither warm nor welcoming, and its service is not friendly. In addition, Dunkin' Donuts appeals to clientele with low to midrange income. Sorelle's has a great location for pedestrian traffic but has difficulty attracting commuter traffic. In addition, its coffee is midlevel in quality, and its service is slow.

Exhibit 6 illustrates the high price differential between Sorelle's and Dunkin' Donuts. Sorelle's pricing reflects a narrow market, high-priced positioning. Incidentally, Sorelle's prices are nearly identical to those of a Back Bay Starbucks. BeanTown prices will be slightly lower than Sorelle's and higher than Dunkin' Donuts.

Comment: Who is your competition? What are the alternatives to your business? You must be realistic in this section and position yourself relative to those options. Citing traffic patterns, BeanTown Coffee is able to explain which coffee shop it competes with and why. Again, this gives credence to the founders' understanding of the market and helps to validate their ability to capture market share. However, they might be naïve in assuming that once BeanTown is established, no other competitors will enter the market. We hope they are correct, but you have to be careful about making such assumptions.

5.0 Marketing Channels and Mix

5.1 Direct Sales Effort

BeanTown Coffee's staff will be well trained and will possess extensive product knowledge and professional selling skills. Ordering coffee beverages in high-end cafés can be confusing and overwhelming for some people. BeanTown's store manager and associates will have four-color, glossy menus with pictures and descriptions, enabling them to quickly educate customers on the options and preparation methods for each beverage type. This will help build customer loyalty and drive revenues by encouraging customers to taste more expensive premium beverages.

To complement sales associates' product knowledge, a library of books devoted to the history of coffee, coffee traditions, and preparation techniques (roasting, grinding, and brewing) will be displayed in the lounge areas.

(Continued on next page.)

BeanTown will also sell coffee preparation merchandise and supplies by partnering with select espresso machine manufacturers and accessory suppliers, including Giotto, Nuova, and Alma. Additionally, BeanTown will carry grinders by La Pavoni and high-end commercial grade blenders for at-home preparation of crushed iced coffee and espresso drinks.

5.2 Advertising

BeanTown Coffee will run a series of print advertisements in the local weekly *Charlestown Patriot* newspaper, for $500 per week. The advertisements will contain a coupon offering a free cup of coffee and an incentive to visit BeanTown repeatedly, i.e., a frequent drinker's card. The same artwork developed for the print ad will be used in a brochure distributed to local businesses and tourist attractions.

In a small community like Charlestown, word of mouth is the most effective form of advertising. BeanTown's core customer base will become loyal because of BeanTown's quality, convenience, and commitment to the local community. This loyalty will provide a viral marketing effect as "the word spreads."

Tickets at the U.S.S. *Constitution*, Bunker Hill Museum, and Freedom Trail will have an offer for a free cup of coffee printed on the backside. In addition, BeanTown brochures will be displayed in the tourist brochure racks at these locations. Employees at these tourist sites will be entitled to one free cup of coffee per day at BeanTown, in order to build goodwill in return for recommendations.

5.3 Web Strategy and Online Marketing Efforts

BeanTown Coffee's Web site will be simple and informational in nature. It will provide contact information, directions, and a description of the products, services, and store environment. It will also contain general information about coffee roasting and the coffee industry. BeanTown will host a second site on its server, called "Charlestown.com." This P.R. site will be a community-centered site, providing residents with a forum to place personal ads, sell vehicles, rent and sublet apartments, post news, and so on. The goal of the site is to provide a range of free services that will be of interest to Charlestown's community. The site will have only one unobtrusive advertiser, BeanTown Coffee! When a visitor clicks on the link, he or she will be sent to BeanTown's information Web site. However, even if users do not click on the banner ad, they will be exposed to the name "BeanTown Coffee" repeatedly. Charlestown.com will also be advertised in the *Charlestown Patriot*.

5.4 Business Partnerships and Marketing Alliances

The BeanTown Coffee brand will soon be known for its high quality and fresh roasted flavors. The brand will be promoted at Boston's high-end restaurants and bars as a featured product. BeanTown will attempt to gain commitment from several Boston restaurants to carry the brand by the end of 2003.

BeanTown will borrow the "Boston Duck Tours" marketing idea by sharing lead generation with several Boston tourist establishments. BeanTown will try to organize partnerships with establishments such as the Boston Aquarium, in order to cross-promote both businesses.

BeanTown will offer premium baked goods from Montilio's Bakery and will proudly display Montilio's name on a printed plaque. In addition, Montilio's will carry BeanTown fresh-roasted coffees and display its name in the bakery.

5.5 PR Efforts

BeanTown will flood the local newspapers and circulars with press releases announcing the opening of its business. BeanTown will provide a public relations packet including a picture of the storefront, a view of Boston's skyline at night from inside the café, an interview with the store manager, and a product lineup. In addition, *Boston Magazine* will publish a feature article on BeanTown Coffee, focusing on why on-premises fresh roasting provides a unique coffee-drinking experience, and how the attention to detail offered by a small, locally owned business makes a noticeable difference.

Channel 7's weekly entertainment program *Chronicle* has agreed to do a feature article on BeanTown Coffee.

The *Charlestown Patriot* has agreed to publish a biweekly column entitled "Uncommon Grounds," intended to promote education and understanding of coffee and coffee-making principles, along with accessory updates and reviews.

BeanTown will offer seasonal special roasted coffee flavors on a quarterly basis. To introduce the new flavors to the local community, BeanTown will deliver samples to the staff of the top 10 morning radio programs in Boston in hopes of getting a 20-second free P.R. spot. The

(Continued on next page.)

objective is to inform the greater Boston community about a one-of-a-kind café located in Charlestown.

BeanTown will be active within the local Charlestown residential community. For example, BeanTown will promote and host individual neighborhood block parties in order to provide a venue for neighbors and friends to get together over a cup of coffee and share stories with one another. Each block party will be announced on invitations to local residents. Revenues from these events will be donated to local youth organizations, sports activities, and community scholarship programs. BeanTown will be an active, responsible member of the Charlestown community.

Comment: How will you carry out your plan? This section shows what you need to do to capture the market. For example, BeanTown recognizes the importance of educating its staff and its customers on the options and preparation methods for each beverage type. As a premium provider, its affiliations and partnerships are important, and the perception of it in the community is critical. Its strategies are strongly aligned with its customers' needs and its unique core competencies.

6.0 Sales Planning Process and Analysis

BeanTown Coffee will derive $740,000 in annual sales from approximately 500 customers per day. Commercial traffic and resident commuters will spend the least, primarily because they will spend less time in the store. Resident pedestrians and tourists will spend the most per visit because they will have more time to spend in the store and are looking for a "café experience." Exhibit 7 illustrates how sales forecasts are derived based on 500 customers per day. The "average daily purchase" figures are based on watching both Starbucks and Sorelle's customers and making educated assumptions about the buying habits of the different target segments.

Cost of goods sold will be 20 percent of total sales, a standard industry figure based on purchasing coffee and supplies at wholesale prices. BeanTown will run three working shifts and staff three counter servers in the morning, two in the afternoon, and three in the evening. In addition, a full-time store manager will be employed. The counter servers will earn $8.00 to $10.00 per hour, and the store manager will earn $40,000 per year plus benefits. Based on these assumptions, BeanTown will earn nearly $80,000 after taxes in its first year. Breakeven will occur with revenue of $610,750. These estimates are based on conservative assumptions regarding the number of people served per day and their average daily purchases, and liberal estimations of business expenses.

Resident commuters and pedestrians will have the highest lifetime value to BeanTown because they "live next door." Commercial traffic and tourists come and go and cannot be relied upon for repeat business. Therefore, marketing efforts will focus on attracting and keeping resident customers. The lifetime value of a resident commuter is $4.00 per day times 250 days per year times 5 years, which equals $5,000. The lifetime value of a resident pedestrian is $5.00 per day times 100 days per year times 5 years, which equals $2,500.

Charlestown is a small, close-knit community; therefore referrals are very important to the growth of BeanTown Coffee. Given the high lifetime value of a satisfied local customer, a single referral is valuable and will be sought through various promotions.

Comment: The owners of BeanTown Coffee clearly have a strong expertise in sales planning and analysis. They understand the lifetime value of a satisfied customer and realize that referrals are critical to their success. They have calculated the numbers and understand which customers are critical to them. This aligns with their marketing strategy and partnership goals.

7.0 Infrastructure and Support System

During the first six months of operation, all three partners will be responsible for managing the day-to-day operations. Ed Urquhart's main focus will be on BeanTown's investors and the Charlestown community and business relationships. Justin Trembath will have primary responsibility for the supply chain and staffing. Brian Sullivan will focus on BeanTown's customers by developing sales and marketing strategies, implementing new customer growth strategies, and developing customer retention programs.

BeanTown will retain a renowned industry consultant who has worked with thousands of entrepreneurs and successfully launched coffee shops, coffee drive-thrus, and espresso carts and kiosks across North America. This consultant will assist BeanTown in quickly qualifying the best green coffee bean wholesalers, identifying other useful supply-chain partners, and providing experienced counsel in order to avoid common start-up mistakes. His retainer will include a three-day training seminar.

(Continued on next page.)

Start-up expenses include stationery and office supplies, prepaid insurance and rent, and legal expenses, along with a $25,000 marketing budget. Remodeling expenses will be significant because of the atmosphere required to differentiate BeanTown from its competition. Also significant will be the expenses for furnishing the three separate lounging areas, each with a different theme. Operating capital must be sufficient to cover employees' salaries, expenses, and cash reserves for the first three months of operation. An investment in start-up inventory of green coffee beans, filters, baked goods, and retail supplies will also be required. Two coffeemakers, two espresso machines, two grinders, various items of food-service equipment (microwave, toaster, dishwasher, refrigerator, blenders, and so on), and retail and service counter equipment will also be purchased.

Comment: Your infrastructure must support your business model. If the partners' expertise and experience isn't in sync with the business's goals, then the execution will be poor, and the business won't grow. Each partner brings his own unique experience to the business, and it's essential that their expertise is used wisely to launch the business model rapidly.

9.0 Budget

$25,000 Marketing Promotion Budget

Trifold Brochure

Design & creative fee	4,000
Print & paper cost per 1,000	1,500
4,000 copies	x4
	6,000
	10,000

Coffee Cart Rental

Cost per cart per week	1,000
Number of carts	x2
Number of weeks	x2
	4,000

Coffee Cart Giveaways

Cost per cup of coffee	50 cents
Number of cups per cart	x500
Number of carts	x2
Number of days	x10
	5,000

Local Sponsorship of Teams

Girls' soccer	1,500
Boys' baseball	1,500
	3,000

Charlestown Patriot Advertisement/Coupon

Add cost per week	500
Number of weeks	x4
	2,000

Coupon Free Giveaway

Average cost of beverage	1
Number of weeks	x4
Response per week	x250
	1,000
Total:	$25,000

Comment: The bottom line is always essential in your planning. I required my students to create a marketing program with only $25,000 (a true entrepreneurial challenge that requires ingenuity and careful planning). Be realistic about how much money you have and how much it will cost to launch your business.

FINAL WORD ON YOUR PLAN

Ask most experienced investors which is more important, a great idea or an experienced, passionate team, and most will say the latter. Skilled execution is the key to success. A great idea without a passionate team is likely to flounder. Therefore, make sure your team has the experience, expertise, and passion to carry your business forward. The next chapter explores the notion of passion as a powerful strategy

(Worksheets start on next page.)

WORKSHEET 20.1

MARKETING PLAN OUTLINE AND MILESTONES FOR COMPLETION

1. Executive Summary; Completion Deadline _____

   1.1 Business vision

   1.2 Growth opportunities

   1.3 Goals of the business

2. Client Profile; Completion Deadline _____

   2.1 Customer demographics

   2.2 Client needs

   2.3 Segmentation of target markets

3. Market Opportunity and Challenges; Completion Deadline _____

   3.1 Industry profile

   3.2 Demand analysis

   3.3 Market penetration

4. Competitive Assessment; Completion Deadline _____

   4.1 Competitors and substitutes

   4.2 Competitive advantage

5. Marketing Channels and Mix; Completion Deadline _____

   5.1 Collateral development

   5.2 Image, logo, and ID package development

   5.3 Advertising, radio, and TV

   5.4 PR efforts

   5.5 Direct mail

5.6 Web strategy and online marketing efforts

5.7 Conference attendance and networking opportunities

5.8 Business partnerships and alliances

6. Sales Planning Process and Analysis; Completion Deadline _____

6.1 Breakeven analysis

6.2 Lifetime value of a client

6.3 Referral patterns

6.4 Sales cycles

7. Infrastructure and Support System; Completion Deadline _____

8. Timetable for Implementation and Milestones; Completion Deadline

_____

9. Budget; Completion Deadline _____

10. Methodologies to Measure Success; Completion Deadline _____

11. Management Team

12. Appendix/Supporting Documents

WORKSHEET 20.2

MARKETING BUDGET WORKSHEET

Anticipated revenue for 20____: $_____

REVENUE MIX

Revenue from present clients: _____% of total revenue = $_____

Revenue from new clients: _____% of total revenue = $_____

Marketing budget _____

Marketing Mix	Percent of Budget	Number of Customers Generated	Marketing Budget	Source
TOTAL	100%		$	
Sales literature				
Logo design and branding				
Direct mail				
Conference exhibiting/sponsorship				
Speaking opportunities/seminars				
Public relations				
E-mail and interactive marketing				
Partner marketing strategies				
Print advertising				
Radio				
TV				
Telemarketing				
Giveaways and promotional items				
Web site design and development				
Direct sales force				

Please note: your percentages of budget will not necessarily reflect direct generation of customers, since not all marketing activities have measurable results.

CHAPTER 21

PASSION AS A STRATEGY

Do not stop thinking of life as an adventure. You have no security unless you can live bravely, excitingly, imaginatively, unless you can choose a challenge instead of a competence.

—**Eleanor Roosevelt**

Does a business need passion in order to thrive? Why do companies with a leader who is truly passionate about the business fail, while others with the same level of passion and a less compelling business model prosper and grow? Is there a magical formula that makes one business successful while another fails? What separates the winners from the losers, and what role does passion play?

There are several ingredients that go into a winning business, including a great idea, a great team, great passion, and great leadership. All are important, but great passion can be the fire that helps fuel the success. It can also destroy the business when it is misguided.

WATCH THE FIRE

Like all fires, passions can spark other flames and become contagious, igniting the passion of investors, business partners, and customers, as well as employees. If left uncontrolled, passion can consume, destroy, and leave a business with an empty dream. However, when controlled, directed, and focused, it can boost a business's chance for success.

It isn't, however, the only important ingredient. In fact, time after time, when I've asked many venture capitalists and business professionals to identify the most critical factor, they've responded, "It's the team that makes the difference." A great business idea alone will not make a business profitable, but a passionate team that has the vision and the ability to execute the idea, even if the idea is only pretty good, can help a company achieve success. A winning team has a passionate leader and a team that is equally committed to achieving success. Your business idea doesn't have to be the most ingenious or creative—just a solid concept that will satisfy a need.

So is there a magic formula? Is it 50 percent passionate team and 50 percent concept? What's missing in this formula? It's the team's ability to execute on the idea. This ability is fueled by passion, vision, experience, and the ability to focus on customer needs. It's the use of basic business principles that makes the difference when this is done properly. Therefore, in order to be successful in business, you don't have to come up with the most ingenious and creative business concept. You must have a solid concept that satisfies a need, and you must be able to properly funnel your passion to execute the plan. There's no magic, but these elements must exist.

THE APPRENTICE: A CASE STUDY IN THE FAILURE OF PASSION

Sometimes passion can backfire. I'm not a big fan of reality TV, but I found myself fascinated by NBC's show *The Apprentice*, and I even began using it to teach a class on business consulting at Brandeis International Business School. It wasn't just good TV—it was a perfect way to illustrate how talented, smart people can be so blinded by their passion to win that they completely botch basic business challenges.

As you might know, the basic premise of the show is to bring together 15 to 20 aspiring entrepreneurs and have them compete to become Donald Trump's apprentice in his real estate empire.

During the first show of the first season, the competitors were split into two teams and given a very basic task: sell lemonade on the streets of New York City. The men and women were divided into separate teams. The women set up their lemonade stand in midtown, a location with tons of potential customers. The men headed downtown to an area by the fish market, where there was minimal foot traffic. Each team bickered about pricing, location, and sales strategies.

Who won? The women, who had chosen the best location and priced the product correctly (the men actually tried to sell a cup of lemonade for $1,000). The men were so caught up in their passion for what they personally wanted to achieve that they lost sight of one of the most important principles of business: know who your customers are; then find them. Classic business mistakes are made by smart, successful, deeply passionate entrepreneurs all the time. And it is usually because they get so consumed with their passion.

BASIC BUSINESS PRINCIPLES

Setting up a successful lemonade stand incorporates all the principles of good business practice. You have to start by identifying who your customers are, determine the value of the product to the customers, and figure out how best to reach them.

The failure to fuel your passion, however, can cause you to skip or dismiss one of these basic principles. In fact, that's where you see really smart businesspeople with good intentions make fatal errors in judgment. The difference lies in the use of the passion. It must be directed constructively, with the business in mind and not individual desires and goals.

philoSophie's®

Passion can also be misdirected when you're caught up in the day-to-day activities of your business and don't take the opportunity to sit back and think about how to focus your energy. Joanna Alberti's business, philoSophie's® (www.sophiesphilosophies.com), is a good example of the importance of taking time to reflect on your business goals and where you want to direct your passion. In fact, philoSophie's is a successful start-up greeting card company launched by owner and entrepreneur Joanna Alberti. In 2005, at the age of 24, Joanna was recognized by *BusinessWeek* as one of the top five young entrepreneurs under 25. Known for her whimsical designs and her humorous illustrations depicting women and their interests, Joanna's style and creativity fueled her passion to launch a greeting card business just one year after receiving her college degree.

As a business mentor to Joanna (a 2003 graduate of the BU School of Management), I had the unique opportunity to work with her as she developed her business model. I also watched her struggle as she worked 20-hour days at her business, often coming into my office covered in glitter from the greeting cards she had hand-embellished. She was doing it all, but was she doing *too much*?

Joanna was trying to launch her business in so many venues that she was not taking the time to determine who her customers were, why they were buying from her, and what need she satisfied. This knowledge could help her focus on which strategies were the best use of her time. She was trying to get into as many markets as possible without thinking about which of them made the most sense for her limited budget and time. She was clearly spread too thin and was unable to prioritize her marketing efforts and focus on growing fast and efficiently and on targeting the most likely prospects with the least amount of money. She became overwhelmed by the day-to-day aspects of the business and lost sight of the big picture. Not all of her customers were desirable, but her passion to become known in the industry and reach as much of the market as possible, and not necessarily the right parts of the market, led to her overlooking the best opportunities for sales and growth. In stepping back to look at the big picture, she soon found where she excelled and brought in a team to help her with both product development and business decisions.

With the support of MBA students at Brandeis International Business School participating in my consulting course, the team launched a marketing research project to help Joanna determine which strategies would generate the greatest revenue for her business. The goal of the team's research was to assess the effectiveness of her current strategy for expanding philoSophie's in both new and existing markets and to identify how to most efficiently allocate her time and maximize the available sales channels and products to get the greatest return on her time and money.

The students uncovered the following information in their research efforts:

■ The greeting card industry is quite competitive. This $7.5 billion industry is divided roughly into two segments—established players targeting the majority of the market, and smaller businesses that target niche markets (like Joanna's focus on the female market).

■ Smaller card designers compete with one another by offering price, quality, and product differentiations and are able to wrest market share away from the larger players by being able to respond more rapidly to trends in the market.

■ Customers purchase cards primarily for friends and family members. The most important traits they look for in a greeting card are high quality, unique design, and the message.

■ Birthday, anniversary, and get well cards are the most sought after year-round; the most sought after seasonal cards are Christmas, Valentine's Day, and Mother's Day cards.

■ The three top places that sell cards are drug and grocery stores, retail gift stores, and bookstores.

How did philoSophie's measure up to the market? It was generating revenue of less than $100,000 annually, and although Joanna earned a solid profit margin by tightly controlling her costs, she was burning candles at both ends by serving as designer, marketer, salesperson, and creator, plus a dozen other roles. Her cards were sold through multiple channels, including online, in person, and through retail stores. The majority of her orders were custom work and retail, followed by Web.

The team did a complete analysis of her sales and discovered that her Web site orders were the most profitable. This information was important in determining Joanna's strategy because she had a bias toward the less profitable but, to her, more interesting retail boutique market.

Was her passion for the business preventing her from seeing where the most profit was to be gained? Unfortunately, yes. With a relatively small market presence, low brand recognition, diluted market strategy, and capital and labor constraints serving as barriers to future expansion, the team recommended the following strategies to Joanna to grow her business:

- Tailor search engine results so that philoSophie's Web site shows up more frequently on Web site searches.

- Spend your most precious resource, your time, contacting and submitting your cards to large national greeting card distributors to expand your scope and visibility.

- Spend less time contacting hundreds of small boutiques because this use of your time isn't justified in terms of bottom-line revenue.

- Pursue networking opportunities at the large industry trade shows to gain a better understanding of the greeting card industry.

- Consider expansion into additional markets such as minority characters and more mass marketing (less high-end operation such as selling through boutiques only).

- Outsource the hand-embellishing jobs to free up time for the development of the products and marketing.

THE TEAM'S INSIGHT

What allowed the team of business students to provide this already successful entrepreneur with insight concerning her business? First, the team members were removed from the passion and thrill of the business and were able to review the data objectively and figure out what made the most sense to get Joanna to the next level of business success. Next, they had the time to conduct the research. When you're a young entrepreneur and you're in the thick of the business, you usually don't get the opportunity to sit back and reflect—you're just doing, doing, doing. That can be dangerous because you lose sight of the forest for the trees. In this case, Joanna was literally doing everything, from operations to design to sales, marketing, and glittering the cards herself. She was spending a lot of time approaching small boutiques, yet this was not where the profit for her business was being generated. She needed to focus on what made most business sense for philoSophie's rather than on what interested her more. Here's what Joanna had to say:

> I initially approached so many small boutiques because I wanted to generate sales and support from a niche of women who shopped with the sense of purchasing a product that is special and unique—my passion for my product

had blinded me. In stepping back and researching boutiques nationally, I found high-end, independent chains (more than two stores), which eliminated the need to go to each small boutique and generated sales equivalent to three small stores, allowing more time and money to be spent working on Web development and total revenue and profit generated.

Most business owners don't get the unique opportunity to have an objective team of students help them focus their business strategy. Therefore, you have to take ownership and find a team to help you think objectively about your business. Having unbiased, skilled advisors is critical to every business owner's success. These can be colleagues or trusted business partners or even friends with the right experience and insight to truly help you. If you seek out these advisors and use the marketing principles discussed throughout this book, your path should be smoother, and you should reach your destination more rapidly, more efficiently, and with greater overall success.

(Worksheets start on next page.)

WORKSHEET 21.1

ADVISOR LIST

List potential advisors who can play an important role in helping you shape your company vision and focus your passion. Note each person's area of expertise to ensure that you have a variety of experiences to rely upon.

Advisor Name and Company	Expertise and Experience
1.	
2.	
3.	
4.	
5.	
6.	
7.	
8.	
9.	
10.	

WORKSHEET 21.2

MARKETING EXECUTION STRATEGY

List 10 strategies that can be acted upon that you are committed to launching in the next six months and the goals they are designed to achieve. Note the individual(s) responsible, your measurement of success, and the deadline for completion. Write these dates in your day planner and make sure you review them throughout the next six months to grow your business.

Goal	Action(s) Required to Achieve Goal	Deadline	Measurement of Success	Individual(s) Responsible
1.				
2.				
3.				
4.				
5.				
6.				
7.				
8.				
9.				
10.				

WORKSHEET 21.3

PASSION AS A STRATEGY

—There is no end. There is no beginning. There is only the passion of life.

Federico Fellini (Italian film director)

Even the most successful companies have their share of business ups and downs. How will you use your passion to get through the rough patches and continue to grow? Now is the time to think about your passion for your business. What do you love about it? Why are you starting it, or why did you start it?

List 10 reasons why you feel passionate about your business. Post this in your office or someplace where you will see it every day to remind yourself why you're getting up each morning and going to work (even if that's just down the hall). These 10 reasons will keep you motivated on the good days as well as the bad ones!

1.

2.

3.

4.

5.

6.

7.

8.

9.

10.

CONCLUSION

You miss 100% of the shots you never take.
—**Wayne Gretzky, hockey player**

Now that you've got the tools and the plan, how do you put it all together to succeed? There is one final ingredient that we talked about at the beginning of this book—it's *you*. *You* have to be ready to devote your heart and your mind and your *passion* to making your business come alive. There will be challenges and setbacks along the way that cannot be anticipated, and that can be survived only if you believe in your business and work to make it happen. Success takes hard work, commitment, and real sweat equity.

BUSINESS IS A MARATHON, NOT A SPRINT

If you were training for a marathon, you wouldn't start off by running 50 miles on the first day. To improve your chances for success and minimize the likelihood of failure, you might begin your training by working on strength and speed exercises, then progress to endurance and aerobic capacity. Operating your business is like training for a marathon. When the shot is fired (whatever those moments are in your business), you use everything that you've learned up to that point and start running. In a business, there are many starts and many guns going off, sometimes at the same time. You must create a plan, determine your finances, look for customers, and search for strategic partners. You may train slowly for some of these activities, but at the end of the day, you have to begin running in order to succeed and complete the race.

TURN YOUR BUSINESS VISION INTO REALITY

Now is the point in time when all your planning, preparation, worrying, thinking, talking, wishing, and dreaming must be interrupted with a strong dose of reality. Virtual planning ceases, and execution, simply doing it, must begin. You must channel your passion and the knowledge you have gained and put them into action. Otherwise, you will have wasted your time and energy on the dream.

DON'T FEAR FAILURE

Malcolm Forbes once said, "Failure is success if we learn from it." Use what you've learned from this book and from all of your past business experiences to move forward. Don't fear failing—fear inertia. There are many ways to move forward and seize an opportunity to realize a dream. I've designed this book to support your vision. Use it like a traditional toolkit: if the small wrench doesn't work, try something different until you solve the problem. You've done your homework. Now you simply need to get out there and make it happen, keeping this toolkit by your side as a steadfast resource to help you plan and develop your business strategy. Good luck. Remember, execution is the only way to turn your business vision into reality.

INDEX

Customer relationship management (CRM), 19, 135, 272–274
Customers
  behavior-based products, research, 61
  business vision, 2–17
  customer profile surveys, 23–27
  defined, 259
  differentiation worksheets, 49
  focus on, Seven Strategies, 8–9, 15
  growth projection worksheets, 47–48
  information worksheets, 66–68
  needs checklist, 229
  questions to ask worksheets, 33

Data for decision-making, 85
  (See also Primary research and surveys)
Database workarounds, research, 63–64
Delivery, of elevator pitch, 249–251, 255–256
  (See also Sales contact strategies)
Demographic information, surveys, 57, 83–84
Design
  literature, 183
  logo, 167–170, 184
  survey worksheets, 80
Differentiation, customer lifetime value, 40–42, 49
Direct-mail checklist, 203
Direct-mail marketing, 188–193
Direction and goals, Seven Strategies, 6, 13
Discipline, selling skills, 223
Drive, business vision, 3
Driving traffic to Web sites, 211

E-mail, as marketing tool, 205–207
Education of prospects, 170–173
Elevator pitch, 246–255
  delivery, 249–251, 255–256
  elements of, 249
  practice, 249
  preparation, 248
  "so what" factor, 247
  stimulate interest, 246–247
  tagline, 252
  template for, 251
  worksheets, 253–255
Entrepreneurial spirit, partnership strategies, 151–152
External factors (opportunities), SWOT, 137, 145, 147–148
Eye contact, elevator pitch, 250–251

Face-to-face contact, 76–77, 262–263
Facial expression, elevator pitch, 251

Failure
  business vision, 2–3
  fear of, 315
  partnership strategies, 158–159
Feasibility, 8, 15, 165–166
Filemaker, 272
Financial requirements (See Budgeting)
Finding right partnership, 152–153
First-mover competitive advantage, 123–124
Flexibility, Seven Strategies, 10, 16–17
Follow-up, 88–89, 265–266
Forbes, Malcolm, 315
Formulas
  customer lifetime value, 38–40
  sales objective formulas, 276–278
Friendship vs. networking, 230–232

Gift ideas, survey participation, 85–88
Goals, Seven Strategies, 6, 13
Golden rules for networking, 232–234

Horn, Paul, 232
Hot buttons, sales contact strategies, 266–267

Ideal customer, customer lifetime value, 35–36
Image (See Brands, building)
Improvement of Web sites, 211–212
In-person contacts, 76–77, 262–263
Individual cycles, sales cycle management, 275–278
Industry
  analysis/strategy worksheets, 113–115
  data sources, secondary research, 103–112
  knowledge of, and selling skills, 226–227
Inequality, customer lifetime value, 34–35
Inertia, and competition, 125–127
Information sources and customer profiles, 18–21, 29
Interest stimulation of, elevator pitch, 246–247
Internet
  banner and online advertising, 207–208
  e-mail push strategies, 205–207
  online social networks, 208
  online surveys, 77–79
  as part of marketing program, 204
  power of Web, 204–205
  SWOT perspective, 138–140
  Web site pull strategies, 208–212
  worksheets, 213–215
  (See also Web sites)
Investigation, partnership strategies, 157

ABOUT THE AUTHOR

Beth Goldstein got her first taste of entrepreneurship in the 1970s at the ripe old age of 10, when she heard an announcement on her favorite children's TV show, *Wonderama*, promoting the opportunity to run a backyard carnival to raise money for a muscular dystrophy charity. Thinking it sounded like a cool project, she sent for the starter kit. She quickly discovered that it was a lot more work than she had imagined—not that dissimilar to the revelation most entrepreneurs have when they start their own businesses. In fact, this carnival involved all of the basic elements of launching a business, from establishing an operating plan to worrying about financial issues like how much to charge for tickets and entrance fees. The carnival also required partners (to donate giveaways) and a solid marketing strategy to target the local kids in the neighborhood. It took a lot of hard work and planning, but the experience was invaluable, and her career as an entrepreneur was born.

Beth is now a consultant, entrepreneur, and adjunct professor of marketing. She founded her consulting firm, Marketing Edge Consulting Group, LLC, in 1999 with the goal of providing creative marketing, sales, and business solutions to organizations that were challenged by limited time and financial resources. With locations in Massachusetts and New York, as well as partner offices in Argentina and Germany, her clients include not only individual entrepreneurs but also American and European small to mid-sized companies in industries ranging from finance and high-tech to academia, medical technology, and engine components. She helps these businesses develop and implement solid marketing strategies and lead-generating sales programs.

In addition to consulting, Beth works with entrepreneurs at the Institute for Technology Entrepreneurship & Commercialization at Boston University and runs the university's Annual $30K Business Plan Competition. She also teaches courses on Strategic Business Consulting and Entrepreneurial Sales and Marketing at Boston University's School of Management and the Brandeis International Business School.

Beth has more than 22 years of sales, marketing, and business development experience and holds an MBA from Boston University and a degree in economics and sociology from Brandeis University. In her spare time, Beth can be found hanging out with her two children (both budding entrepreneurs) and their 80-pound lapdog, Biscotti.